# ARCHITECTURE
## Form, Space, & Order
### Second Edition

# ARCHITECTURE
## Form, Space, & Order
### Second Edition

Francis D.K. Ching

A VNR Book

JOHN WILEY & SONS, INC.

New York  Chichester  Weinheim  Brisbane  Singapore  Toronto

Interior Design: Frank Ching
Page Composition: Theo Coates Design

This publication is designed to provide accurate and authoritative information in regard to the subject matter covered. It is sold with the understanding that the publisher is not engaged in rendering professional services. If professional advice or other expert assistance is required, the services of a competent professional person should be sought.

**Library of Congress Cataloging-in-Publication Data:**

Ching, Francis D.K. 1943-
  Architecture: Form, Space, & Order / Francis D.K. Ching.—2nd Ed.
    p.  cm.
  Includes bibliographical references and index.
  ISBN 0-471-28616-8
  1. Architecture-Composition, proportion, etc. 2. Space
  (Architecture)   I. Title.
NA2760.C46  1996
720'.1—dc20                                              95-38133
                                                              CIP

Printed in the United States of America

10  9

# CONTENTS

The original edition of this study introduced the student of architecture to form and space and the principles that guide their ordering in the built environment. Form and space are the critical means of architecture that comprise a design vocabulary that is both elemental and timeless. While this revision continues to be a comprehensive primer on the ways form and space are interrelated and organized in the shaping of our environment, it has been refined by editing the text and incorporating diagrams for greater clarity, adding selected examples of architectural works, expanding the sections on openings, stairways and scale, and finally, by including a glossary and an index to designers.

This work continues to illustrate the ways the fundamental elements and principals of architectural design manifest themselves over the course of human history. These historical models span time and cross cultural boundaries. While the juxtaposition of styles may appear to be abrupt at times, the diverse range of examples is deliberate. The collage is intended to persuade the reader to look for likenesses among seemingly unlike constructions and bring into sharper focus the critical distinctions that reflect the time and place of their making. Readers are encouraged to take note of additional examples encountered or recalled within the context of their individual experiences. As the design elements and principles become more familiar, new connections, relationships, and levels of meaning may be established.

The illustrated examples are neither exhaustive nor necessarily the prototypes for the concepts and principles discussed. Their selection merely serves to illuminate and clarify the formal and spatial ideas being explored. These seminal ideas transcend their historical context and encourage speculation: How might they be analyzed, perceived, and experienced? How might they be transformed into coherent, useful, and meaningful structures of space and enclosure? How might they be reapplied to a range of architectural problems? This manner of presentation attempts to promote a more evocative understanding of the architecture one experiences, the architecture one encounters in literature, and the architecture one imagines while designing.

# ACKNOWLEDGMENTS

I am indebted to the following people for their valuable contributions to the original edition of this work: Forrest Wilson, whose insights into the communication of design principles helped clarify the organization of the material, and whose support made its publication possible; James Tice, whose knowledge and understanding of architectural history and theory strengthened the development of this study; Norman Crowe, whose diligence and skill in the teaching of architecture encouraged me to pursue this work; Roger Sherwood, whose research into the organizational principles of form fostered the development of the chapter on ordering principles; Daniel Friedman, for his enthusiasm and careful editing of the final copy; Diane Turner and Philip Hamp, for their assistance in researching material for the illustrations; and to the editorial and production staff at Van Nostrand Reinhold, for their exceptional support and service during the making of this book.

For this second edition, I want to express my appreciation to the many students and their teachers who have used this book over the years and offered suggestions for its improvement as a reference and tool for study and teaching. I want to especially thank the following educators for their careful and thoughtful critique of the first edition: L. Rudolph Barton, Laurence A. Clement, Jr., Kevin Forseth, Simon Herbert, Jan Jennings, Marjorie Kriebel, Thomas E. Steinfeld, Cheryl Wagner, James M. Wehler, and Robert L. Wright. While I have attempted to incorporate much of their wise counsel for enhancing this second edition, I remain solely responsible for any of its deficiencies.

*To Debra, Emily, and Andrew, for their love of life,*
*which ultimately it is the role of architecture to house.*

Architecture is generally conceived—designed—and realized—built—in response to an existing set of conditions. These conditions may be purely functional in nature, or they may also reflect in varying degrees the social, political, and economic climate. In any case, it is assumed that the existing set of conditions—the problem—is less than satisfactory and that a new set of conditions—a solution—would be desirable. The act of creating architecture, then, is a problem-solving or design process.

The initial phase of any design process is the recognition of a problematic condition and the decision to find a solution to it. Design is above all a willful act, a purposeful endeavor. A designer must first document the existing conditions of a problem, define its context, and collect relevant data to be assimilated and analyzed. This is the critical phase of the design process since the nature of a solution is inexorably related to how a problem is perceived, defined, and articulated. Piet Hein, the noted Danish poet and scientist, puts it this way: "Art is solving problems that cannot be formulated before they have been solved. The shaping of the question is part of the answer."

Designers inevitably and instinctively prefigure solutions to the problems they are confronted with, but the depth and range of their design vocabulary influence both their perception of a question and the shaping of its answer. If one's understanding of a design language is limited, then the range of possible solutions to a problem will also be limited. This book focuses, therefore, on broadening and enriching a vocabulary of design through the study of its essential elements and principles and the exploration of a wide array of solutions to architectural problems developed over the course of human history.

As an art, architecture is more than satisfying the purely functional requirements of a building program. Fundamentally, the physical manifestations of architecture accommodate human activity. However, the arrangement and ordering of forms and spaces also determine how architecture might promote endeavors, elicit responses, and communicate meaning. So while this study focuses on formal and spatial ideas, it is not intended to diminish the importance of the social, political, or economic aspects of architecture. Form and space are presented not as ends in themselves but as means to solve a problem in response to conditions of function, purpose, and context—that is, architecturally.

The analogy may be made that one must know and understand the alphabet before words can be formed and a vocabulary developed; one must understand the rules of grammar and syntax before sentences can be constructed; one must understand the principles of composition before essays, novels, and the like can be written. Once these elements are understood, one can write poignantly or with force, call for peace or incite to riot, comment on trivia or speak with insight and meaning. In a similar way, it might be appropriate to be able to recognize the basic elements of form and space and understand how they can be manipulated and organized in the development of a design concept, before addressing the more vital issue of meaning in architecture.

# INTRODUCTION

In order to place this study in proper context, the following is an overview of the basic elements, systems, and orders that constitute a work of architecture. All of these constituents can be perceived and experienced. Some may be readily apparent while others are more obscure to our intellect and senses. Some may dominate while others play a secondary role in a building's organization. Some may convey images and meaning while others serve as qualifiers or modifiers of these messages.

In all cases, however, these elements and systems should be interrelated to form an integrated whole having a unifying or coherent structure. Architectural order is created when the organization of parts makes visible their relationships to each other and the structure as a whole. When these relationships are perceived as mutually reinforcing and contributing to the singular nature of the whole, then a conceptual order exists—an order that may well be more enduring than transient perceptual visions.

## Architectural Systems

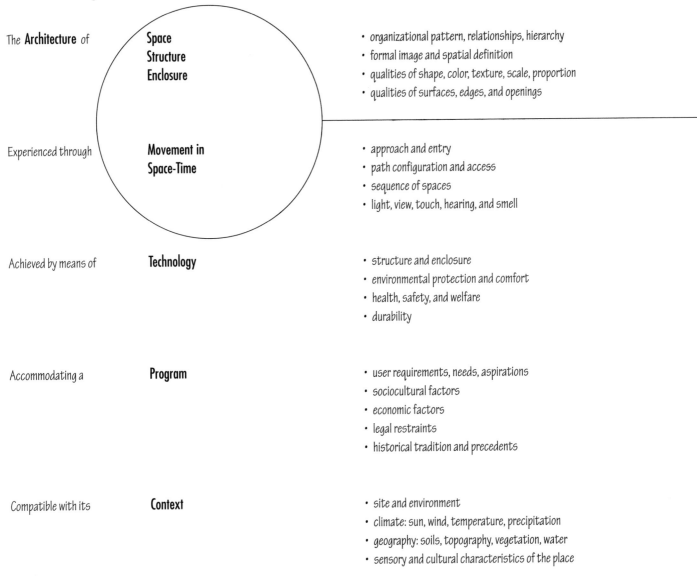

The **Architecture** of

**Space**
**Structure**
**Enclosure**

- organizational pattern, relationships, hierarchy
- formal image and spatial definition
- qualities of shape, color, texture, scale, proportion
- qualities of surfaces, edges, and openings

Experienced through

**Movement in Space-Time**

- approach and entry
- path configuration and access
- sequence of spaces
- light, view, touch, hearing, and smell

Achieved by means of

**Technology**

- structure and enclosure
- environmental protection and comfort
- health, safety, and welfare
- durability

Accommodating a

**Program**

- user requirements, needs, aspirations
- sociocultural factors
- economic factors
- legal restraints
- historical tradition and precedents

Compatible with its

**Context**

- site and environment
- climate: sun, wind, temperature, precipitation
- geography: soils, topography, vegetation, water
- sensory and cultural characteristics of the place

## ...& Orders

**Physical** — **Form and Space**
- solids and voids
- interior and exterior

Systems and organizations of
- space
- structure
- enclosure
- machines

**Perceptual** — Sensory perception and recognition of the physical elements by experiencing them sequentially in time

- approach and departure
- entry and egress
- movement through the order of spaces
- functioning of and activities within spaces
- qualities of light, color, texture, view, and sound

**Conceptual** — Comprehension of the ordered or disordered relationships among a building's elements and systems, and responding to the meanings they evoke

- images
- patterns
- signs
- symbols
- context

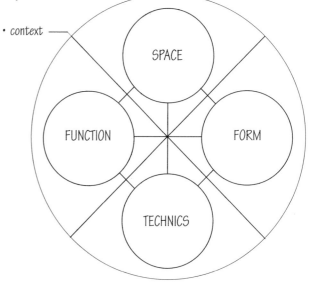

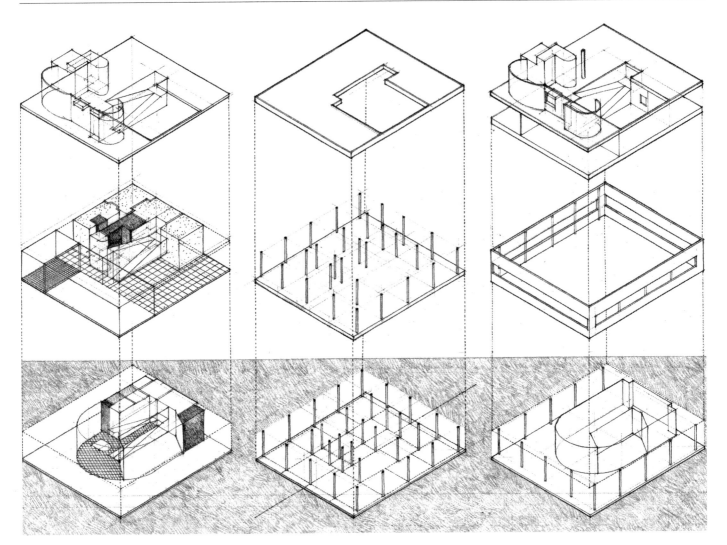

## Spatial System
- The three-dimensional integration of program elements and spaces accommodates the multiple functions and relationships of a house.

## Structural system
- A grid of columns supports horizontal beams and slabs.
- The cantilever acknowledges the direction of approach along the longitudinal axis.

## Enclosure system
- Four exterior wall planes define a rectangular volume that contains the program elements and spaces.

**Villa Savoye**, Poissy, east of Paris, 1923–31, Le Corbusier

This graphic analysis illustrates the way architecture embodies the harmonious integration of interacting and interrelated parts into a complex and unified whole.

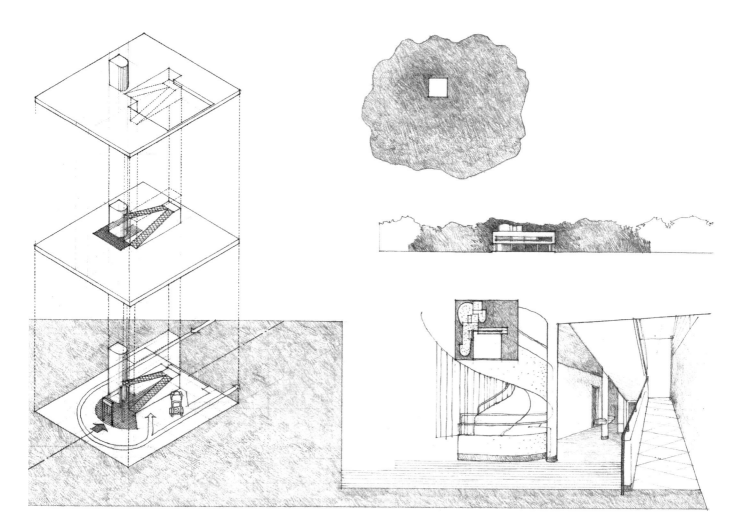

## Circulation system

- The stair and ramp penetrate and link the three levels, and heighten the viewer's perception of forms in space and light.
- The curved form of the entrance foyer reflects the movement of the automobile.

## Context

- A simple exterior form wraps around a complex interior organization of forms and spaces.
- Elevating the main floor provides a better view and avoids the humidity of the ground.
- A garden terrace distributes sunlight to the spaces gathered around it.

"Its severe, almost square exterior surrounds an intricate interior configuration glimpsed through openings and from protrusions above. . . . Its inside order accommodates the multiple functions of a house, domestic scale, and partial mystery inherent in a sense of privacy. Its outside order expresses the unity of the idea of house at an easy scale appropriate to the green field it dominated and possibly to the city it will one day be part of."
Robert Venturi, *Complexity and Contradiction in Architecture,* 1966

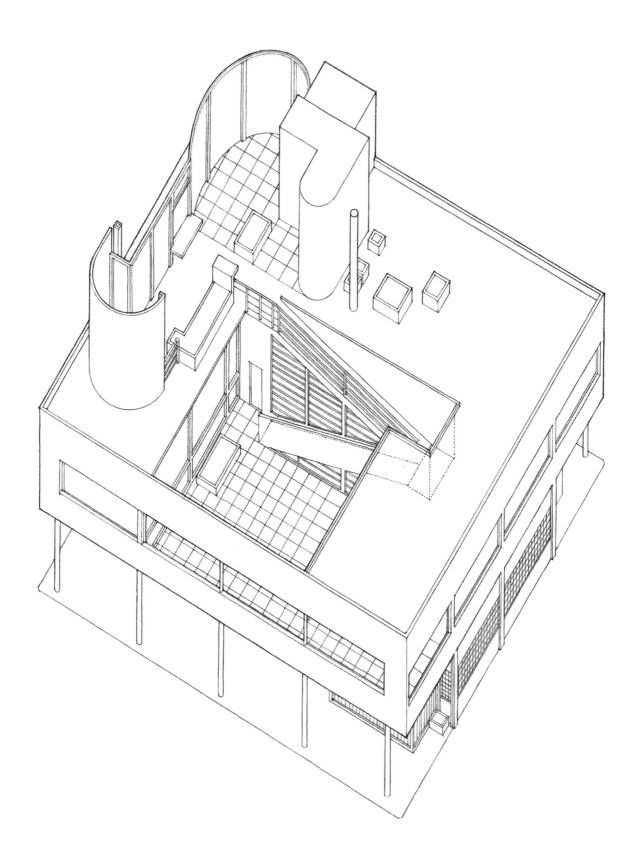

# 1
# Primary Elements

"All pictorial form begins with the point that sets itself in motion...
The point moves ... and the line comes into being—the first dimension.
If the line shifts to form a plane, we obtain a two-dimensional element.
In the movement from plane to spaces, the clash of planes gives rise to
body (three-dimensional) ... A summary of the kinetic energies
which move the point into a line, the line into a plane,
and the plane into a spatial dimension."

Paul Klee
*The Thinking Eye: The Notebooks of Paul Klee*
*(English translation)*
1961

This opening chapter presents the primary elements of form in the order of their growth from the point to a one-dimensional line, from the line to a two-dimensional plane, and from the plane to a three-dimensional volume. Each element is first considered as a conceptual element, then as a visual element in the vocabulary of architectural design.

As conceptual elements, the point, line, plane, and volume are not visible except to the mind's eye. While they do not actually exist, we nevertheless feel their presence. We can sense a point at the meeting of two lines, a line marking the contour of a plane, a plane enclosing a volume, and the volume of an object that occupies space.

When made visible to the eye on paper or in three-dimensional space, these elements become form with characteristics of substance, shape, size, color, and texture. As we experience these forms in our environment, we should be able to perceive in their structure the existence of the primary elements of point, line, plane, and volume.

As the prime generator of form, the

**Point**   indicates a position in space.   •

A point extended becomes a
**Line**   with properties of:
• length
• direction
• position

A line extended becomes a
**Plane**   with properties of:
• length and width
• shape
• surface
• orientation
• position

A plane extended becomes a
**Volume**   with properties of:
• length, width, and depth
• form and space
• surface
• orientation
• position

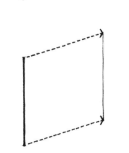

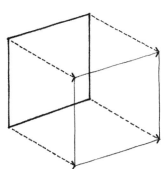

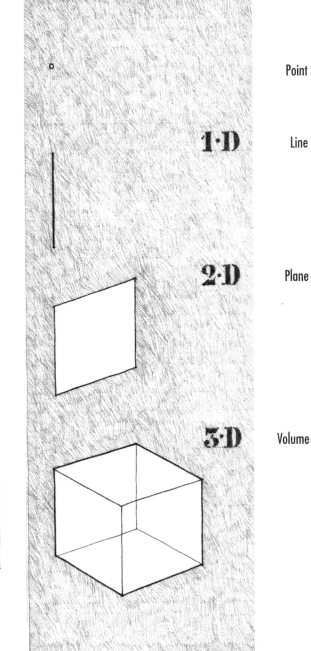

Point

**1·D**   Line

**2·D**   Plane

**3·D**   Volume

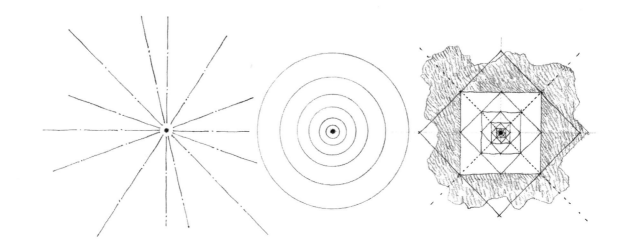

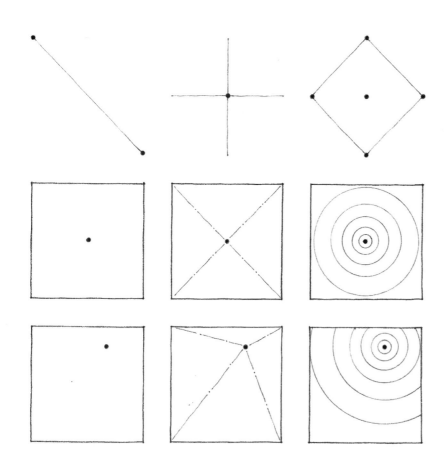

A point marks a position in space. Conceptually, it has no length, width, or depth, and is therefore static, centralized, and directionless.

As the prime element in the vocabulary of form, a point can serve to mark:

- the two ends of a line
- the intersection of two lines
- the meeting of lines at the corner of a plane or volume
- the center of a field

Although a point theoretically has neither shape nor form, it begins to make its presence felt when placed within a visual field. At the center of its environment, a point is stable and at rest, organizing surrounding elements about itself and dominating its field.

When the point is moved off-center, however, its field becomes more aggressive and begins to compete for visual supremacy. Visual tension is created between the point and its field.

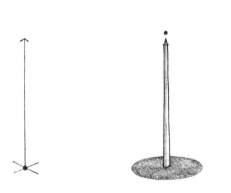

A point has no dimension. To visibly mark a position in space or on the ground plane, a point must be projected vertically into a linear form, as a column, obelisk, or tower. Any such columnar element is seen in plan as a point and therefore retains the visual characteristics of a point. Other point-generated forms that share these same visual attributes are the:

**Piazza del Campidoglio**, Rome, c. 1544, Michelangelo.
The equestrian statue of Marcus Aurelius marks the center of this urban space.

- circle

**Tholos of Polycleitos**, Epidauros, Greece, c. 350 B.C.

- cylinder

**Baptistery at Pisa**, Italy, 1153–1265, Dioti Salvi

- sphere

**Cenotaph for Sir Isaac Newton**, Project, 1784, Étienne-Louis Boulé

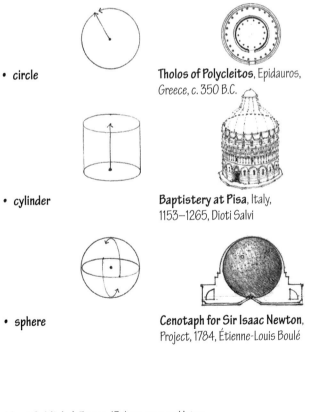

**Mont S. Michel**, France, 13th century and later.
The pyramidal composition culminates in a spire that serves to establish this fortified monastery as a specific place in the landscape.

Two points describe a line that connects them. Although the points give this line finite length, the line can also be considered a segment of an infinitely longer path.

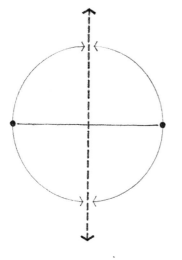

Two points further suggest an axis perpendicular to the line they describe and about which they are symmetrical. Because this axis may be infinite in length, it can be at times more dominant than the described line.

In both cases, however, the described line and the perpendicular axis are optically more dominant than the infinite number of lines that may pass through each of the individual points.

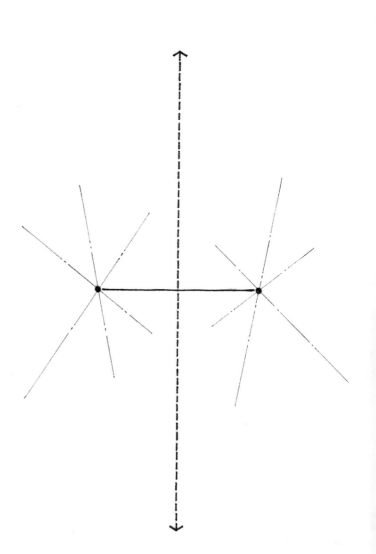

Two points established in space by columnar elements or centralized forms can define an axis, an ordering device used throughout history to organize building forms and spaces.

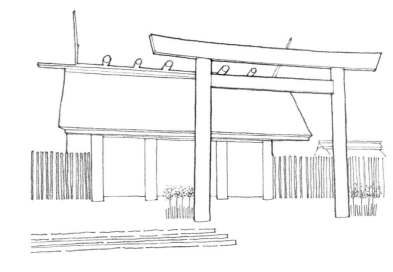

**Torii, Ise Shrine**, Mie Prefecture, Japan, A.D. 690

In plan, two points can denote a gateway signifying passage from one place to another. Extended vertically, the two points define both a plane of entry and an approach perpendicular to it.

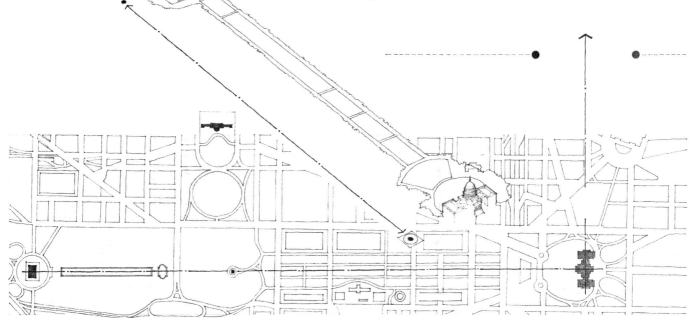

**The Mall, Washington, D.C.**, lies along the axis established by the Lincoln Memorial, the Washington Monument, and the United States Capitol building.

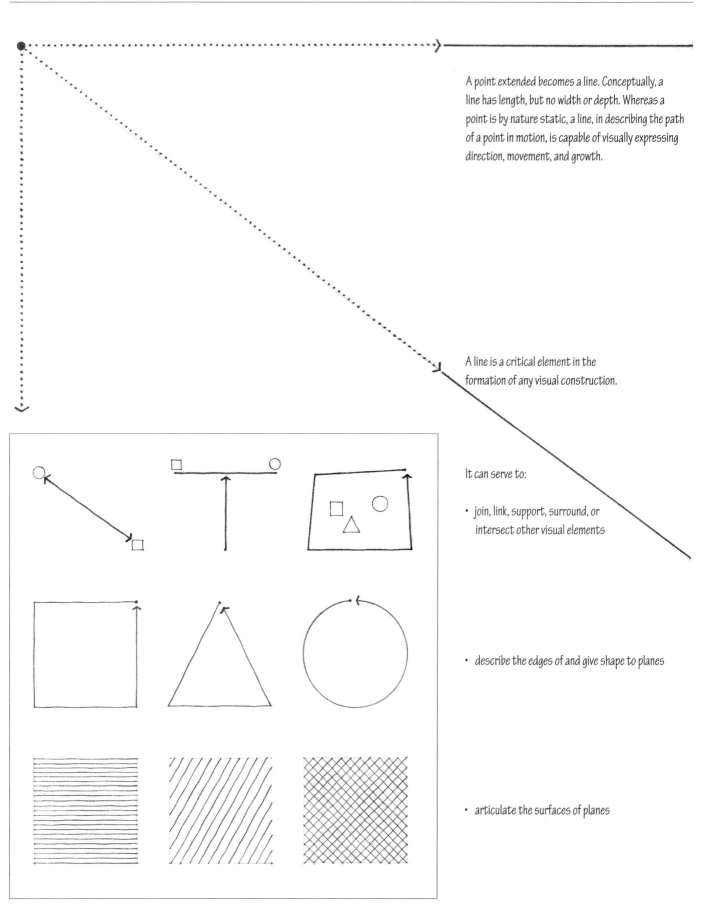

A point extended becomes a line. Conceptually, a line has length, but no width or depth. Whereas a point is by nature static, a line, in describing the path of a point in motion, is capable of visually expressing direction, movement, and growth.

A line is a critical element in the formation of any visual construction.

It can serve to:

• join, link, support, surround, or intersect other visual elements

• describe the edges of and give shape to planes

• articulate the surfaces of planes

Although a line theoretically has only one dimension, it must have some degree of thickness to become visible. It is seen as a line simply because its length dominates its width. The character of a line, whether taut or limp, bold or tentative, graceful or ragged, is determined by our perception of its length–width ratio, its contour, and its degree of continuity.

Even the simple repetition of like or similar elements, if continuous enough, can be regarded as a line. This type of line has significant textural qualities.

abcddefgghhijklmnopqrstuvwxyz(&!?$.1234567890

The orientation of a line affects its role in a visual construction. While a vertical line can express a state of equilibrium with the force of gravity, symbolize the human condition, or mark a position in space, a horizontal line can represent stability, the ground plane, the horizon, or a body at rest.

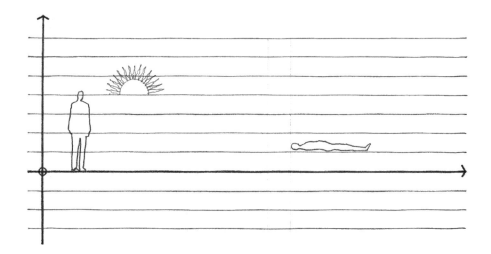

An oblique line is a deviation from the vertical or horizontal. It `may be seen as a vertical line falling or a horizontal line rising. In either case, whether it is falling toward a point on the ground plane or rising to a place in the sky, it is dynamic and visually active in its unbalanced state.

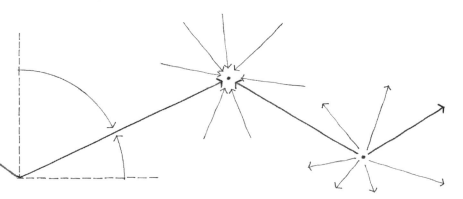

# LINEAR ELEMENTS

Vertical linear elements, such as columns, obelisks, and towers, have been used throughout history to commemorate significant events and establish particular points in space.

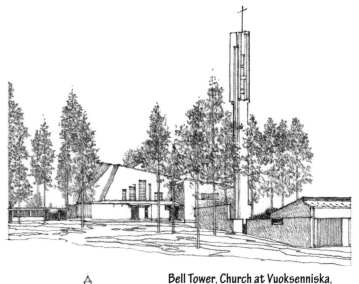

**Bell Tower**, Church at Vuoksenniska, Finland, 1956, Alvar Aalto

**Menhir,**
a prehistoric monument consisting of an upright megalith, usually standing alone but sometimes aligned with others.

**Column of Marcus Aurelius,**
Piazza Colonna, Rome, A.D. 174. This cylindrical shaft commemorates the emperor's victory over Germanic tribes north of the Danube.

**Obelisk,**
Place de la Concorde, Paris

Vertical linear elements can also define a transparent volume of space. In the example illustrated to the left, four minaret towers outline a spatial field from which the dome of Hagia Sophia rises in splendor.

**Sultan Selin Mosque,** Builder: Sinan. Edirne, Turkey. A.D. 1569–75

Linear members that possess the necessary material strength can perform structural functions. In these three examples, linear elements:

• express movement across space
• provide support for an overhead plane
• form a three-dimensional structural frame for architectural space

**Salginatobel Bridge**, Switzerland, 1929–30, Robert Maillart. Beams and girders have the bending strength to span the space between their supports and carry transverse loads.

**Caryatid Porch**, The Erechtheion, Athens, 421–405 B.C., Mnesicles. The sculptured female figures stand as columnar supports for the entablature.

**Katsura Palace**, Kyoto, Japan, 17th century.
Linear columns and beams together form a three-dimensional framework for architectural space.

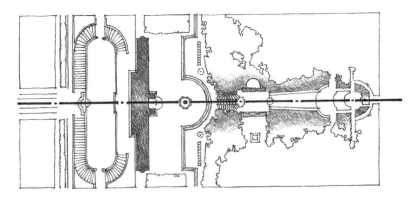

A line can be an imagined element rather than a visible one in architecture. An example is the axis, a regulating line established by two distant points in space and about which elements are symmetrically arranged.

**Villa Aldobrandini**, Italy, 1598–1603, Giacomo Della Porta

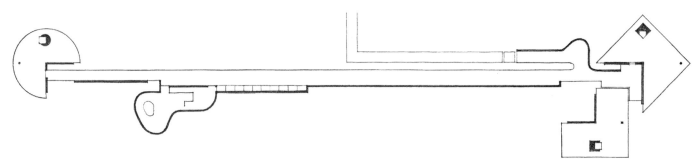

**House 10**, 1966, John Hejduk

Although architectural space exists in three dimensions, it can be linear in form to accommodate the path of movement through a building and link its spaces to one another.

Buildings also can be linear in form, particularly when they consist of repetitive spaces organized along a circulation path. As illustrated here, linear building forms have the ability to enclose exterior spaces as well as adapt to the environmental conditions of a site.

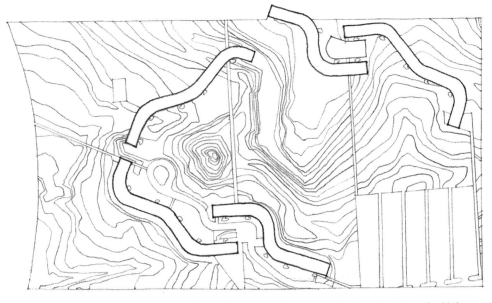

**Cornell University Undergraduate Housing**, Ithaca, New York, 1974, Richard Meier

**Town Hall, Säynätsalo**, Finland, 1950–52, Alvar Aalto

At a smaller scale, lines articulate the edges and surfaces of planes and volumes. These lines can be expressed by joints within or between building materials, by frames around window or door openings, or by a structural grid of columns and beams. How these linear elements affect the texture of a surface will depend on their visual weight, spacing, and direction.

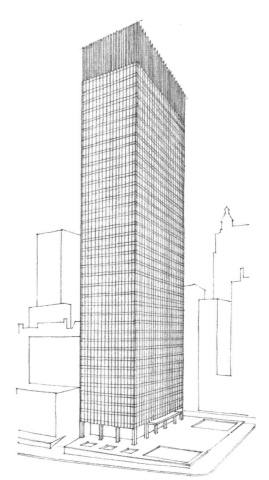

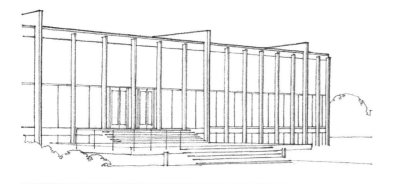

**Crown Hall**, School of Architecture and Urban Design, Illinois Institute of Technology, Chicago, 1956, Mies van der Rohe

**Seagram Building**, New York City, 1956–58, Mies van de Rohe and Philip Johnson

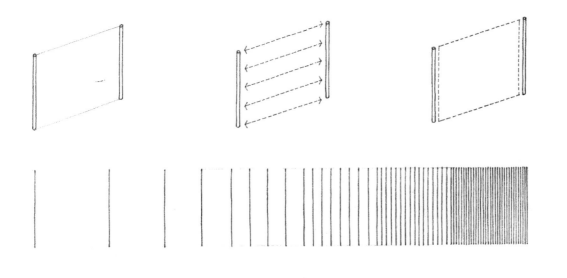

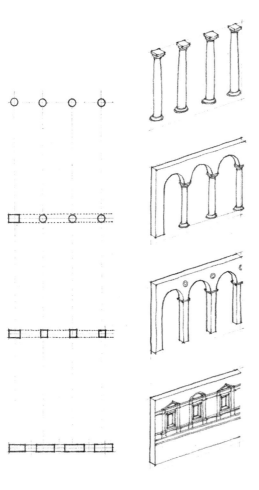

Two parallel lines have the ability to visually describe a plane. A transparent spatial membrane can be stretched between them to acknowledge their visual relationship. The closer these lines are to each other, the stronger will be the sense of plane they convey.

A series of parallel lines, through their repetitiveness, reinforces our perception of the plane they describe. As these lines extend themselves along the plane they describe, the implied plane becomes real and the original voids between the lines revert to being mere interruptions of the planar surface.

The diagrams illustrate the transformation of a row of round columns, initially supporting a portion of a wall, then evolving into square piers which are an integral part of the wall plane, and finally becoming pilasters—remnants of the original columns occurring as a relief along the surface of the wall.

"The column is a certain strengthened part of a wall, carried up perpendicular from the foundation to the top . . . A row of columns is indeed nothing but a wall, open and discontinued in several places." *Leon Battista Alberti*

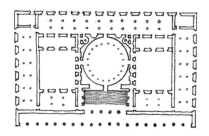

**Altes Museum**, Berlin, 1823–30, Karl Friedrich von Schinkel

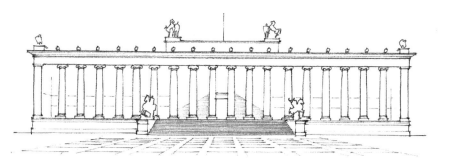

A row of columns supporting an entablature—a colonnade—is often used to define the public face or facade of a building, especially one that fronts on a major civic space. A colonnaded facade can be penetrated easily for entry, offers a degree of shelter from the elements, and forms a semi-transparent screen that unifies individual building forms behind it.

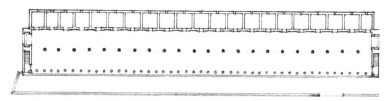

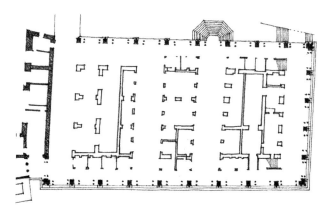

**The Basilica**, Vicenza, Italy.
Andrea Palladio designed this two-story loggia in 1545 to wrap around an existing medieval structure. This addition not only buttressed the existing structure but also acted as a screen that disguised the irregularity of the original core and presented a uniform but elegant face to the Piazza del Signori.

**Stoa of Attalus** fronting the Agora, Athens

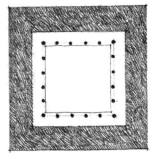

**Cloister of Moissac Abbey**, France, c. 1100

In addition to the structural role columns play in supporting an overhead floor or roof plane, they can articulate the penetrable boundaries of spatial zones which mesh easily with adjacent spaces.

These two examples illustrate how columns can define the edges of an exterior space defined within the mass of a building as well as articulate the edges of a building mass in space.

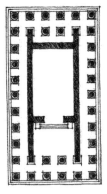

**Temple of Athena Polias**, Priene, c. 334 B.C., Pythius

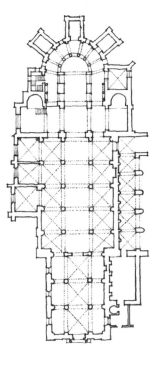

**St. Philibert**, Tournus, France, 950–1120. This view of the nave shows how rows of columns can provide a rhythmic measure of space.

**Cary House**, Mill Valley, California, 1963, Joseph Esherick

**Trellised Courtyard**, Georgia O'Keefe Residence, Abiquiu, northwest of Sante Fe, New Mexico

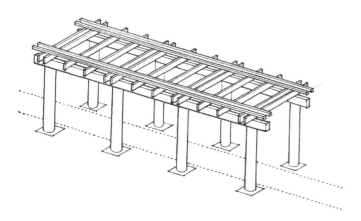

The linear members of trellises and pergolas can provide a moderate degree of definition and enclosure for outdoor spaces while allowing filtered sunlight and breezes to penetrate.

Vertical and horizontal linear elements together can define a volume of space such as the solarium illustrated to the right. Note that the form of the volume is determined solely by the configuration of the linear elements.

**Solarium of Condominium Unit 1, Sea Ranch**, California, 1966, MLTW

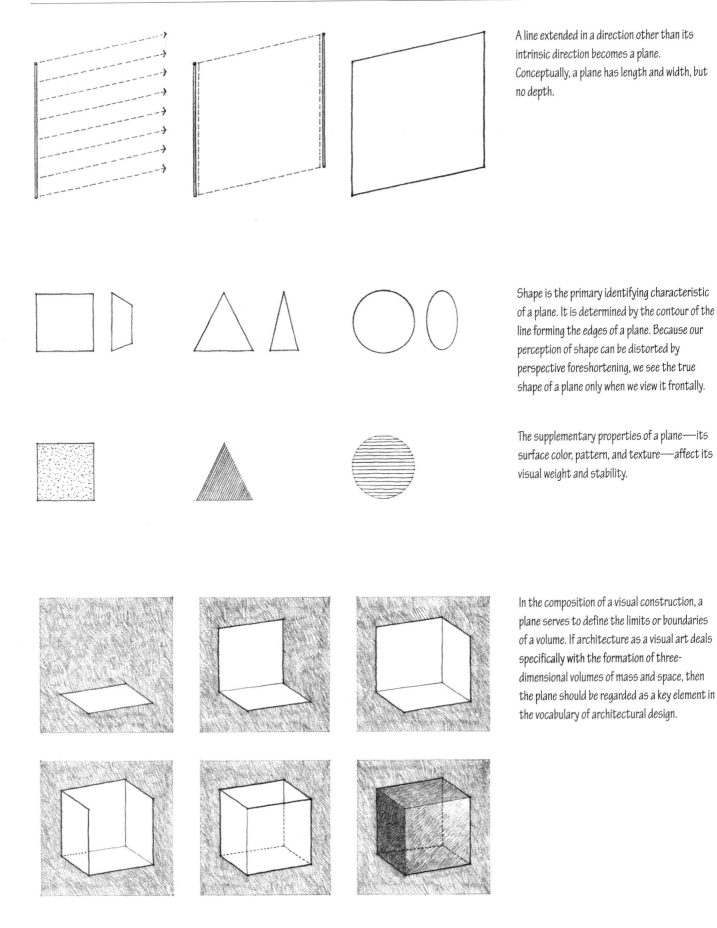

A line extended in a direction other than its intrinsic direction becomes a plane. Conceptually, a plane has length and width, but no depth.

Shape is the primary identifying characteristic of a plane. It is determined by the contour of the line forming the edges of a plane. Because our perception of shape can be distorted by perspective foreshortening, we see the true shape of a plane only when we view it frontally.

The supplementary properties of a plane—its surface color, pattern, and texture—affect its visual weight and stability.

In the composition of a visual construction, a plane serves to define the limits or boundaries of a volume. If architecture as a visual art deals specifically with the formation of three-dimensional volumes of mass and space, then the plane should be regarded as a key element in the vocabulary of architectural design.

Planes in architecture define three-dimensional volumes of mass and space. The properties of each plane—size, shape, color, texture —as well as their spatial relationship to one another ultimately determine the visual attributes of the form they define and the qualities of the space they enclose.

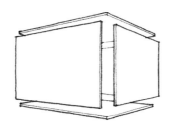

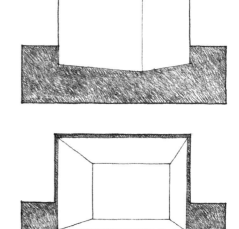

In architectural design, we manipulate three generic types of planes:

## Overhead Plane

The overhead plane can be either the roof plane that shelters the interior spaces of a building from the climatic elements, or the ceiling plane that forms the upper enclosing surface of a room.

## Wall Plane

The wall plane, because of its vertical orientation, is active in our normal field of vision and vital to the shaping and enclosure of architectural space.

## Base Plane

The base plane can be either the ground plane that serves as the physical foundation and visual base for building forms, or the floor plane that forms the lower enclosing surface of a room upon which we walk.

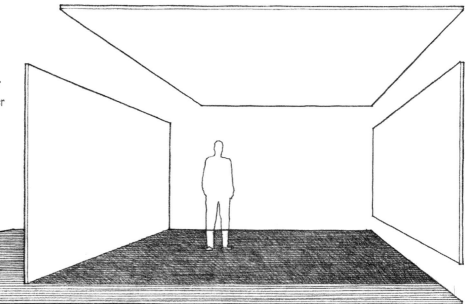

The ground plane ultimately supports all architectural construction. Along with climate and other environmental conditions of a site, the topographical character of the ground plane influences the form of the building that rises from it. The building can merge with the ground plane, rest firmly on it, or be elevated above it.

The ground plane itself can be manipulated as well to establish a podium for a building form. It can be elevated to honor a sacred or significant place; bermed to define outdoor spaces or buffer against undesirable conditions; carved or terraced to provide a suitable platform on which to build; or stepped to allow changes in elevation to be easily traversed.

**Scala de Spagna (Spanish Steps)**, Rome, 1721–25.
Alessandro Specchi designed this civic project to connect the Piazza di Spagna with SS. Trinita de' Monti; completed by Francesco de Sanctis.

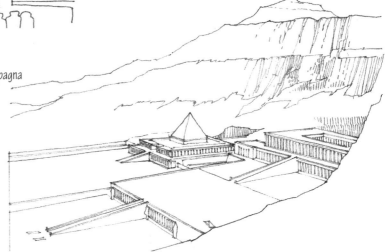

**Mortuary Temple of Queen Hatshepsut**,
Dêr el-Bahari, Thebes,1511–1480 B.C., Senmut.
Three terraces approached by ramps rise toward the base of the cliffs where the chief sanctuary is cut deep into the rock.

**Machu Picchu**, an ancient Incan city established c.1500 in the Andes Mountains on a saddle between two peaks, 8000 ft. above the Urubamba River in south-central Peru.

**Sitting Area, Lawrence House,**
Sea Ranch, California, 1966,
MLTW/Moore-Turnbull

The floor plane is the horizontal element that sustains the force of gravity as we move around and place objects for our use on it. It may be a durable covering of the ground plane or a more artificial, elevated plane spanning the space between its supports. In either case, the texture and density of the flooring material influences both the acoustical quality of a space and how we feel as we walk across its surface.

While the pragmatic, supportive nature of the floor plane limits the extent to which it can be manipulated, it is nonetheless an important element of architectural design. Its shape, color, and pattern determine to what degree it defines spatial boundaries or serves as a unifying element for the different parts of a space.

Like the ground plane, the form of a floor plane can be stepped or terraced to break the scale of a space down to human dimensions and create platforms for sitting, viewing, or performing. It can be elevated to define a sacred or honorific place. It can be rendered as a neutral ground against which other elements in a space are seen as figures.

**Emperor's Seat, Imperial Palace, Kyoto,** Japan, 17th century

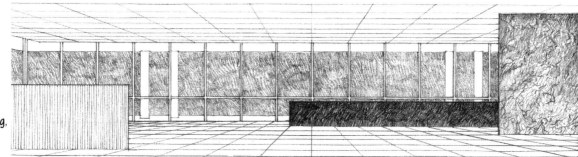

**Bacardi Office Building,**
Santiago de Cuba, 1958,
Mies van der Rohe

**S. Maria Novella**, Florence, 1456–70.
The Renaissance facade by Alberti presents a public face to a square.

Exterior wall planes isolate a portion of space to create a controlled interior environment. Their construction provides both privacy and protection from the climatic elements for the interior spaces of a building, while openings within or between their boundaries reestablish a connection with the exterior environment. As exterior walls mold interior space, they simultaneously shape exterior space and describe the form, massing, and image of a building in space.

As a design element, the plane of an exterior wall can be articulated as the front or primary facade of a building. In urban situations, these facades serve as walls that define courtyards, streets, and such public gathering places as squares and marketplaces.

**Uffizi Palace**, 1560–65, Giorgio Vasari.
This Florentine street defined by the two wings of the Uffizi Palace links the Piazza della Signoria with the River Arno.

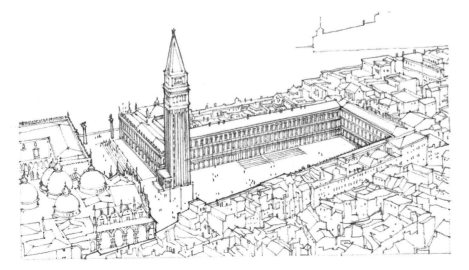

**Piazza of San Marco**, Venice.
The continuous facades of buildings form the "walls" of the urban space.

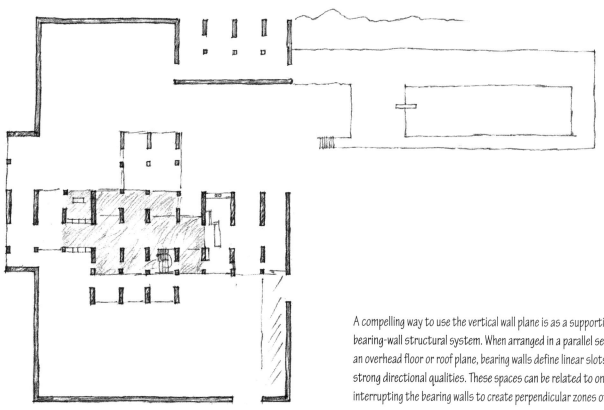

**Peyrissac Residence**, Cherchell, North Africa, 1942, Le Corbusier

A compelling way to use the vertical wall plane is as a supporting element in the bearing-wall structural system. When arranged in a parallel series to support an overhead floor or roof plane, bearing walls define linear slots of space with strong directional qualities. These spaces can be related to one another only by interrupting the bearing walls to create perpendicular zones of space.

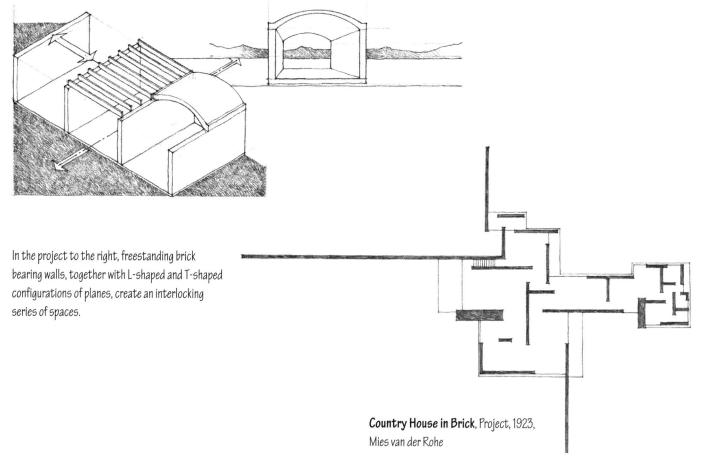

In the project to the right, freestanding brick bearing walls, together with L-shaped and T-shaped configurations of planes, create an interlocking series of spaces.

**Country House in Brick**, Project, 1923, Mies van der Rohe

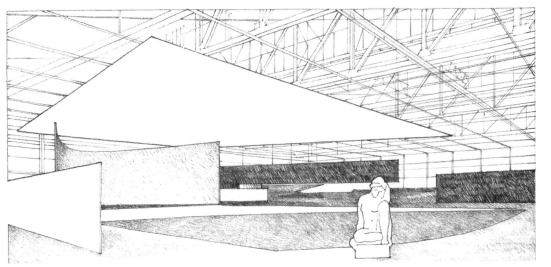

**Concert Hall**, Project, 1942, Mies van der Rohe

Interior wall planes govern the size and shape of the internal spaces or rooms within a building. Their visual properties, their relationship to one another, and the size and distribution of openings within their boundaries determine both the quality of the spaces they define and the degree to which adjoining spaces relate to one another.

As a design element, a wall plane can merge with the floor or ceiling plane, or be articulated as an element isolated from adjacent planes. It can be treated as a passive or receding backdrop for other elements in the space, or it can assert itself as a visually active element within a room by virtue of its form, color, texture, or material.

While walls provide privacy for interior spaces and serve as barriers that limit our movement, doorways and windows reestablish continuity with neighboring spaces and allow the passage of light, heat, and sound. As they increase in size, these openings begin to erode the natural sense of enclosure walls provide. Views seen through the openings become part of the spatial experience.

**Finnish Pavilion**, New York World's Fair, 1939, Alvar Aalto

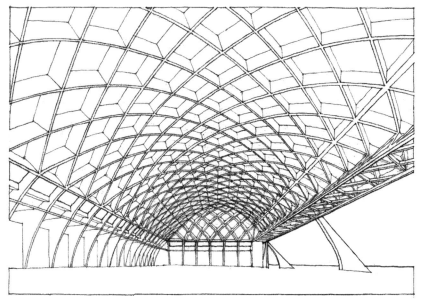

**Hangar**, **Design I**, 1935, Pier Luigi Nervi.
The lamella structure expresses the way forces are resolved and channeled down to the roof supports.

**Brick House**, New Canaan, Connecticut, 1949, Philip Johnson. The detached vaulted ceiling plane appears to float above the bed.

While we walk on a floor and have physical contact with walls, the ceiling plane is usually out of our reach and is almost always a purely visual event in a space. It may be the underside of an overhead floor or roof plane and express the form of its structure as it spans the space between its supports, or it may be suspended as the upper enclosing surface of a room or hall.

As a detached lining, the ceiling plane can symbolize the sky vault or be the primary sheltering element that unifies the different parts of a space. It can serve as a repository for frescoes and other means of artistic expression or be treated simply as a passive or receding surface. It can be raised or lowered to alter the scale of a space or to define spatial zones within a room. Its form can be manipulated to control the quality of light or sound within a space.

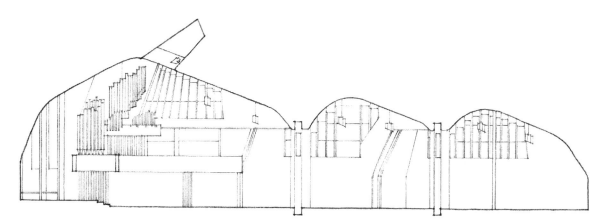

**Church at Vuoksenniska**, Finland, 1956, Alvar Aalto.
The form of the ceiling plane defines a progression of spaces and enhances their acoustical quality.

The roof plane is the essential sheltering element that protects the interior of a building from the climatic elements. The form and geometry of its structure is established by the manner in which it spans across space to bear on its supports and slopes to shed rain and melting snow. As a design element, the roof plane is significant because of the impact it can have on the form and silhouette of a building within its setting.

**Dolmen**, a prehistoric monument consisting of two or more large upright stones supporting a horizontal stone slab, found especially in Britain and France and usually regarded as a burial place for an important person.

The roof plane can be hidden from view by the exterior walls of a building or merge with the walls to emphasize the volume of the building mass. It can be expressed as a single sheltering form that encompasses a variety of spaces beneath its canopy, or comprise a number of hats that articulate a series of spaces within a single building.

A roof plane can extend outward to form overhangs that shield door and window openings from sun or rain, or continue downward further still to relate itself more closely to the ground plane. In warm climates, it can be elevated to allow cooling breezes to flow across and through the interior spaces of a building.

**Robie House**, Chicago, 1909, Frank Lloyd Wright.
The low sloping roof planes and broad overhangs are characteristic of the Prairie School of Architecture.

**Shodhan House**, Ahmedabad, India, 1956, Le Corbusier.
A grid of columns elevates the reinforced concrete roof slab above the main volume of the house.

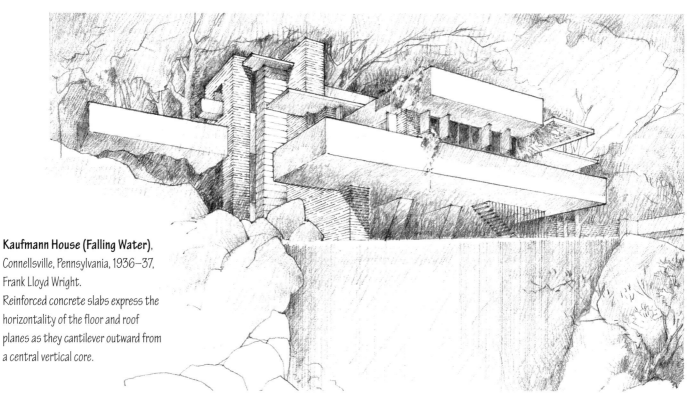

**Kaufmann House (Falling Water)**,
Connellsville, Pennsylvania, 1936–37,
Frank Lloyd Wright.
Reinforced concrete slabs express the
horizontality of the floor and roof
planes as they cantilever outward from
a central vertical core.

The overall form of a building can be endowed with a distinctly planar
quality by carefully introducing openings which expose the edges of
vertical and horizontal planes. These planes can be further differentiated
and accentuated by changes in color, texture, or material.

**Schröder House**, Utrecht, 1924–25, Gerrit Thomas Rietveld.
Asymmetrical compositions of simple rectangular forms and primary
colors characterized the de Stijl school of art and architecture.

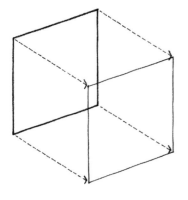

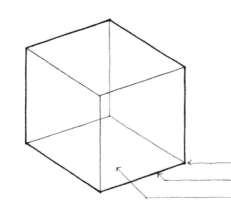

A plane extended in a direction other than its intrinsic direction becomes a volume. Conceptually, a volume has three dimensions: length, width, and depth.

All volumes can be analyzed and understood to consist of:

- points or vertices where several planes come together
- lines or edges where two planes meet
- planes or surfaces which define the limits or boundaries of a volume

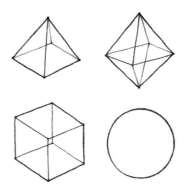

Form is the primary identifying characteristic of a volume. It is established by the shapes and interrelationships of the planes that describe the boundaries of the volume.

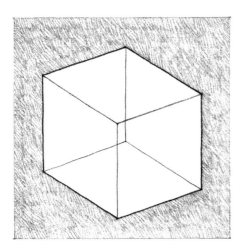

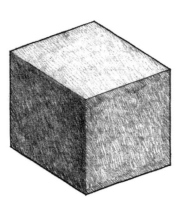

As the three-dimensional element in the vocabulary of architectural design, a volume can be either a solid—space displaced by mass—or a void—space contained or enclosed by planes.

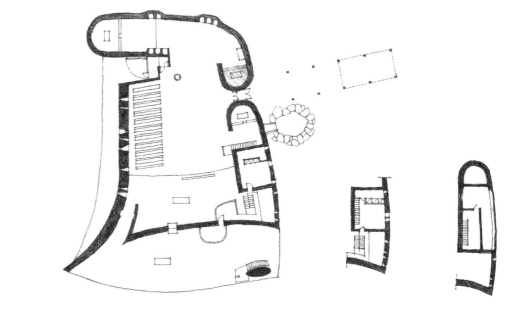

### Plan and Section
Space defined by wall, floor, and ceiling or roof planes

In architecture, a volume can be seen to be either a portion of space contained and defined by wall, floor, and ceiling or roof planes, or a quantity of space displaced by the mass of a building. It is important to perceive this duality, especially when reading orthographic plans, elevations, and sections.

### Elevation
Space displaced by
the mass of a building

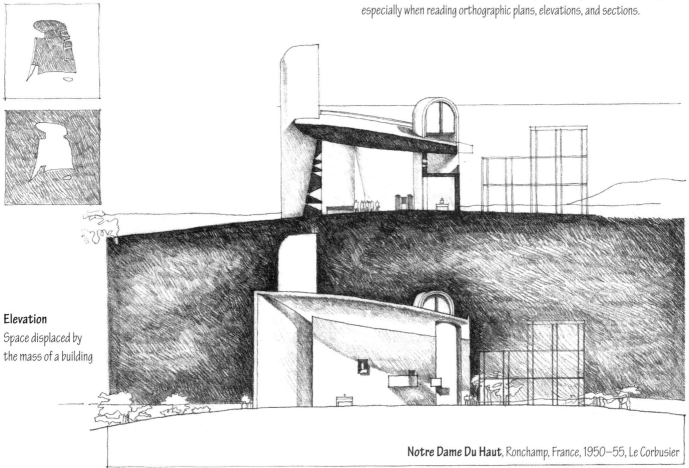

**Notre Dame Du Haut**, Ronchamp, France, 1950–55, Le Corbusier

# VOLUMETRIC ELEMENTS

Building forms that stand as objects in the landscape
can be read as occupying volumes in space.

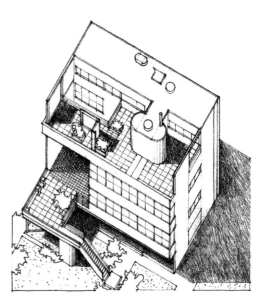

**Doric Temple at Segesta**, Sicily, c. 424–416 B.C.

**Villa Garches**, Vaucresson, France, 1926–27, Le Corbusier

**Barn in Ontario**, Canada

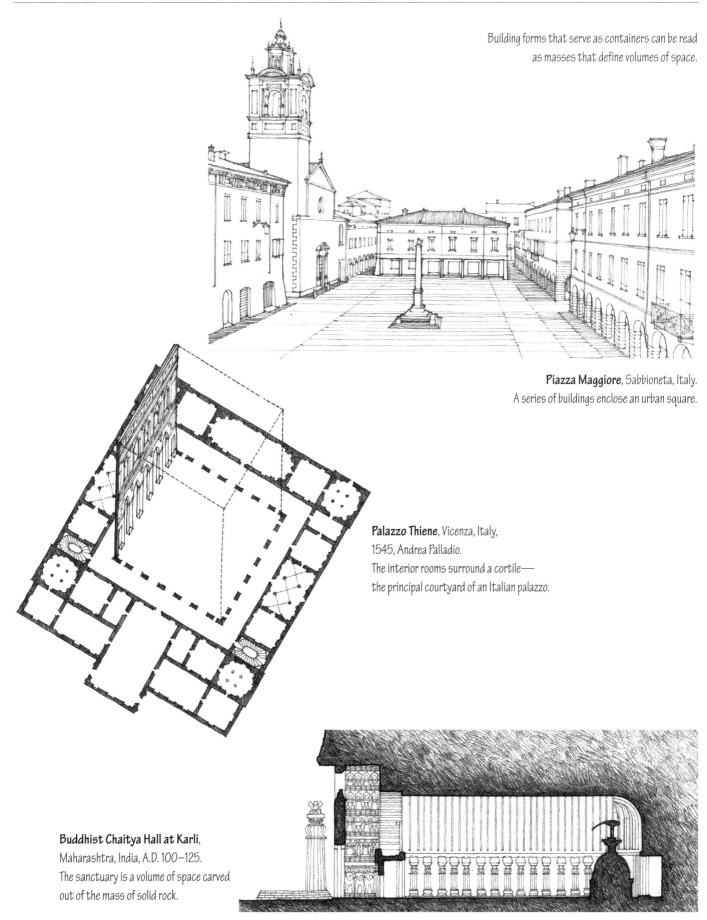

Building forms that serve as containers can be read as masses that define volumes of space.

**Piazza Maggiore**, Sabbioneta, Italy.
A series of buildings enclose an urban square.

**Palazzo Thiene**, Vicenza, Italy,
1545, Andrea Palladio.
The interior rooms surround a cortile—
the principal courtyard of an Italian palazzo.

**Buddhist Chaitya Hall at Karli**,
Maharashtra, India, A.D. 100–125.
The sanctuary is a volume of space carved
out of the mass of solid rock.

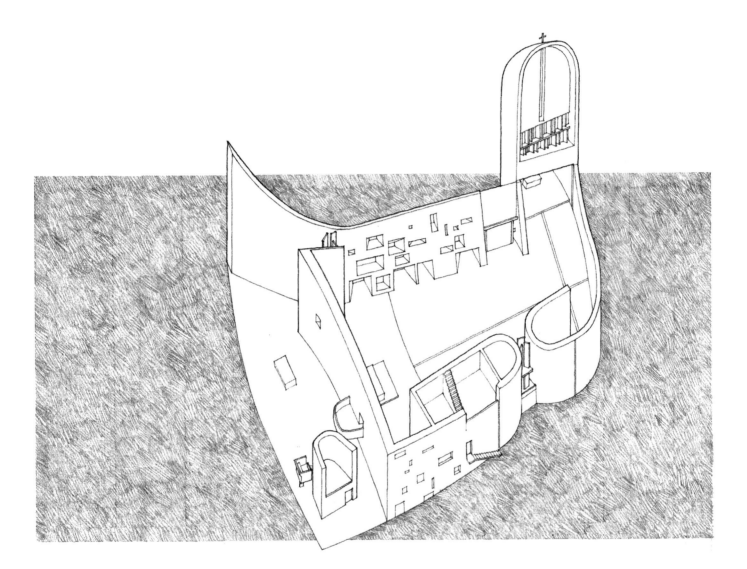

# 2
# Form

"Architectural form is the point of contact between mass and space . . . Architectural forms, textures, materials, modulation of light and shade, color, all combine to inject a quality or spirit that articulates space. The quality of the architecture will be determined by the skill of the designer in using and relating these elements, both in the interior spaces and in the spaces around buildings."

Edmund N. Bacon
*The Design of Cities*
1974

Form is an inclusive term that has several meanings. It may refer to an external appearance that can be recognized, as that of a chair or the human body that sits in it. It may also allude to a particular condition in which something acts or manifests itself, as when we speak of water in the form of ice or steam. In art and design, we often use the term to denote the formal structure of a work—the manner of arranging and coordinating the elements and parts of a composition so as as to produce a coherent image.

In the context of this study, form suggests reference to both internal structure and external outline and the principle that gives unity to the whole. While form often includes a sense of three-dimensional mass or volume, shape refers more specifically to the essential aspect of form that governs its appearance—the configuration or relative disposition of the lines or contours that delimit a figure or form.

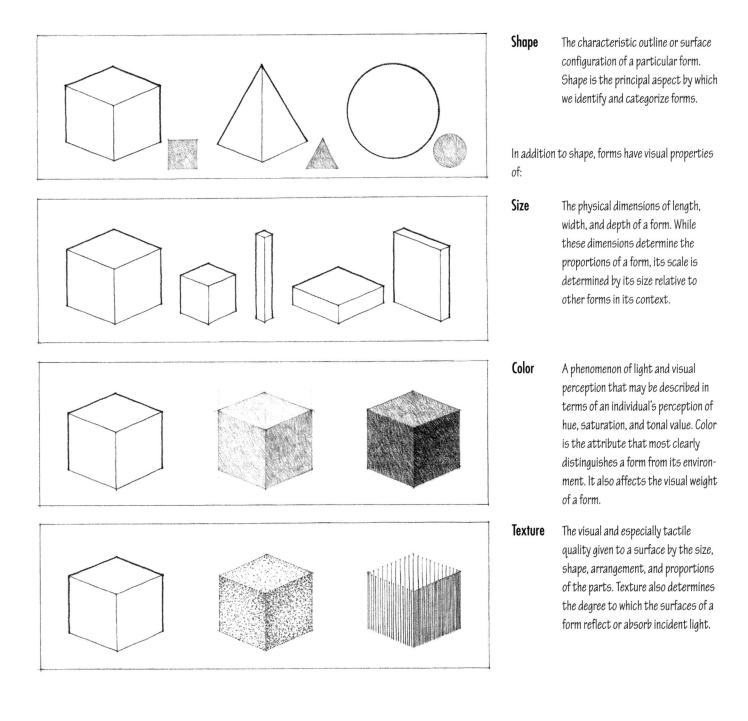

**Shape**   The characteristic outline or surface configuration of a particular form. Shape is the principal aspect by which we identify and categorize forms.

In addition to shape, forms have visual properties of:

**Size**   The physical dimensions of length, width, and depth of a form. While these dimensions determine the proportions of a form, its scale is determined by its size relative to other forms in its context.

**Color**   A phenomenon of light and visual perception that may be described in terms of an individual's perception of hue, saturation, and tonal value. Color is the attribute that most clearly distinguishes a form from its environment. It also affects the visual weight of a form.

**Texture**   The visual and especially tactile quality given to a surface by the size, shape, arrangement, and proportions of the parts. Texture also determines the degree to which the surfaces of a form reflect or absorb incident light.

Forms also have relational properties which govern the pattern and composition of elements:

**Position**  The location of a form relative to its environment or the visual field within which it is seen.

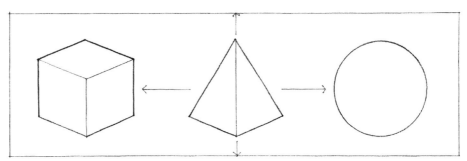

**Orientation**  The direction of a form relative to the ground plane, the compass points, other forms, or to the person viewing the form.

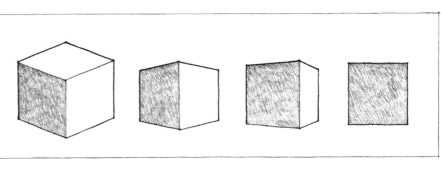

**Visual Inertia**  The degree of concentration and stability of a form. The visual inertia of a form depends on its geometry as well as its orientation relative to the ground plane, the pull of gravity, and our line of sight.

All of these properties of form are in reality affected by the conditions under which we view them.

- A changing perspective or angle of view presents different shapes or aspects of a form to our eyes.
- Our distance from a form determines its apparent size.
- The lighting conditions under which we view a form affects the clarity of its shape and structure.
- The visual field surrounding a form influences our ability to read and identify it.

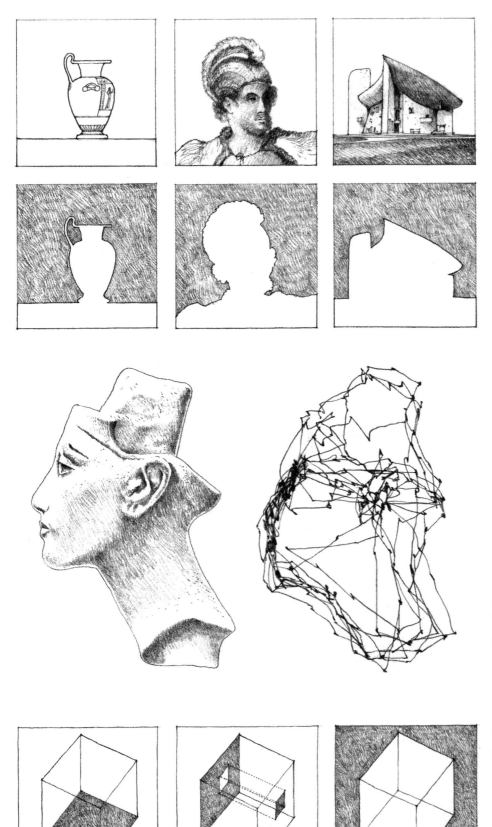

Shape refers to the characteristic outline of a plane figure or the surface configuration of a volumetric form. It is the primary means by which we recognize, identify, and categorize particular figures and forms. Our perception of shape depends on the degree of visual contrast that exists along the contour separating a figure from its ground or between a form and its field.

**Bust of Queen Nefertiti**
The pattern of eye movement of a person viewing the figure, from research by Alfred L. Yarbus of the Institute for Problems of Information Transmission in Moscow.

In architecture, we are concerned with the shapes of:

- floor, wall, and ceiling planes that enclose space
- door and window openings within a spatial enclosure
- silhouettes and contours of building forms

These examples illustrate how shaping the juncture between mass and space expresses the manner in which the contours of a building mass rise from the ground plane and meet the sky.

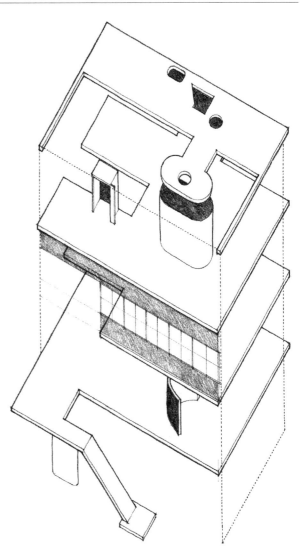

**Central Pavilion, Horyu-Ji Temple**, Nara, Japan, A.D. 607

**Villa Garches**, Vaucresson, France, 1926–27, Le Corbusier.
This architectural composition illustrates the interplay between the shapes of planar solids and voids.

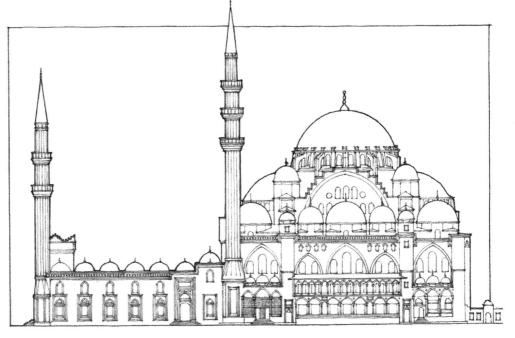

**Suleymaniye Mosque**,
Constantinople (Istanbul), 1551–58, Sinan

Gestalt psychology affirms that the mind will simplify the visual environment in order to understand it. Given any composition of forms, we tend to reduce the subject matter in our visual field to the simplest and most regular shapes. The simpler and more regular a shape is, the easier it is to perceive and understand.

From geometry we know the regular shapes to be the circle, and the infinite series of regular polygons that can be inscribed within it. Of these, the most significant are the primary shapes: the circle, the triangle, and the square.

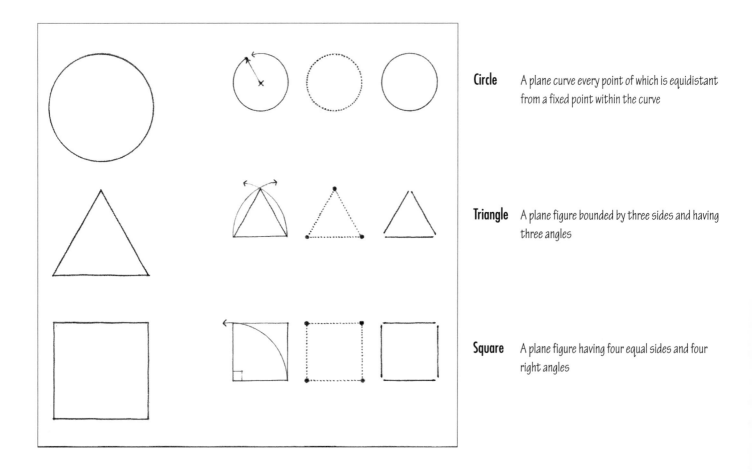

**Circle**    A plane curve every point of which is equidistant from a fixed point within the curve

**Triangle**    A plane figure bounded by three sides and having three angles

**Square**    A plane figure having four equal sides and four right angles

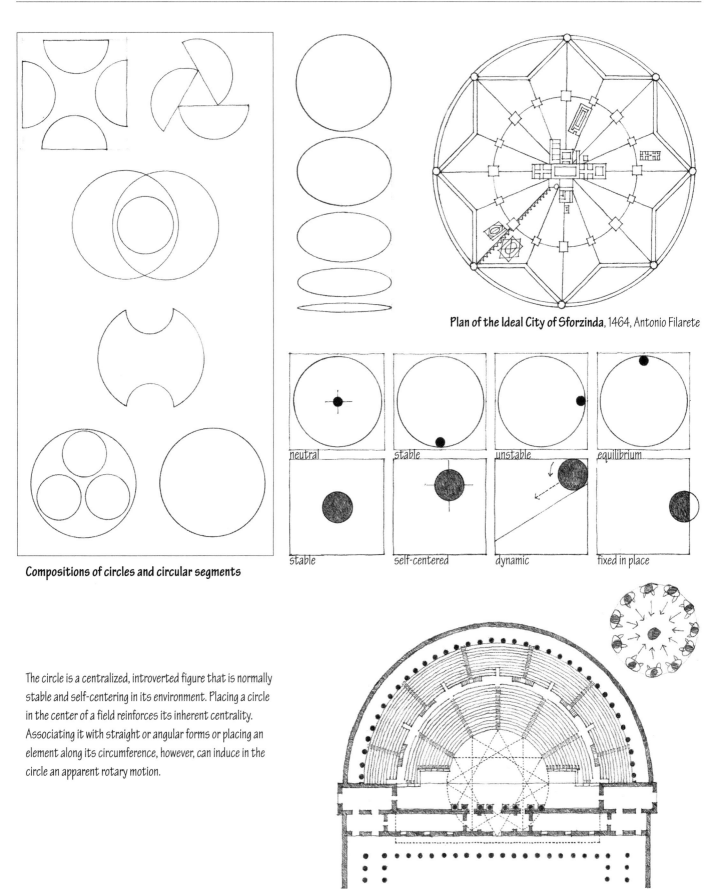

Compositions of circles and circular segments

**Plan of the Ideal City of Sforzinda**, 1464, Antonio Filarete

neutral          stable          unstable          equilibrium

stable          self-centered          dynamic          fixed in place

The circle is a centralized, introverted figure that is normally stable and self-centering in its environment. Placing a circle in the center of a field reinforces its inherent centrality. Associating it with straight or angular forms or placing an element along its circumference, however, can induce in the circle an apparent rotary motion.

**Roman Theater** according to Vitruvius

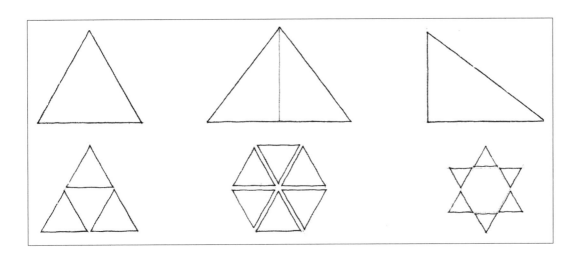

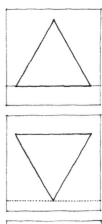

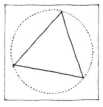

The triangle signifies stability. When resting on one of its sides, the triangle is an extremely stable figure. When tipped to stand on one of its vertices, however, it can either be balanced in a precarious state of equilibrium or be unstable and tend to fall over onto one of its sides.

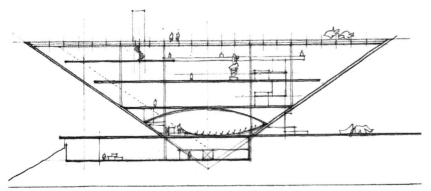

**Modern Art Museum, Caracas**, Venezuela, 1955, Oscar Niemeyer

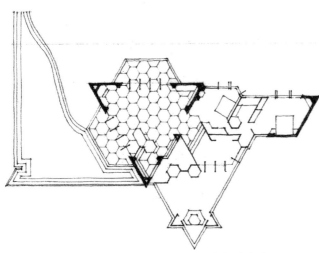

**Vigo Sundt House**, Madison, Wisconsin, 1942, Frank Lloyd Wright

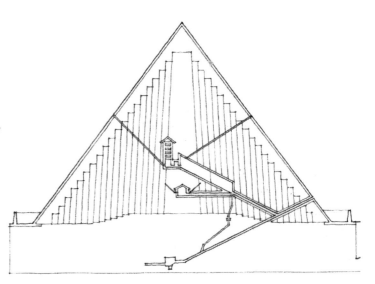

**Great Pyramid of Cheops at Giza**, Egypt, c. 2500 B.C.

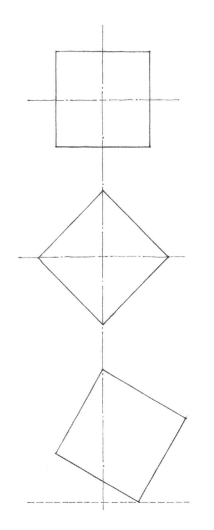

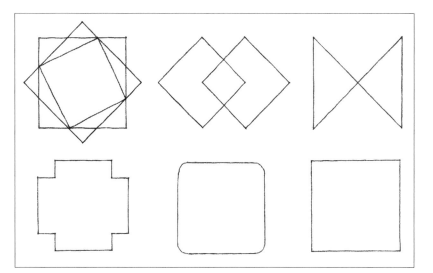

**Compositions resulting from the rotation and modification of the square**

The square represents the pure and the rational. It is a static and neutral figure having no preferred direction. All other rectangles can be considered variations of the square—deviations from the norm by the addition of height or width. Like the triangle, the square is stable when resting on one of its sides, and dynamic when standing on one its corners.

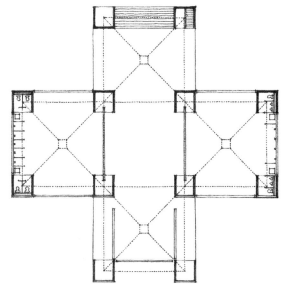

**Bathhouse, Jewish Community Center**, Trenton, New Jersey, 1954—59, Louis Kahn

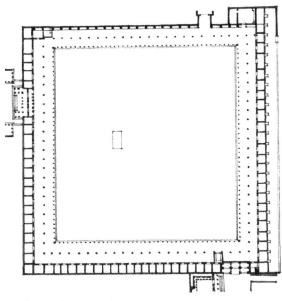

**Agora of Ephesus**, Asia Minor

"...cubes, cones, spheres, cylinders, or pyramids are the great primary forms that light reveals to advantage; the image of these is distinct and tangible within us and without ambiguity. It is for this reason that these are beautiful forms, the most beautiful forms." *Le Corbusier*

The primary shapes can be extended or rotated to generate volumetric forms or solids which are distinct, regular, and easily recognizable. Circles generate spheres and cylinders; triangles generate cones and pyramids; squares generate cubes. In this context, the term solid does not refer to firmness of substance but rather to a three-dimensional geometric body or figure.

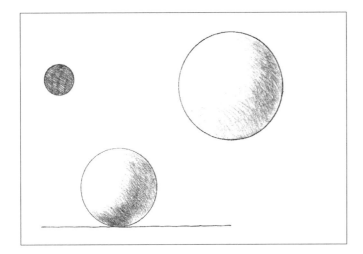

**Sphere**   A solid generated by the revolution of a semicircle about its diameter, whose surface is at all points equidistant from the center. A sphere is a centralized and highly concentrated form. Like the circle from which it is generated, it is self-centering and normally stable in its environment. It can be inclined toward a rotary motion when placed on a sloping plane. From any viewpoint, it retains its circular shape.

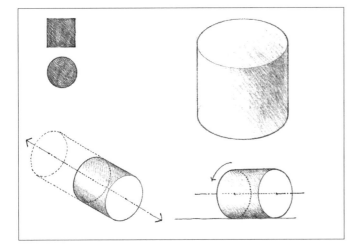

**Cylinder**   A solid generated by the revolution of a rectangle about one of its sides. A cylinder is centralized about the axis passing through the centers of its two circular faces. Along this axis, it can be easily extended. The cylinder is stable if it rests on one of its circular faces; it becomes unstable when its central axis is inclined from the vertical.

**Cone**   A solid generated by the revolution of a right triangle about one of its sides. Like the cylinder, the cone is a highly stable form when resting on its circular base, and unstable when its vertical axis is tipped or overturned. It can also rest on its apex in a precarious state of balance.

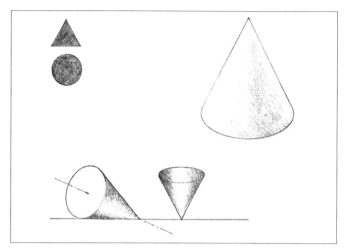

**Pyramid**   A polyhedron having a polygonal base and triangular faces meeting at a common point or vertex. The pyramid has properties similar to those of the cone. Because all of its surfaces are flat planes, however, the pyramid can rest in a stable manner on any of its faces. While the cone is a soft form, the pyramid is relatively hard and angular.

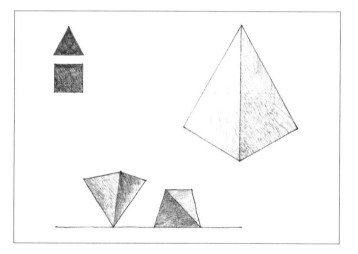

**Cube**   A prismatic solid bounded by six equal square sides, the angle between any two adjacent faces being a right angle. Because of the equality of its dimensions, the cube is a static form that lacks apparent movement or direction. It is a stable form except when it stands on one of its edges or corners. Even though its angular profile is affected by our point of view, the cube remains a highly recognizable form.

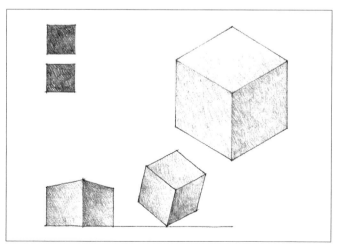

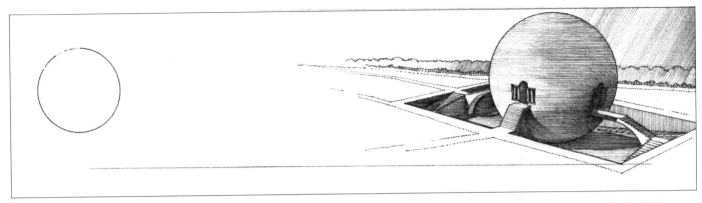

**Maupertius, Project for an Agricultural Lodge**, 1775, Claude-Nicolas Ledoux

**Chapel, Massachusetts Institute of Technology**, Cambridge, Massachusetts, 1955, Eero Saarinen and Associates

**Project for a Conical Cenotaph**, 1784, Étienne-Louis Boulée

**Pyramids of Cheops, Chephren, and Mykerinos** at Giza, Egypt, c. 2500 B.C.

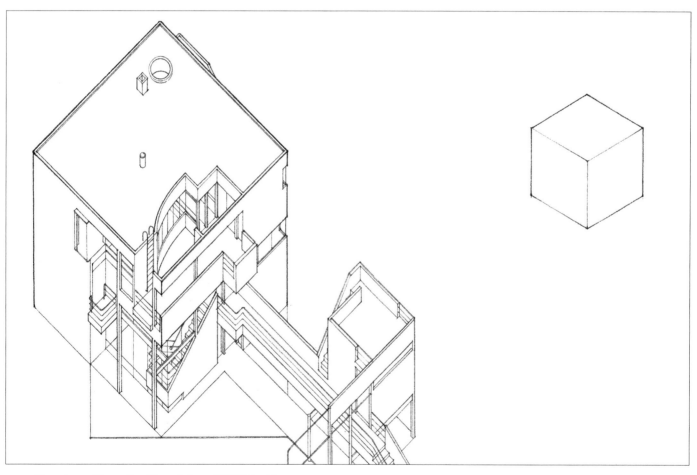

**Hanselmann House**, Fort Wayne, Indiana, 1967, Michael Graves

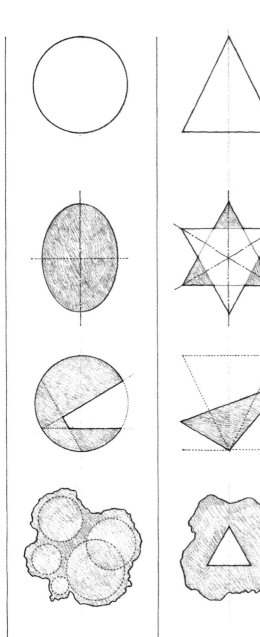

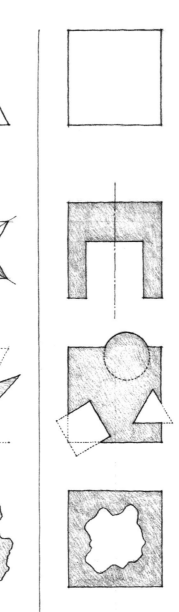

Regular forms refer to those whose parts are related to one another in a consistent and orderly manner. They are generally stable in nature and symmetrical about one or more axes. The sphere, cylinder, cone, cube, and pyramid are prime examples of regular forms.

Forms can retain their regularity even when transformed dimensionally or by the addition or subtraction of elements. From our experiences with similar forms, we can construct a mental model of the original whole even when a fragment is missing or another part is added.

Irregular forms are those whose parts are dissimilar in nature and related to one another in an inconsistent manner. They are generally asymmetrical and more dynamic than regular forms. They can be regular forms from which irregular elements have been subtracted or result from an irregular composition of regular forms.

Since we deal with both solid masses and spatial voids in architecture, regular forms can be contained within irregular forms. In a similar manner, irregular forms can be enclosed by regular forms.

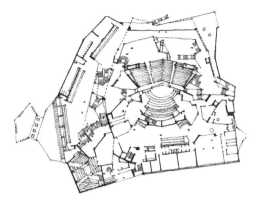

**Irregular Forms:**
Philharmonic Hall, Berlin, 1956–63, Hans Scharoun

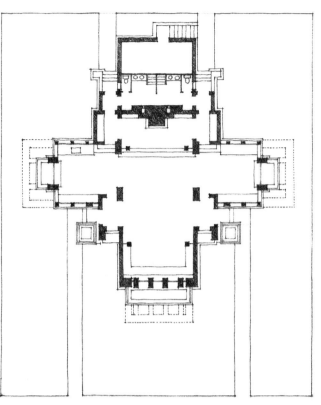

**A Regular Composition of Regular Forms:**
Coonley Playhouse, Riverside, Illinois, 1912, Frank Lloyd Wright

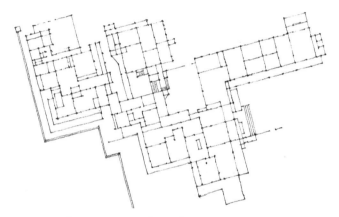

**An Irregular Composition of Regular Forms:**
Katsura Palace, Kyoto, Japan, 17th century

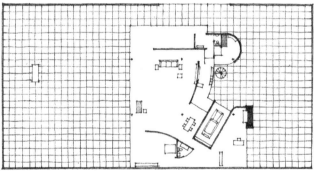

**Irregular Forms within a Regular Field:**
Courtyard House Project, 1934, Mies van de Rohe

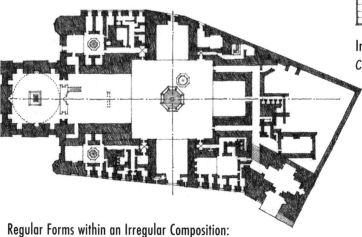

**Regular Forms within an Irregular Composition:**
Mosque of Sultan Hasan, Cairo, Egypt, 1356–63

All other forms can be understood to be transformations of the primary solids, variations which are generated by the manipulation of one or more dimensions or by the addition or subtraction of elements.

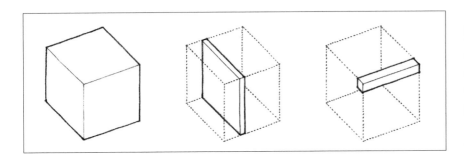

### Dimensional Transformation

A form can be transformed by altering one or more of its dimensions and still retain its identity as a member of a family of forms. A cube, for example, can be transformed into similar prismatic forms through discrete changes in height, width, or length. It can be compressed into a planar form or be stretched out into a linear one.

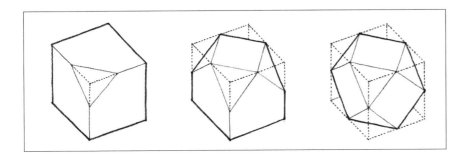

### Subtractive Transformation

A form can be transformed by subtracting a portion of its volume. Depending on the extent of the subtractive process, the form can retain its initial identity or be transformed into a form of another family. For example, a cube can retain its identity as a cube even though a portion of it is removed, or be transformed into a series of regular polyhedrons that begin to approximate a sphere.

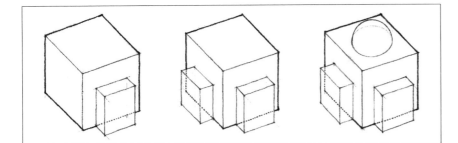

### Additive Transformation

A form can be transformed by the addition of elements to its volume. The nature of the additive process and the number and relative sizes of the elements being attached determine whether the identity of the initial form is altered or retained.

Dimensional Transformation of a Cube into a Vertical Slab:
**Unité d'Habitation**, Firminy-Vert, France, 1963–68, Le Corbusier

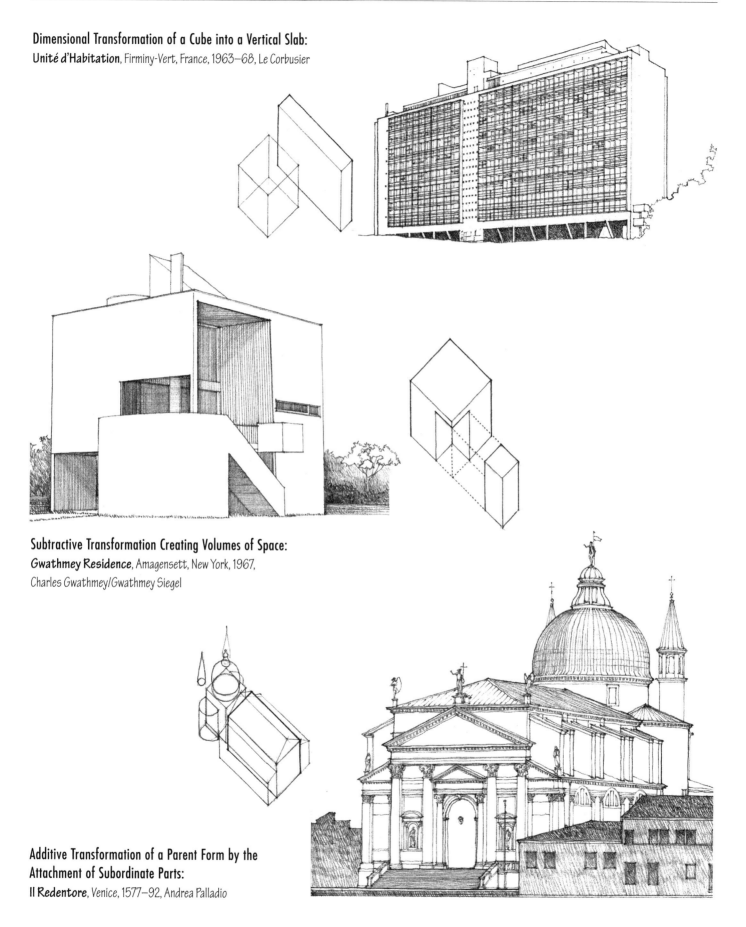

Subtractive Transformation Creating Volumes of Space:
**Gwathmey Residence**, Amagensett, New York, 1967,
Charles Gwathmey/Gwathmey Siegel

Additive Transformation of a Parent Form by the
Attachment of Subordinate Parts:
**Il Redentore**, Venice, 1577–92, Andrea Palladio

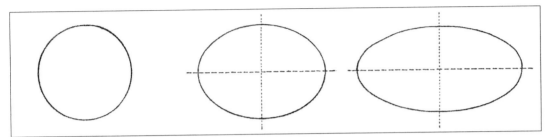

A sphere can be transformed into any number of ovoid or ellipsoidal forms by elongating it along an axis.

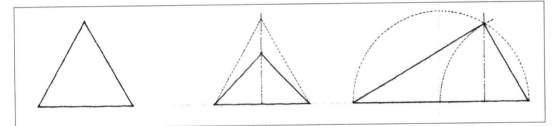

A pyramid can be transformed by altering the dimensions of the base, modifying the height of the apex, or tilting the normally vertical axis.

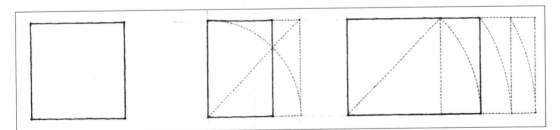

A cube can be transformed into similar prismatic forms by shortening or elongating its height, width, or depth.

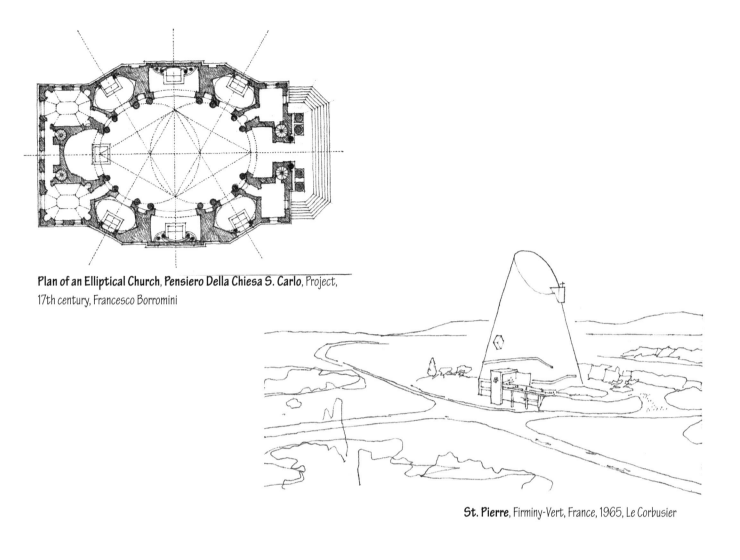

**Plan of an Elliptical Church, Pensiero Della Chiesa S. Carlo**, Project, 17th century, Francesco Borromini

**St. Pierre**, Firminy-Vert, France, 1965, Le Corbusier

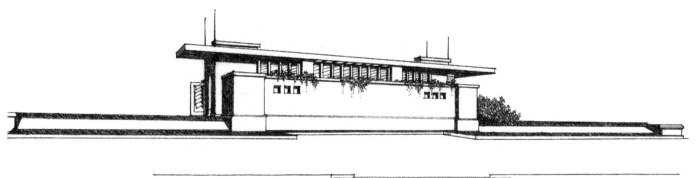

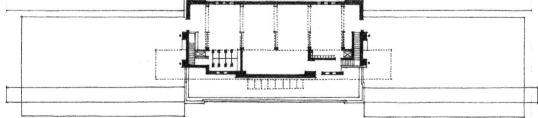

**Project for Yahara Boat Club**, Madison, Wisconsin, 1902, Frank Lloyd Wright

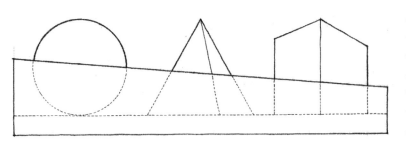

We search for regularity and continuity in the forms we see within our field of vision. If any of the primary solids is partially hidden from our view, we tend to complete its form and visualize it as if it were whole because the mind fills in what the eyes do not see. In a similar manner, when regular forms have fragments missing from their volumes, they retain their formal identities if we perceive them as incomplete wholes. We refer to these mutilated forms as subtractive forms.

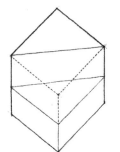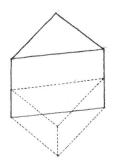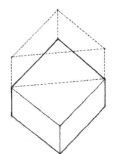

Because they are easily recognizable, simple geometric forms, such as the primary solids, adapt readily to subtractive treatment. These forms will retain their formal identities if portions of their volumes are removed without deteriorating their edges, corners, and overall profile.

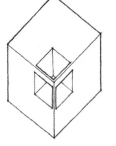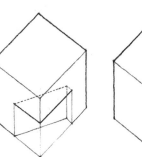

Ambiguity regarding the original identity of a form will result if the portion removed from its volume erodes its edges and drastically alters its profile.

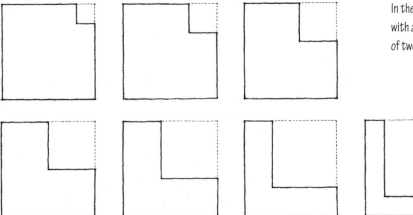

In the series of figures below, at what point does the square shape with a corner portion removed become an L-shaped configuration of two rectangular planes?

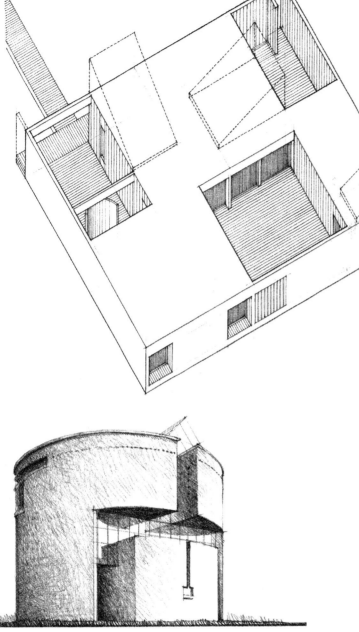

**Gorman Residence**, Amagansett, New York, 1968, Julian and Barbara Neski

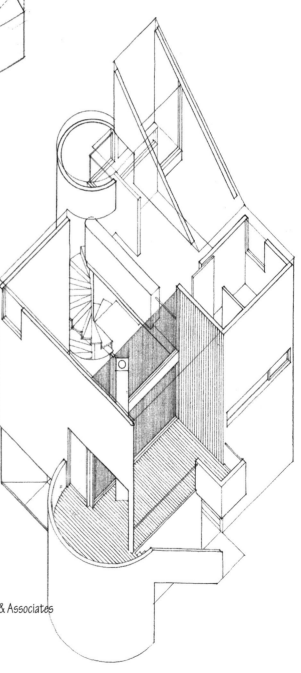

**House at Stabio**, Switzerland, 1981, Mario Botta

Spatial volumes may be subtracted from a form to create recessed entrances, positive courtyard spaces, or window openings shaded by the vertical and horizontal surfaces of the recess.

**Gwathmey Residence**, Amagansett, New York, 1967, Charles Gwathmey/Gwathmey Siegel & Associates

**Shodhan House**, Ahmedabad, India, 1956, Le Corbusier

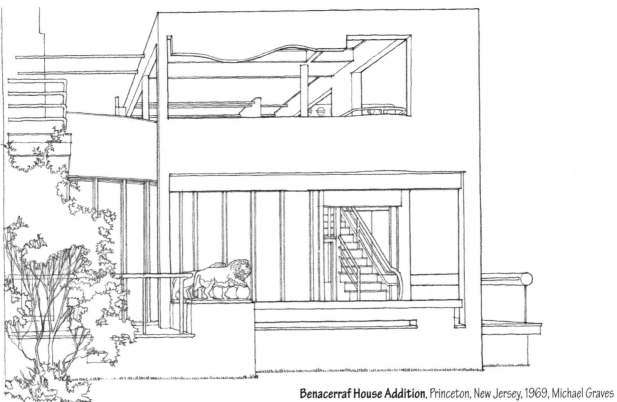

**Benacerraf House Addition**, Princeton, New Jersey, 1969, Michael Graves

Le Corbusier comments on form:

"Cumulative Composition
- additive form
- a rather easy type
- picturesque; full of movement
- can be completely disciplined by classification and
  hierarchy"

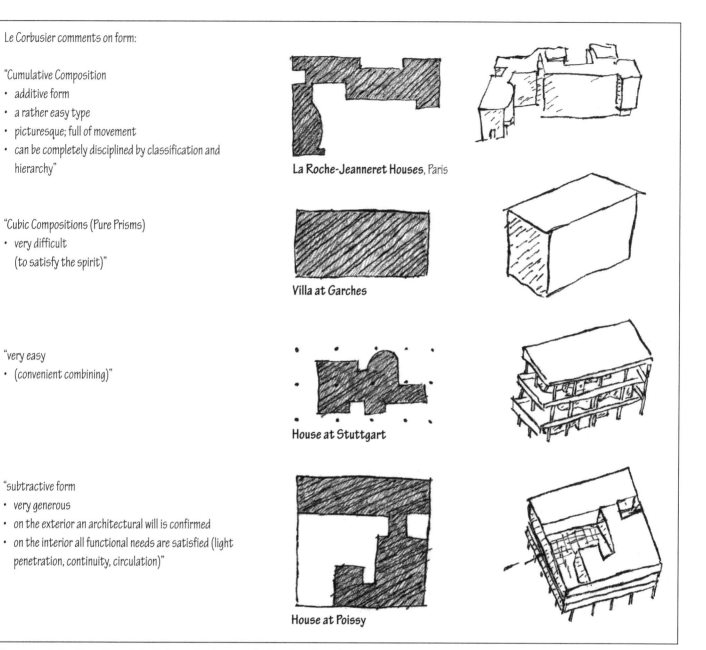

La Roche-Jeanneret Houses, Paris

"Cubic Compositions (Pure Prisms)
- very difficult
  (to satisfy the spirit)"

Villa at Garches

"very easy
- (convenient combining)"

House at Stuttgart

"subtractive form
- very generous
- on the exterior an architectural will is confirmed
- on the interior all functional needs are satisfied (light
  penetration, continuity, circulation)"

House at Poissy

After a sketch, *Four House Forms*, by Le Corbusier for the cover of Volume Two of the *Oeuvre Complète*, published in 1935.

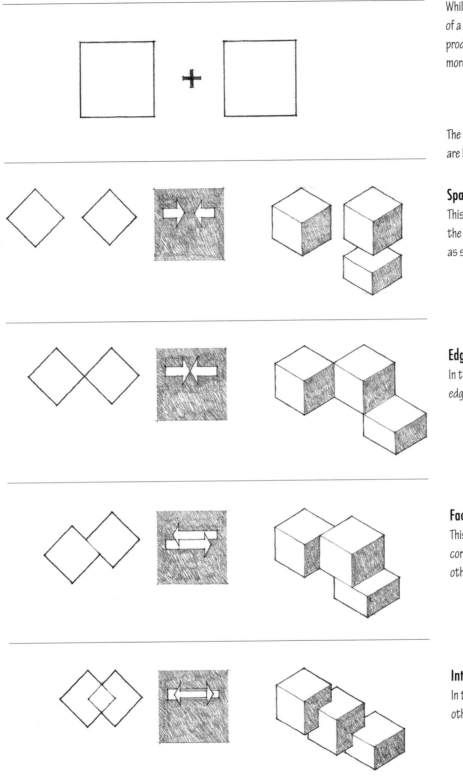

While a subtractive form results from the removal of a portion of its original volume, an additive form is produced by relating or physically attaching one or more subordinate forms to its volume.

The basic possibilities for grouping two or more forms are by:

## Spatial Tension

This type of relationship relies on the close proximity of the forms or their sharing of a common visual trait, such as shape, color, or material.

## Edge-to-edge Contact

In this type of relationship, the forms share a common edge and can pivot about that edge.

## Face-to-face Contact

This type of relationship requires that the two forms have corresponding planar surfaces which are parallel to each other.

## Interlocking Volumes

In this type of relationship, the forms interpenetrate each other's space. The forms need not share any visual traits.

Additive forms resulting from the accretion of discrete elements can be characterized by their ability to grow and merge with other forms. For us to perceive additive groupings as unified compositions of form—as figures in our visual field—the combining elements must be related to one another in a coherent manner.

These diagrams categorize additive forms according to the nature of the relationships that exist among the component forms as well as their overall configurations. This outline of formal organizations should be compared with a parallel discussion of spatial organizations in Chapter 4.

### Centralized Form
A number of secondary forms clustered about a dominant, central parent-form

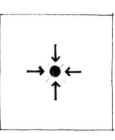

### Linear Form
A series of forms arranged sequentially in a row

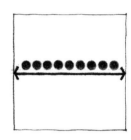

### Radial Form
A composition of linear forms extending outward from a central form in a radial manner

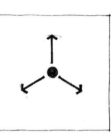

### Clustered Form
A collection of forms grouped together by proximity or the sharing of a common visual trait

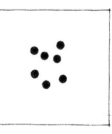

### Grid Form
A set of modular forms related and regulated by a three-dimensional grid

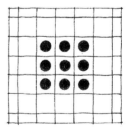

**S. Maria Della Salute**, Venice, 1631–82, Baldassare Longhena

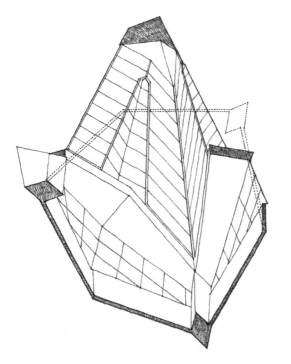

**Beth Sholom Synagogue**, Elkins Park, Pennsylvania, 1959, Frank Lloyd Wright

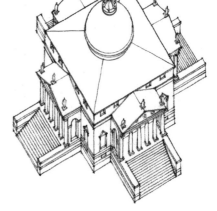

**Villa Capra (The Rotunda)**, Vicenza, Italy, 1552–67, Andrea Palladio

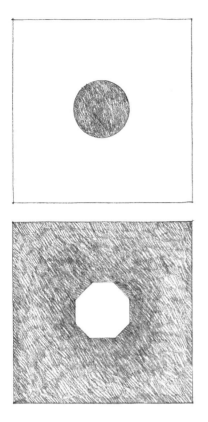

**Tempietto, S. Pietro in Montorio**, Rome, 1502, Donato Bramante

Centralized forms require the visual dominance of a geometrically regular, centrally located form, such as a sphere, cone, or cylinder. Because of their inherent centrality, these forms share the self-centering properties of the point and circle. They are ideal as freestanding structures isolated within their context, dominating a point in space, or occupying the center of a defined field. They can embody sacred or honorific places, or commemorate significant persons or events.

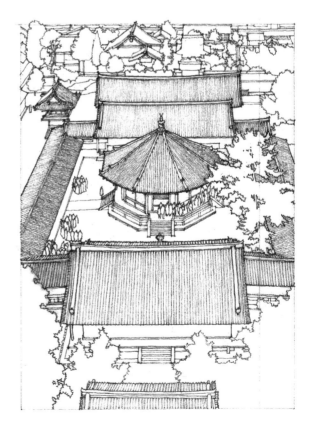

**Yume-Dono, Eastern precinct of Horyu-Ji Temple**, Nara, Japan, A.D. 607

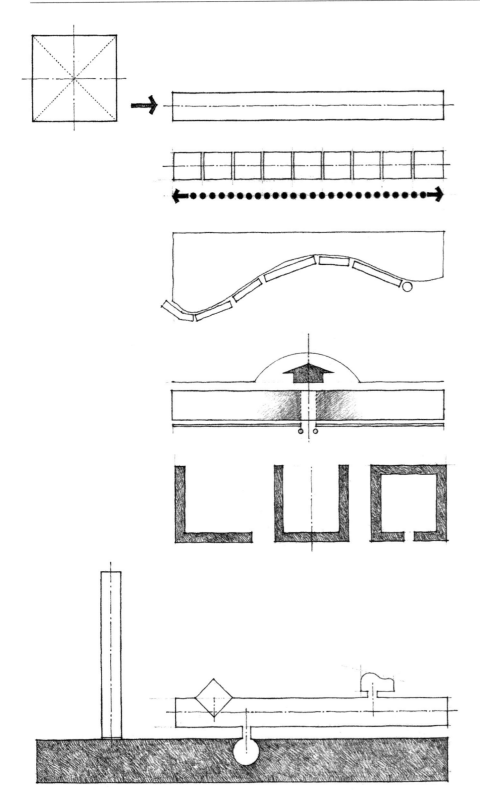

A linear form can result from a proportional change in a form's dimensions or the arrangement of a series of discrete forms along a line. In the latter case, the series of forms may be either repetitive or dissimilar in nature and organized by a separate and distinct element such as a wall or path.

• A linear form can be segmented or curvilinear to respond to topography, vegetation, views, or other features of a site.

• A linear form can front on or define an edge of an exterior space, or define a plane of entry into the spaces behind it.

• A linear form can be manipulated to enclose a portion of space.

• A linear form can be oriented vertically as a tower element to establish or denote a point in space.

• A linear form can serve as an organizing element to which a variety of secondary forms are attached.

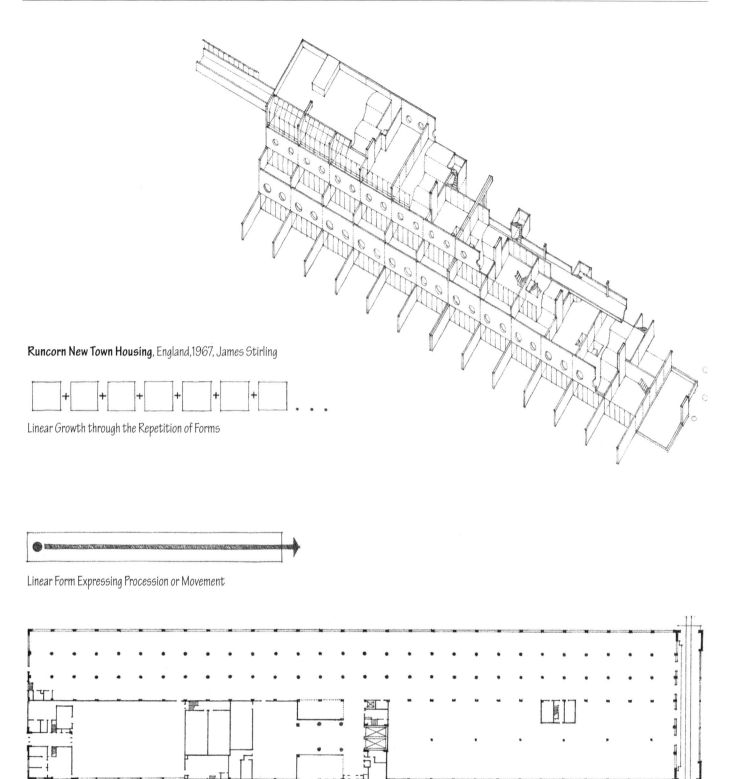

**Runcorn New Town Housing**, England,1967, James Stirling

Linear Growth through the Repetition of Forms

Linear Form Expressing Procession or Movement

**Burroughs Adding Machine Company**, Plymouth, Michigan, 1904, Albert Kahn

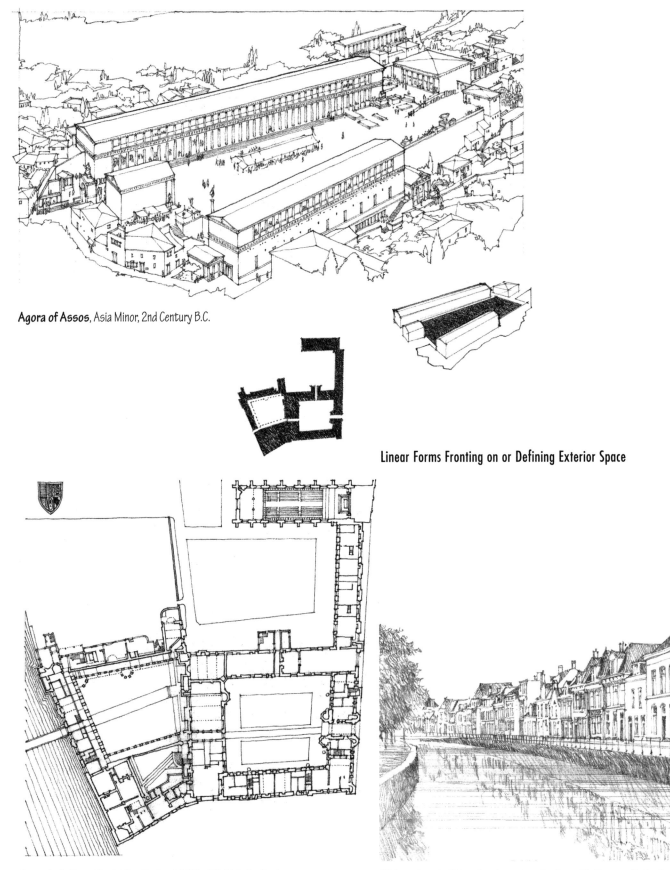

**Agora of Assos**, Asia Minor, 2nd Century B.C.

Linear Forms Fronting on or Defining Exterior Space

**Queen's College**, Cambridge, England, 1709–38, Nicholas Hawksmoor

18th-century buildings fronting a tree-lined canal in Kampen, Holland

**Henry Babson House**, Riverside, Illinois, 1907, Louis Sullivan

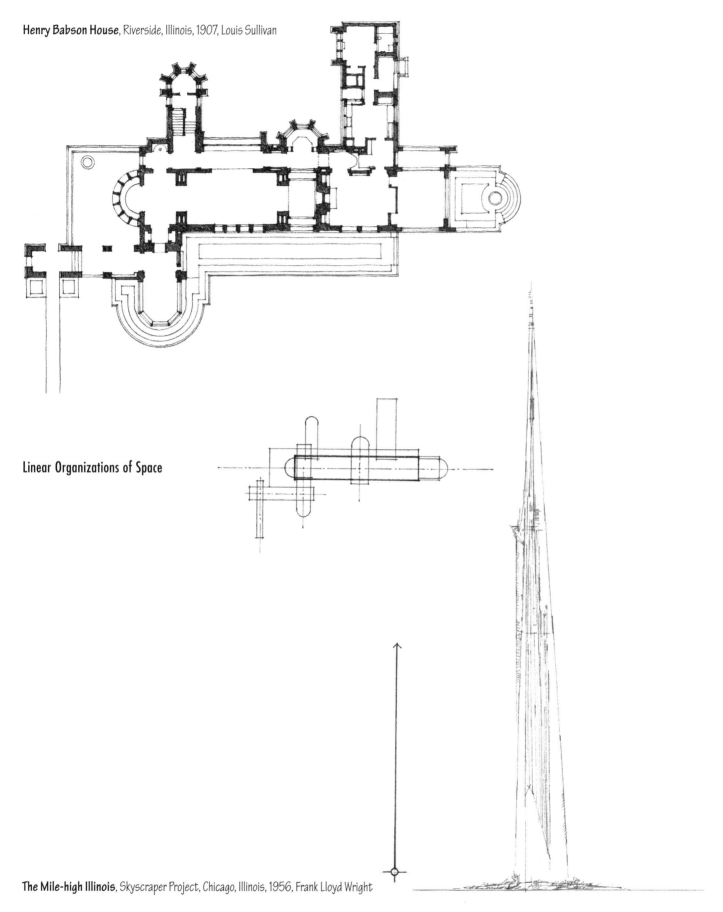

Linear Organizations of Space

**The Mile-high Illinois**, Skyscraper Project, Chicago, Illinois, 1956, Frank Lloyd Wright

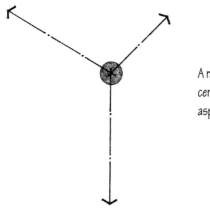

A radial form consists of linear forms that extend outward from a centrally located core element in a radiating manner. It combines the aspects of centrality and linearity into a single composition.

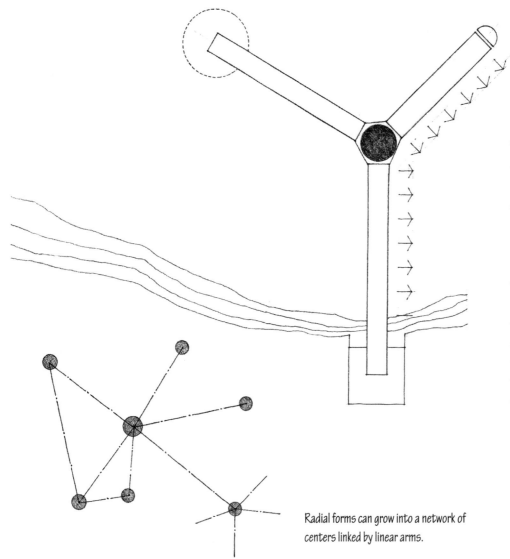

The core is either the symbolic or functional center of the organization. Its central position can be articulated with a visually dominant form, or it can merge with and become subservient to the radiating arms.

The radiating arms, having properties similar to those of linear forms, give a radial form its extroverted nature. They can reach out and relate to or attach themselves to specific features of a site. They can expose their elongated surfaces to desirable conditions of sun, wind, view, or space.

Radial forms can grow into a network of centers linked by linear arms.

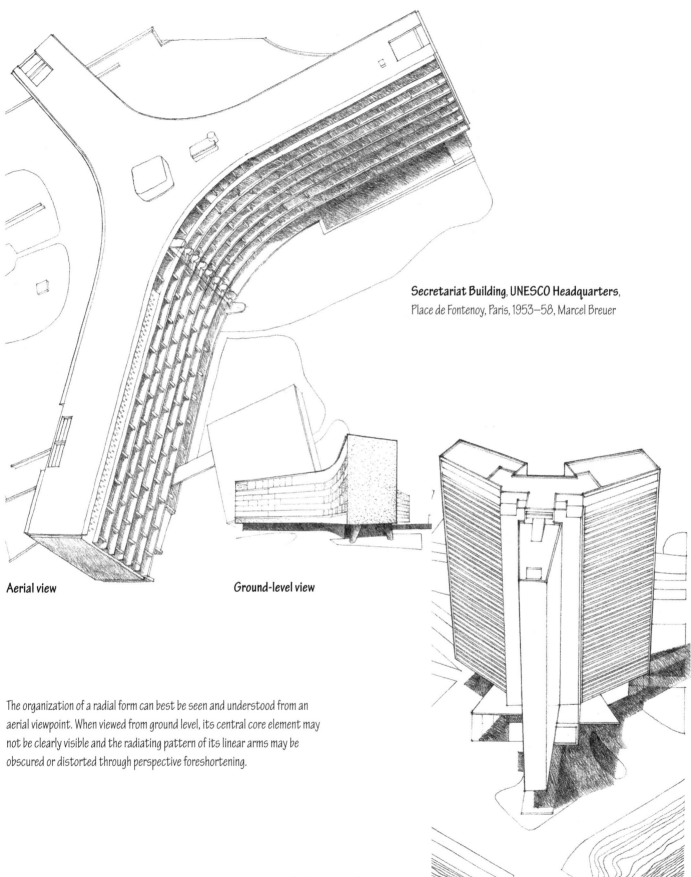

**Secretariat Building**, UNESCO Headquarters, Place de Fontenoy, Paris, 1953–58, Marcel Breuer

**Aerial view**

**Ground-level view**

The organization of a radial form can best be seen and understood from an aerial viewpoint. When viewed from ground level, its central core element may not be clearly visible and the radiating pattern of its linear arms may be obscured or distorted through perspective foreshortening.

**Skyscraper by the Sea**, Project for Algiers, 1938, Le Corbusier

While a centralized organization has a strong geometric basis for the ordering of its forms, a clustered organization groups its forms according to functional requirements of size, shape, or proximity. While it lacks the geometric regularity and introverted nature of centralized forms, a clustered organization is flexible enough to incorporate forms of various shapes, sizes, and orientations into its structure.

Considering their flexibility, clustered organizations of forms may be organized in the following ways:

- They can be attached as appendages to a larger parent form or space.

- They can be related by proximity alone to articulate and express their volumes as individual entities.

- They can interlock their volumes and merge into a single form having a variety of faces.

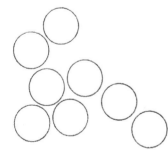

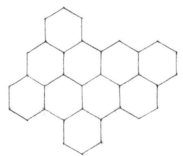

A clustered organization can also consist of forms that are generally equivalent in size, shape, and function. These forms are visually ordered into a coherent, nonhierarchical organization not only by their close proximity to one another, but also by the similarity of their visual properties.

**A Cluster of Forms Attached to a Parent Form:**
**Vacation House, Sea Ranch**, *California, 1968, MLTW/Moore & Turnbull*

**A Cluster of Interlocking Forms:**
**G.N. Black House (Kragsyde)**, *Manchester-by-the-Sea, Massachusetts, 1882–83, Peabody & Stearns*

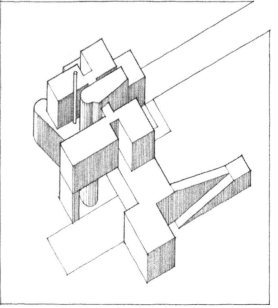

**A Cluster of Articulated Forms:**
**House Study**, *1956, James Stirling & James Gowan*

**Trulli Village**, Alberobello, Italy
Traditional dry-stone shelters in existence since the 17th century.

Numerous examples of clustered housing forms can be found in the vernacular architecture of various cultures. Even though each culture produced a unique style in response to differing technical, climatic, and sociocultural factors, these clustered housing organizations usually maintained the individuality of each unit and a moderate degree of diversity within the context of an ordered whole.

**Taos Pueblo**, New Mexico, 13th century

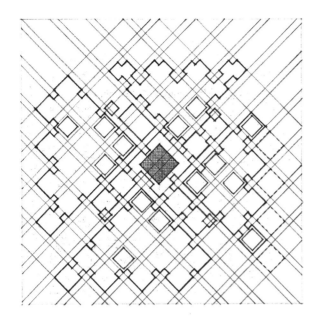

**Centraal Beheer Office Building**, Apeldoorn, The Netherlands, 1972, Herman Hertzberger with Lucas & Niemeyer

**Habitat Israel**, Jerusalem, 1969, Moshe Safdie

Vernacular examples of clustered forms can be readily transformed into modular, geometrically ordered compositions which are related to grid organizations of form.

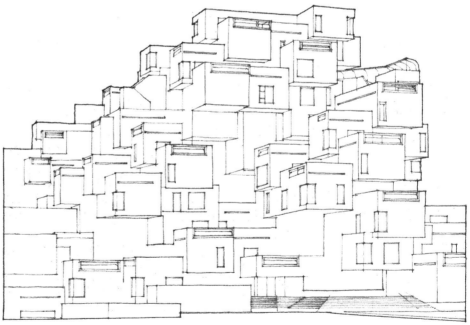

**Habitat Montreal**, 1967, Moshe Safdie

A grid is a system of two or more intersecting sets of regularly spaced parallel lines. It generates a geometric pattern of regularly spaced points at the intersections of the grid lines and regularly shaped fields defined by the grid lines themselves.

The most common grid is based on the geometry of the square. Because of the equality of its dimensions and its bilateral symmetry, a square grid is essentially nonhierarchical and nondirectional. It can be used to break the scale of a surface down into measurable units and give it an even texture. It can be used to wrap several surfaces of a form and unify them with its repetitive and pervasive geometry.

The square grid, when projected into the third dimension, generates a spatial network of reference points and lines. Within this modular framework, any number of forms and spaces can be visually organized.

**Conceptual Diagram, Gunma Prefectural Museum of Fine Arts**, Japan, 1974, Arata Isozaki

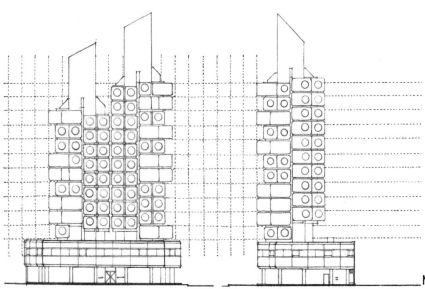

**Nakagin Capsule Building**, Tokyo, 1972, Kisho Kurokawa

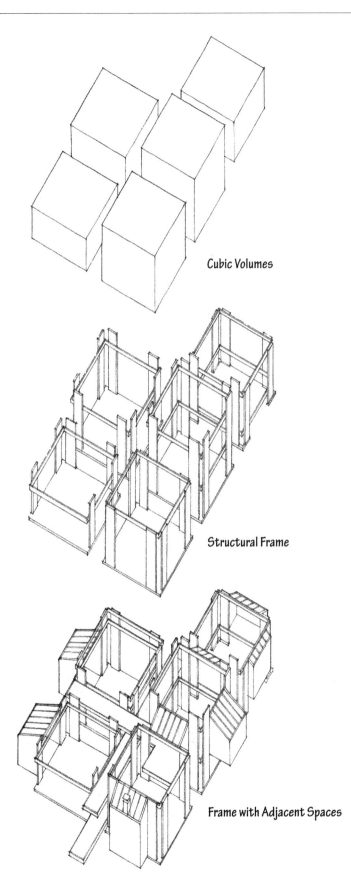

Cubic Volumes

Structural Frame

Frame with Adjacent Spaces

**Hattenbach Residence**, Santa Monica, California, 1971–73, Raymond Kappe

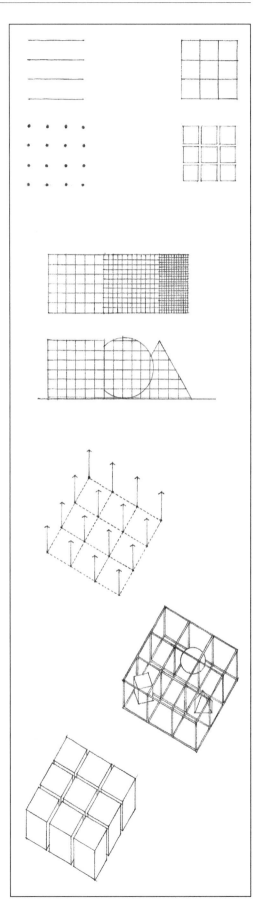

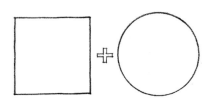

Circle and Square

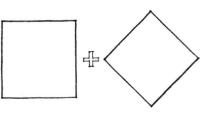

Rotated Grid

When two forms differing in geometry or orientation collide and interpenetrate each other's boundaries, each will vie for visual supremacy and dominance. In these situations, the following forms can evolve:

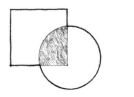

• The two forms can subvert their individual identities and merge to create a new composite form.

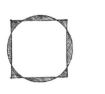

• One of the two forms can receive the other totally within its volume.

• The two forms can retain their individual identities and share the interlocking portion of their volumes.

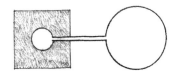

• The two forms can separate and be linked by a third element that recalls the geometry of one of the original forms.

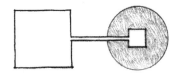

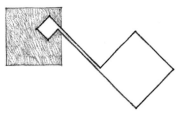

Forms differing in geometry or orientation may be incorporated into a single organization for any of the following reasons:

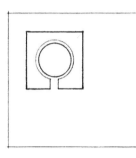
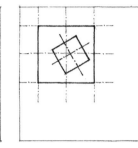
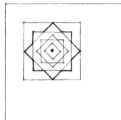

- To accommodate or accentuate the differing requirements of interior space and exterior form
- To express the functional or symbolic importance of a form or space within its context
- To generate a composite form that incorporates the contrasting geometries into its centralized organization

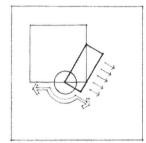
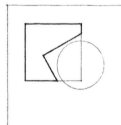
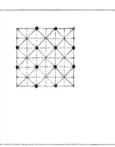

- To inflect a space toward a specific feature of a building site
- To carve a well-defined volume of space from a building form
- To express and articulate the various constructional or mechanical systems that exist within a building form

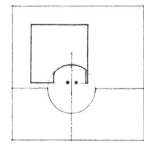
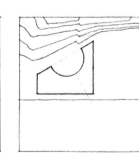
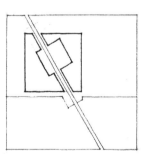

- To reinforce a local condition of symmetry in a building form
- To respond to contrasting geometries of the topography, vegetation, boundaries, or existing structures of a site
- To acknowledge an already existing path of movement through a building site

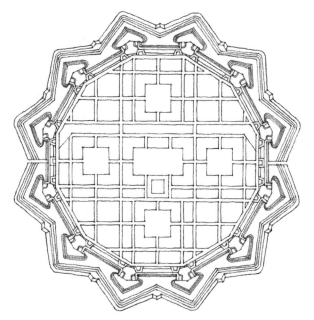

**Plan for an Ideal City**, 1615, Vincenzo Scamozzi

A circular form can be freestanding in its context to express its ideal shape and still incorporate a more functional, rectilinear geometry within its boundaries.

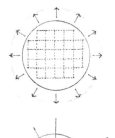

The centrality of a circular form enables it to act as a hub and unify forms of contrasting geometry or orientation about itself.

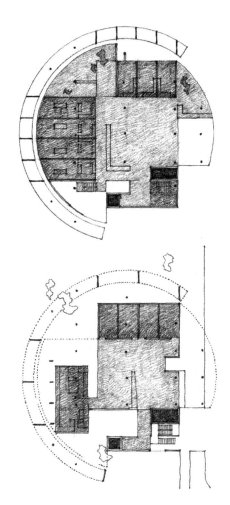

**Chancellery Building, French Embassy**, Brasilia, 1964–65, Le Corbusier

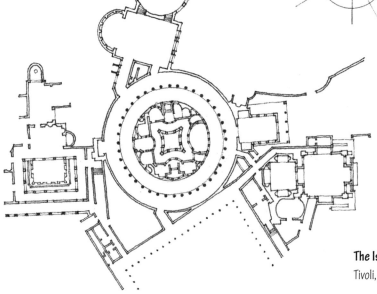

**The Island Villa (Teatro Marittimo)**, Hadrian's Villa, Tivoli, Italy, A.D. 118–125

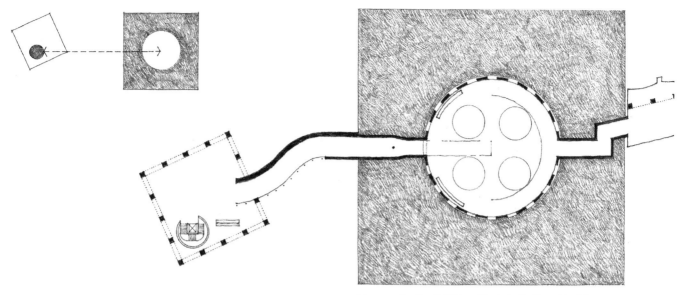

**Museum for North Rhine—Westphalia**, Dusseldorf, Germany, 1975, James Stirling & Michael Wilford

A circular or cylindrical space can serve to organize the spaces within a rectangular enclosure.

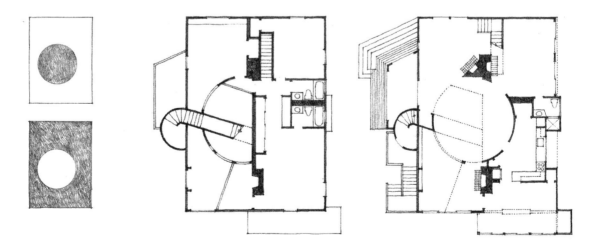

**Murray House,** Cambridge, Massachusetts, 1969, MLTW/Moore-Turnbull

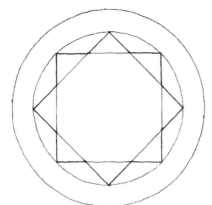

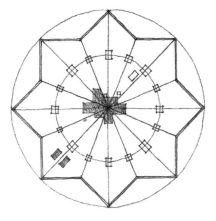

**Plan of the Ideal City of Sforzinda**, 1464, Antonio Filarete

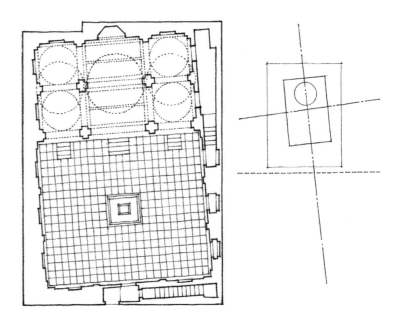

**Pearl Mosque**, within the Red Fort, an imperial palace at Agra, India, 1658–1707, Aurangzib.

The interior space of this mosque is oriented exactly with the cardinal points while its exterior conforms to the existing layout of the fort.

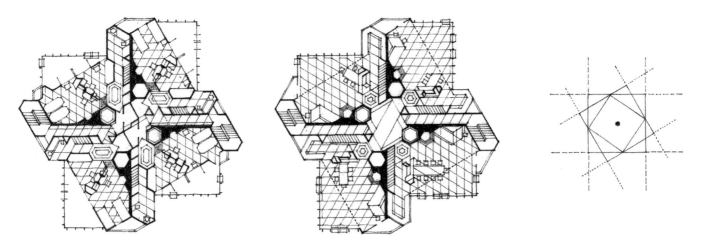

**St. Mark's Tower**, Project, New York City, 1929, Frank Lloyd Wright

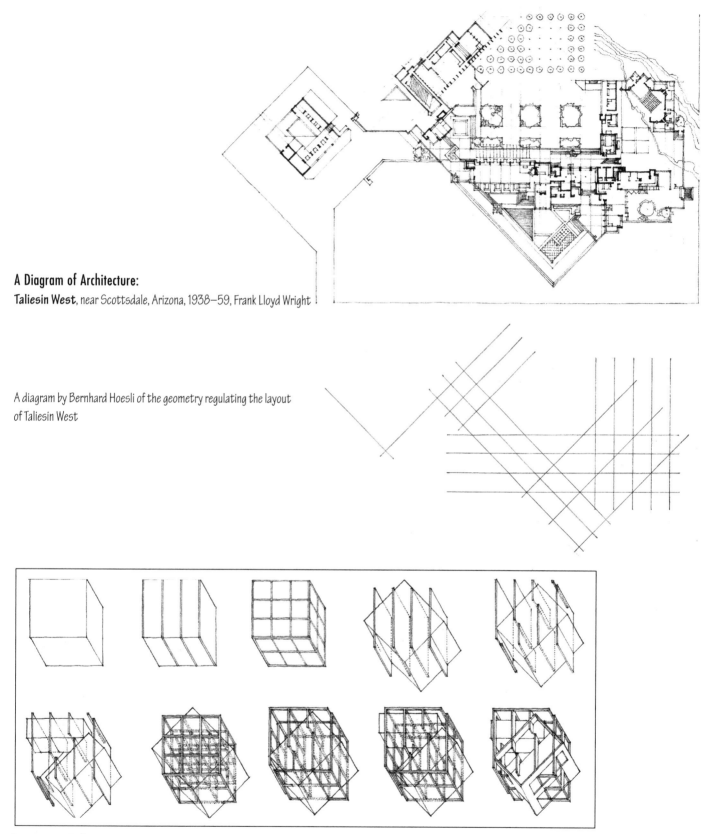

**A Diagram of Architecture:**
**Taliesin West**, near Scottsdale, Arizona, 1938–59, Frank Lloyd Wright

A diagram by Bernhard Hoesli of the geometry regulating the layout
of Taliesin West

**Diagram as Architecture:**
**House III for Robert Miller**, Lakeville, Connecticut, 1971, Design Development Drawings, Peter Eisenman

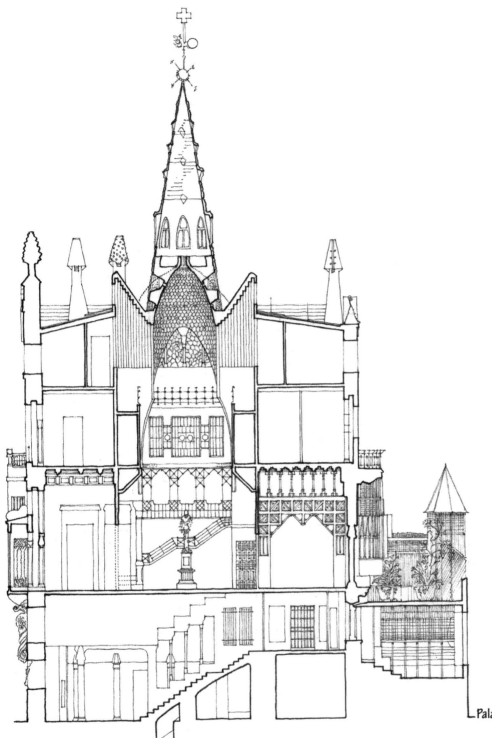

Palacio Güell, Barcelona, 1885–89, Antonio Gaudi

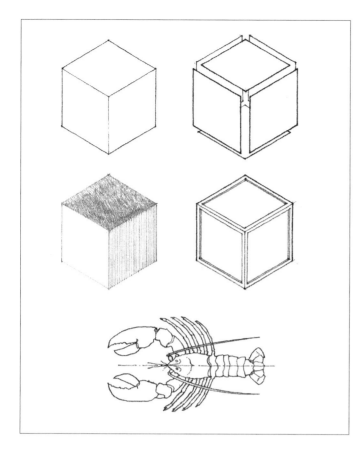

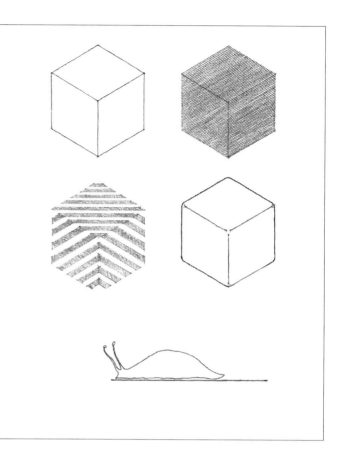

Articulation refers to the manner in which the surfaces of a form come together to define its shape and volume. An articulated form clearly reveals the precise nature of its parts and their relationships to each other and to the whole. Its surfaces appear as discrete planes with distinct shapes and their overall configuration is legible and easily perceived. In a similar manner, an articulated group of forms accentuates the joints between the constituent parts in order to visually express their individuality.

A form can be articulated by:

- differentiating adjoining planes with a change in material, color, texture, or pattern
- developing corners as distinct linear elements independent of the abutting planes
- removing corners to physically separate neighboring planes
- lighting the form to create sharp contrasts in tonal value along edges and corners

In opposition to the above, the corners of a form can be rounded and smoothed over to emphasize the continuity of its surfaces. Or a material, color, texture, or pattern can be carried across a corner onto the adjoining surfaces to de-emphasize the individuality of the surface planes and emphasize instead the volume of a form.

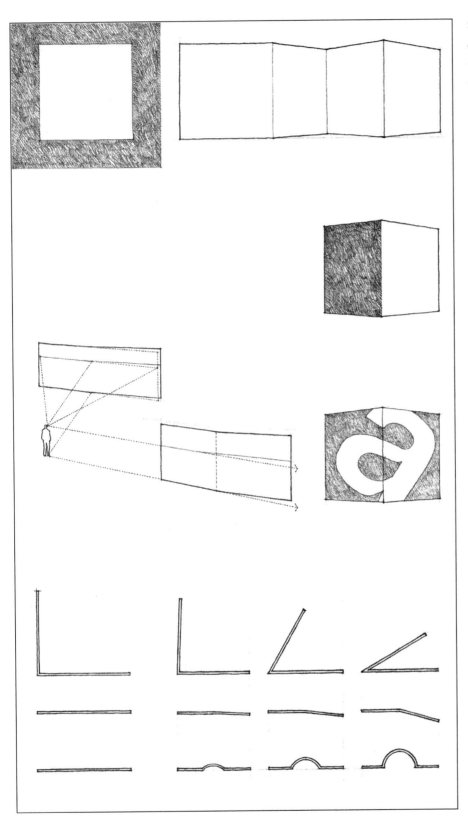

Since the articulation of a form depends to a great degree on how its surfaces meet each other at corners, how these edge conditions are resolved is critical to the definition and clarity of a form.

While a corner can be articulated by simply contrasting the surface qualities of the adjoining planes, or obscured by layering their joining with an optical pattern, our perception of its existence is also affected by the laws of perspective and the quality of light that illuminates the form.

For a corner to be formally active, there must be more than a slight deviation in the angle between the adjoining planes. Since we constantly search for regularity and continuity within our field of vision, we tend to regularize or smooth out slight irregularities in the forms we see. For example, a wall plane that is bent only slightly will appear to be a single flat plane, perhaps with a surface imperfection. A corner would not be perceived.

At what point do these formal deviations become an acute angle? . . . a right angle?

a segmented line? . . . a straight line?

a circular segment? . . . a change in a line's contour?

Corners define the meeting of two planes. If the two planes simply touch and the corner remains unadorned, the presence of the corner will depend on the visual treatment of the adjoining surfaces. This corner condition emphasizes the volume of a form.

A corner condition can be visually reinforced by introducing a separate and distinct element that is independent of the surfaces it joins. This element articulates the corner as a linear condition, defines the edges of the adjoining planes, and becomes a positive feature of the form.

If an opening is introduced to one side of the corner, one of the planes will appear to bypass the other. The opening diminishes the corner condition, weakens the definition of the volume within the form, and emphasizes the planar qualities of the neighboring surfaces.

If neither plane is extended to define the corner, a volume of space is created to replace the corner. This corner condition deteriorates the volume of the form, allows the interior space to leak outward, and clearly reveals the surfaces as planes in space.

Rounding off the corner emphasizes the continuity of the bounding surfaces of a form, the compactness of its volume, and softness of its contour. The scale of the radius of curvature is important. If too small, it becomes visually insignificant; if large, it affects the interior space it encloses and the exterior form it describes.

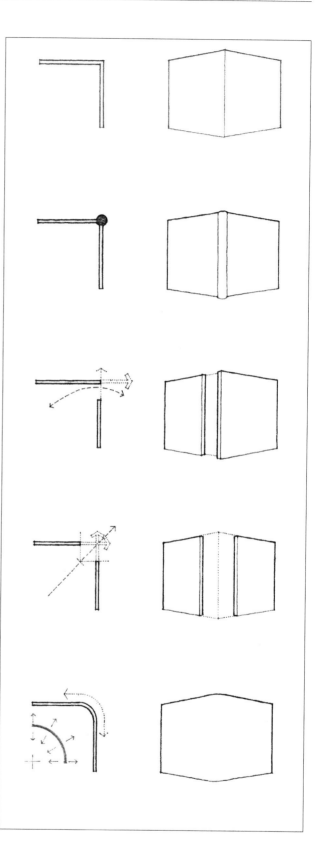

**Everson Museum**, Syracuse, New York, 1968, I.M. Pei.
The unadorned corners of the forms emphasize the volume of their mass.

**Corner Detail, Izumo Shrine**, Shimane Prefecture, Japan, A.D. 717 (last rebuilt in 1744).
The timber joinery articulates the individuality of the members meeting at the corner.

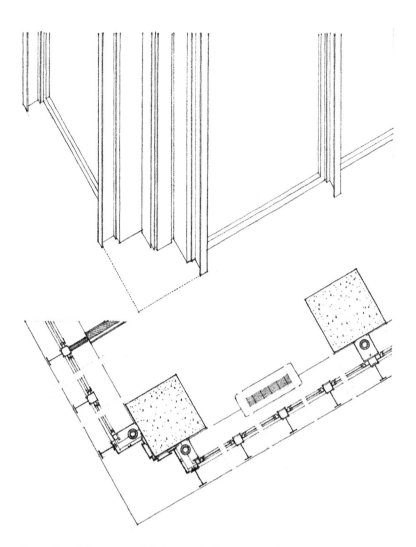

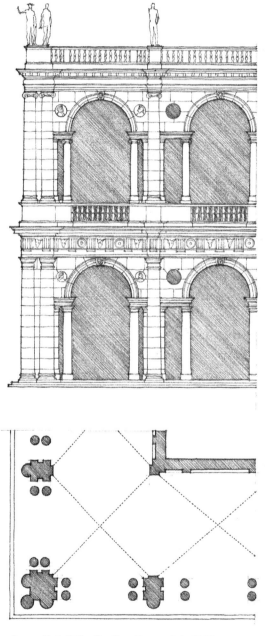

**Corner Detail, Commonwealth Promenade Apartments**, Chicago,
1953–56, Mies van der Rohe.
The corner member is recessed to be independent of the adjoining wall planes.

**Corner Detail, The Basilica**, Vicenza, Italy, 1545,
Andrea Palladio.
The corner column emphasizes the edge of the building form.

**Einstein Tower**, Potsdam, Germany, 1919, Eric Mendelsohn

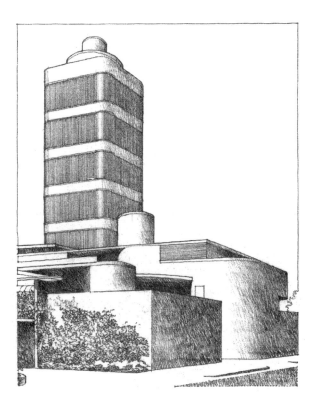

Rounded corners express continuity of surface, compactness of volume, and softness of form.

**Laboratory Tower, Johnson Wax Building**, Racine, Wisconsin, 1950, Frank Lloyd Wright

**Kaufmann Desert House**, Palm Springs, California, 1946, Richard Neutra

Openings at corners emphasize the definition of planes over volume.

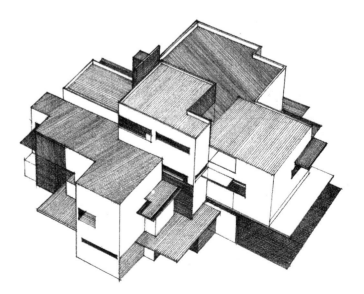

**Architectural Design Study**, 1923, Van Doesburg and Van Esteren

Our perception of the shape, size, scale, proportion, and visual weight of a plane is influenced by its surface properties as well as its visual context.

- A distinct contrast between the surface color of a plane and that of the surrounding field can clarify its shape, while modifying its tonal value can either increase or decrease its visual weight.

- A frontal view reveals the true shape of a plane; oblique views distort it.

- Elements of known size within the visual context of a plane can aid our perception of its size and scale.

- Texture and color together affect the visual weight and scale of a plane and the degree to which it absorbs or reflects light and sound.

- Directional or oversized optical patterns can distort the shape or exaggerate the proportions of a plane.

**Vincent Street Flats**, London, 1928, Sir Edwin Lutyens

**Palazzo Medici-Ricardo**, Florence, Italy, 1444–60, Michelozzi

The color, texture, and pattern of surfaces articulate the existence of planes and influence the visual weight of a form.

**Hoffman House**, East Hampton, New York, 1966–67, Richard Meier

**John Deere & Company Building**, Moline, Illinois, 1961–64, Eero Saarinen & Associates.
The linear sun-shading devices accentuate the horizontality of the building form.

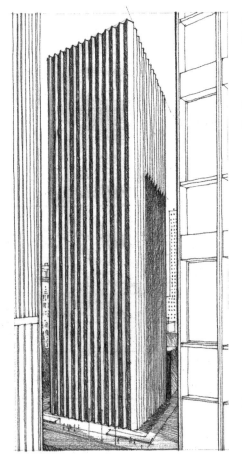

**CBS Building**, New York City, 1962–64, Eero Saarinen & Associates.
Linear columnar elements emphasize the verticality of this high-rise structure.

Linear patterns have the ability to emphasize the height or length of a form,
unify its surfaces, and define its textural quality.

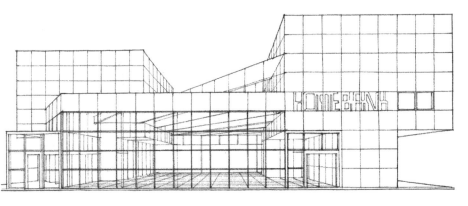

**Fukuoka Sogo Bank**, Study of the Saga Branch, 1971, Arata Isozaki.
A grid pattern unifies the surfaces of the three-dimensional composition.

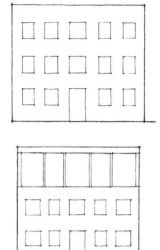

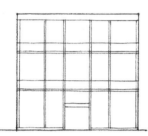

A transformation from a pattern of openings in a plane to an open facade articulated by a linear framework.

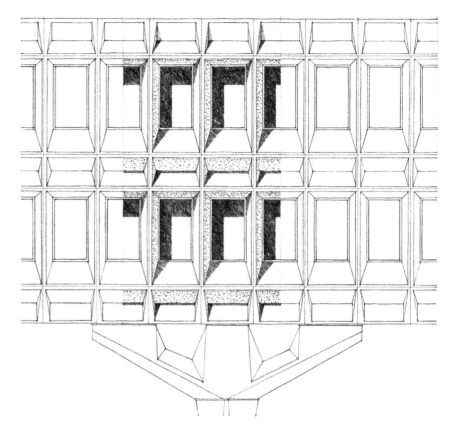

**IBM Research Center**, La Guade, Var, France, 1960–61, Marcel Breuer.
The three-dimensional form of the openings creates a texture of light, shade, and shadows.

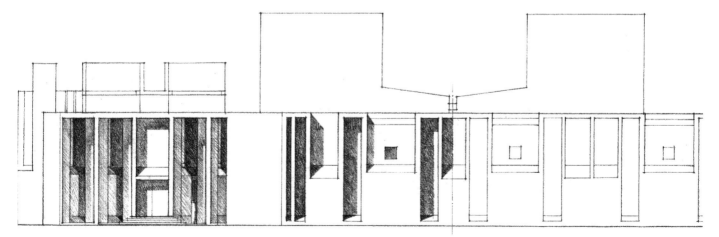

**First Unitarian Church**, Rochester, New York, 1956–67, Louis Kahn.
The pattern of openings and cavities interrupt the continuity of the exterior wall planes.

# 3
# Form & Space

"We put thirty spokes together and call it a wheel;
But it is on the space where there is nothing
that the utility of the wheel depends.
We turn clay to make a vessel;
But it is on the space where there is nothing
that the utility of the vessel depends.
We pierce doors and windows to make a house;
and it is on these spaces where there is nothing
that the utility of the house depends.
Therefore, just as we take advantage of what is,
we should recognize the utility of what is not."

Lao-tzu
*Tao Te Ching*
6th century B.C.

Space constantly encompasses our being. Through the volume of space, we move, see forms, hear sounds, feel breezes, smell the fragrances of a flower garden in bloom. It is a material substance like wood or stone. Yet it is an inherently formless vapor. Its visual form, its dimensions and scale, the quality of its light—all of these qualities depend on our perception of the spatial boundaries defined by elements of form. As space begins to be captured, enclosed, molded, and organized by the elements of mass, architecture comes into being.

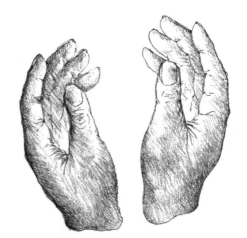

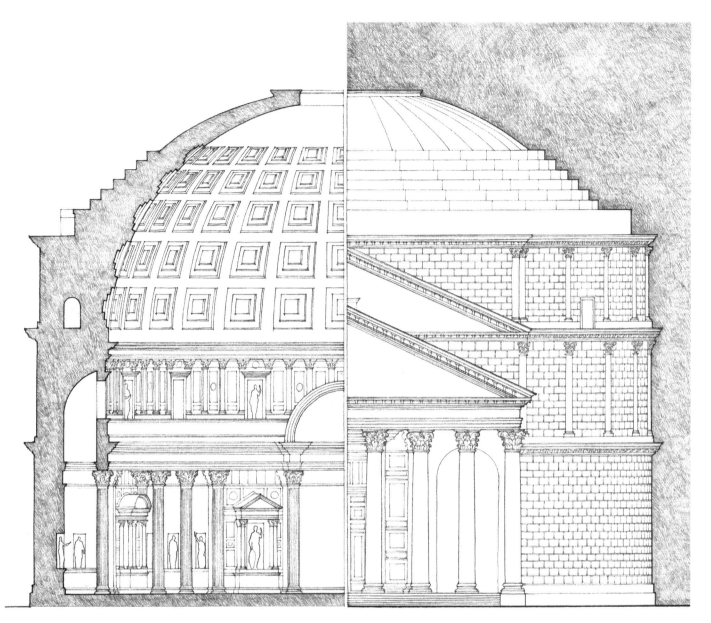

**The Pantheon**, Rome, A.D. 120–124

Our visual field normally consists of heterogeneous elements that differ in shape, size, color, or orientation. To better comprehend the structure of a visual field, we tend to organize its elements into two opposing groups: positive elements which are perceived as figures and negative elements which provide a background for the figures.

Our perception and understanding of a composition depends on how we interpret the visual interaction between the positive and negative elements within its field. On this page, for example, letters are seen as dark figures against the white background of the paper surface. Consequently, we are able to perceive their organization into words, sentences, and paragraphs. In the diagrams to the left, the letter 'a' is seen as a figure not only because we recognize it as a letter in our alphabet but also because its profile is distinct, its value contrasts with that of its background, and its placement isolates it from its context. As it grows in size relative to its field, however, other elements within and around it begin to compete for our attention as figures. At times, the relationship between figures and their background is so ambiguous that we visually switch their identities back and forth almost simultaneously.

**Two Faces or a Vase?**

**White-on-Black or Black-on-White?**

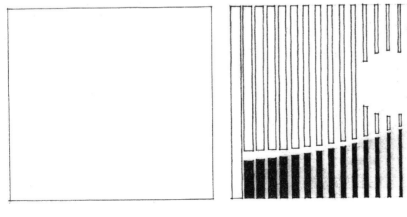

In all cases, however, we should understand that figures, the positive elements that attract our attention, could not exist without a contrasting background. Figures and their background, therefore, are more than opposing elements. Together, they form an inseparable reality—a unity of opposites—just as the elements of form and space together form the reality of architecture.

**Taj Mahal**, Agra, India, 1630–53. Shah Jahan built this white marble mausoleum for his favorite wife, Muntaz Mahal.

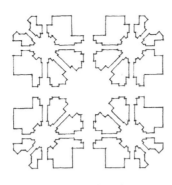 

**A.** Line defining the boundary between solid mass and spatial void

**B.** The form of solid mass rendered as a figure

**C.** The form of the spatial void rendered as figure

Architectural form occurs at the juncture between mass and space. In executing and reading design drawings, we should be concerned with both the form of the mass containing a volume of space as well as the form of the spatial volume itself.

**Fragment of a Map of Rome**, drawn by Giambattista Nolli in 1748

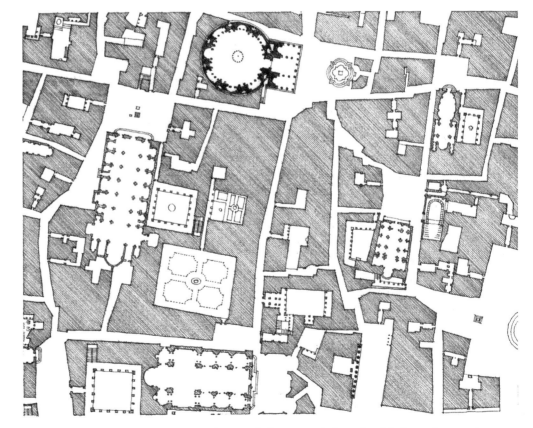

Depending on what we perceive to be positive elements, the figure-ground relationship of the forms of mass and space can be inverted in different parts of this map of Rome. In portions of the map, buildings appear to be positive forms that define street spaces. In other parts of the drawing, urban squares, courtyards, and major spaces within important public buildings read as positive elements seen against the background of the surrounding building mass.

The symbiotic relationship of the forms of mass and space in architecture can be examined and found to exist at several different scales. At each level, we should be concerned not only with the form of a building but also its impact on the space around it. At an urban scale, we should carefully consider whether the role of a building is to continue the existing fabric of a place, form a backdrop for other buildings, or define an urban space, or whether it might be appropriate for it to stand free as a significant object in space.

At the scale of a building site, there are various strategies for relating the form of a building to the space around it. A building can:

A. form a wall along an edge of its site and define a positive outdoor space
B. surround and enclose a courtyard or atrium space within its volume
C. merge its interior space with the private outdoor space of a walled site
D. enclose a portion of its site as an outdoor room
E. stand as a distinct form in space and dominate its site
F. stretch out and present a broad face to a feature of its site
G. stand free within its site but have private exterior spaces be an extension of its interior spaces
H. stand as a positive form in negative space

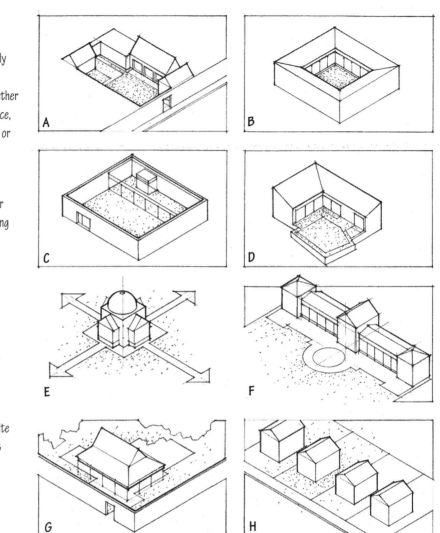

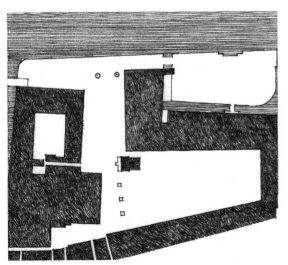

**Piazza of San Marco**, Venice

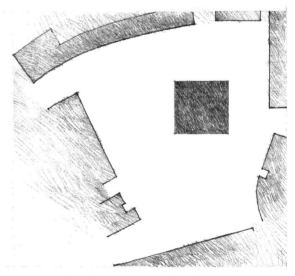

**Boston City Hall**, 1960, Kallmann, McKinnell & Knowles

**Theater in Seinäjoki**, Finland,1968–69,
Alvar Aalto

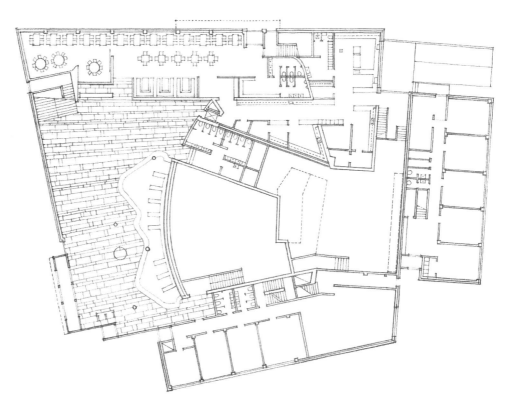

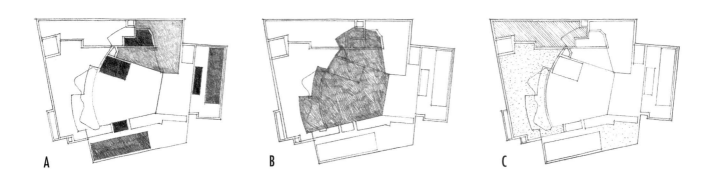

A          B          C

At the scale of a building, we tend to read the configurations of walls as the positive elements of a plan. The white space in between, however, should not be seen simply as background for the walls, but also as figures in the drawing that have shape and form.

The form and enclosure of each space in a building either determines, or is determined by, the form of the spaces around it. In the Theater in Seinäjoki by Alvar Aalto, for example, we can distinguish several categories of spatial forms and analyze how they interact. Each category has an active or passive role in defining space.

A. Some spaces, such as offices, have specific but similar functions and can be grouped into single, linear, or clustered forms.
B. Some spaces, such as concert halls, have specific functional and technical requirements, and require specific forms that will affect the forms of the spaces around them.
C. Some spaces, such as lobbies, are flexible in nature and can therefore be freely defined by the spaces or grouping of spaces around them.

Even at the scale of a room, articles of furnishings can either stand as forms within a field of space or serve to define the form of a spatial field.

**Square in Giron**, **Colombia**, South America

When we place a two-dimensional figure on a piece of paper, it influences the shape of the white space around it. In a similar manner, any three-dimensional form naturally articulates the volume of space surrounding it and generates a field of influence or territory which it claims as its own. The following section of this chapter looks at horizontal and vertical elements of form and presents examples of how various configurations of these formal elements generate and define specific types of space.

### Base Plane

A horizontal plane laying as a figure on a contrasting background defines a simple field of space. This field can be visually reinforced in the following ways.

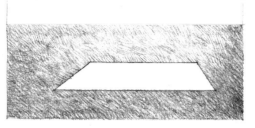 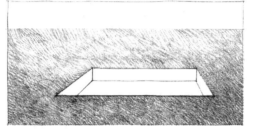

### Elevated Base Plane

A horizontal plane elevated above the ground plane establishes vertical surfaces along its edges that reinforce the visual separation between its field and the surrounding ground.

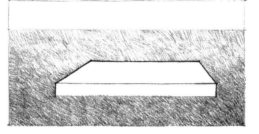 

### Depressed Base Plane

A horizontal plane depressed into the ground plane utilizes the vertical surfaces of the lowered area to define a volume of space.

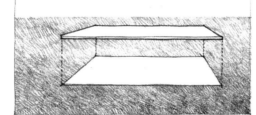 

### Overhead Plane

A horizontal plane located overhead defines a volume of space between itself and the ground plane.

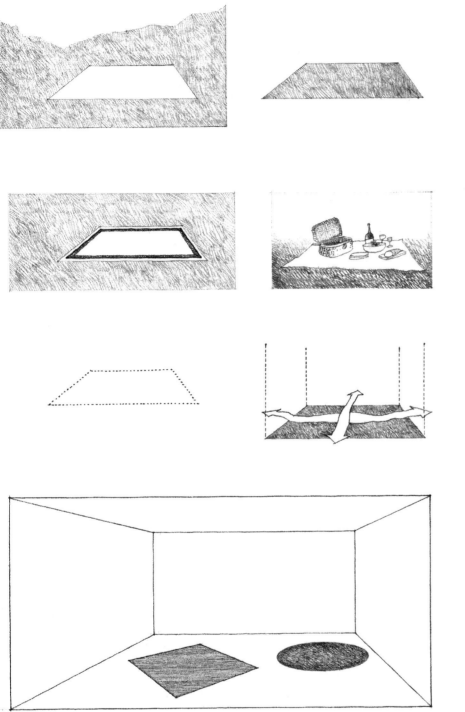

For a horizontal plane to be seen as a figure, there must be a perceptible change in color, tone, or texture between its surface and that of the surrounding area.

The stronger the edge definition of a horizontal plane is, the more distinct will be its field.

Although there is a continuous flow of space across it, the field nevertheless generates a spatial zone or realm within its boundaries.

The surface articulation of the ground or floor plane is often used in architecture to define a zone of space within a larger context. The examples on the facing page illustrate how this type of spatial definition can be used to differentiate between a path of movement and places of rest, establish a field from which the form of a building rises out of the ground, or articulate a functional zone within a one-room living environment.

**Street in Woodstock**, Oxfordshire, England

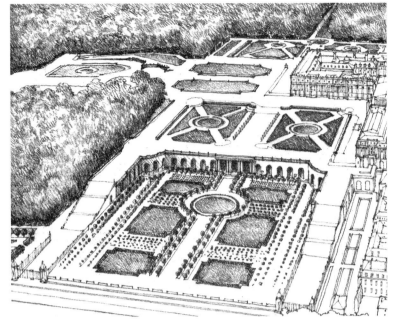

**Parterre de Broderie**, **Versailles**, France, 17th century, André Le Nôtre

**Katsura Palace**, Kyoto, Japan, 17th century

**Interior of Glass House**, New Canaan, Connecticut, 1949, Philip Johnson

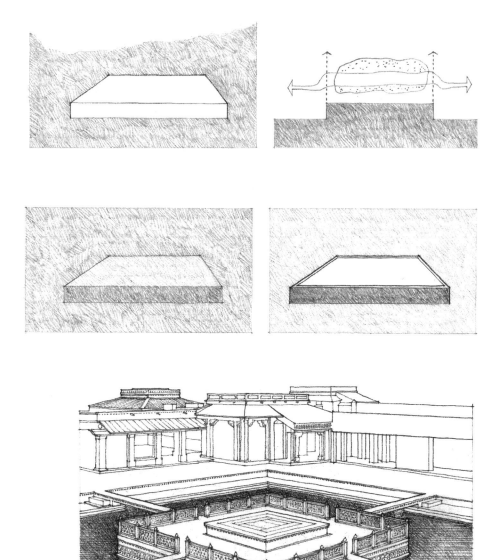

Elevating a portion of the base plane creates a specific domain within a larger spatial context. The changes in level that occur along the edges of the elevated plane define the boundaries of its field and interrupts the flow of space across its surface.

If the surface characteristics of the base plane continues up and across the elevated plane, then the field of the elevated plane will appear to be very much a part of the surrounding space. If, however, the edge condition is articulated by a change in form, color, or texture, then the field will become a plateau that is separate and distinct from its surroundings.

**Fatehpur Sikri**, Palace Complex of Akbar the Great, Mogul Emperor of India, 1569–74.
A special place is established by a platform in an artificial lake surrounded by the emperor's living and sleeping quarters.

The degree to which spatial and visual continuity is maintained between an elevated space and its surroundings depends on the scale of the level change.

1. The edge of the field is well-defined; visual and spatial continuity is maintained; physical access is easily accommodated.

2. Visual continuity is maintained; spatial continuity is interrupted; physical access requires the use of stairs or ramps.

3. Visual and spatial continuity is interrupted; the field of the elevated plane is isolated from the ground or floor plane; the elevated plane is transformed into a sheltering element for the space below.

**The Acropolis**, the citadel of Athens, 5th century B.C.

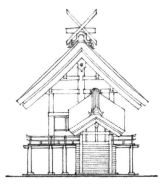
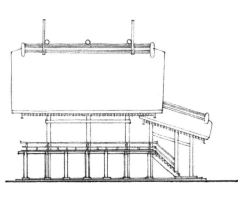

**Izumo Shrine**, Shimane Prefecture, Japan, A. D. 717 (last rebuilt in in 1744)

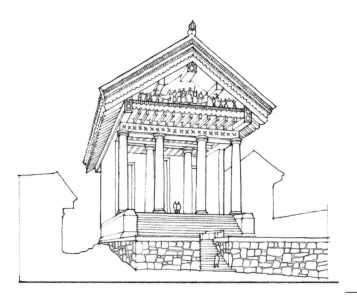

**Temple of Jupiter Capitolinus**, Rome, 509 B.C.

Elevating a portion of the ground plane establishes a platform or podium that structurally and visually supports the form and mass of a building. The elevated ground plane can be a preexisting site condition, or it can be artificially constructed to deliberately raise a building above the surrounding context or enhance its image in the landscape. The examples on these two pages illustrate how these techniques have been used to venerate sacred and honorific buildings.

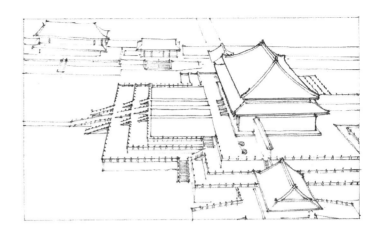

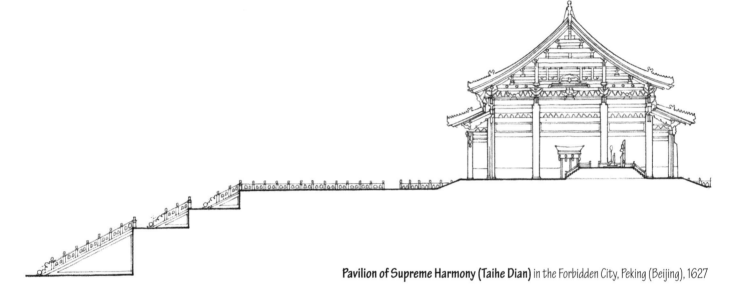

**Pavilion of Supreme Harmony (Taihe Dian)** in the Forbidden City, Peking (Beijing), 1627

**Private Courtyard of the Imperial Palace**, the Forbidden City,
Peking (Beijing), 15th century

An elevated plane can define a transitional space between the interior of a
building and the outdoor environment. Combined with a roof plane, it develops
into the semiprivate realm of a porch or veranda.

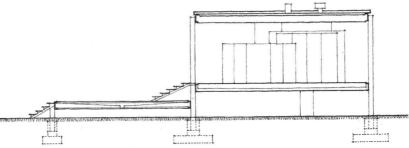

**Section of the Farnsworth House**, Plano, Illinois, 1950, Mies van der Rohe.
The Farnsworth House was constructed to rise above the flood plain of the Fox River. This
elevated floor plane, together with an overhead roof plane, defines a volume of space that
hovers delicately above the surface of its site.

High Altar in the Chapel at the Cistercian Monastery of
**La Tourette**, near Lyons, France, 1956–59, Le Corbusier

A section of the floor plane can be elevated to establish
a singular zone of space within a larger room or hall. This
raised space can serve as a retreat from the activity
around it or be a platform for viewing the surrounding
space. Within a religious structure, it can demarcate a
sacred, holy, or consecrated place.

**East Harlem Preschool**, New York City,
1970, Hammel, Green & Abrahamson

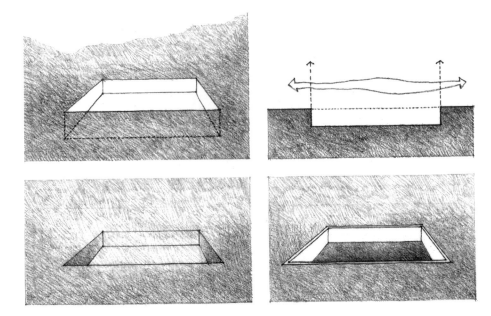

Lowering a portion of the base plane isolates a field of space from a larger context. The vertical surfaces of the depression establish the boundaries of the field. These boundaries are not implied as in the case of an elevated plane, but visible edges that begin to form the walls of the space.

The field of space can be further articulated by contrasting the surface treatment of the lowered area and that of the surrounding base plane.

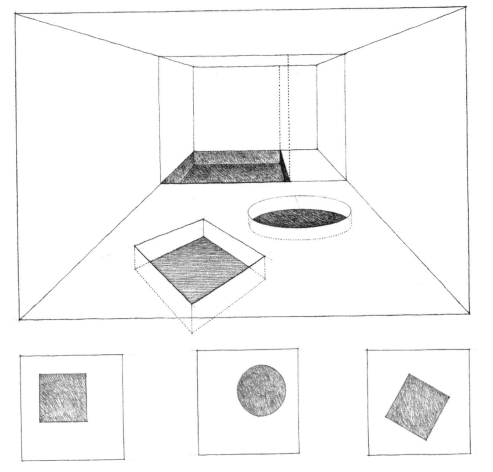

A contrast in form, geometry, or orientation can also visually reinforce the identity and independence of the sunken field from its larger spatial context.

The degree of spatial continuity between a depressed field and the raised area surrounding it depends on the scale of the level change.

- The depressed field can be an interruption of the ground or floor plane and remain an integral part of the surrounding space.

- Increasing the depth of the depressed field weakens its visual relationship with the surrounding space and strengthens its definition as a distinct volume of space.

- Once the original base plane is above our eye-level, the depressed field becomes a separate and distinct room in itself.

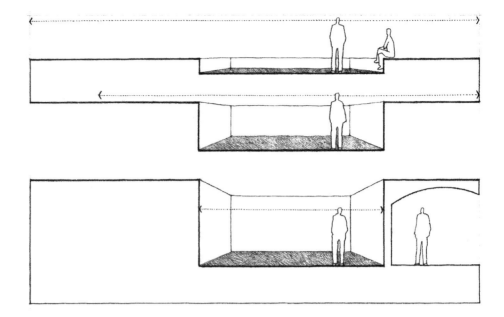

Creating a stepped, terraced, or ramped transition from one level to the next helps promote continuity between a sunken space and the area that rises around it.

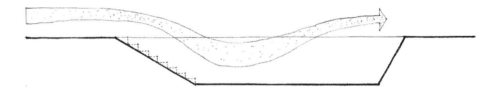

Whereas the act of stepping up to an elevated space might express the extroverted nature or significance of the space, the lowering of a space below its surroundings might allude to its introverted nature or to its sheltering and protective qualities.

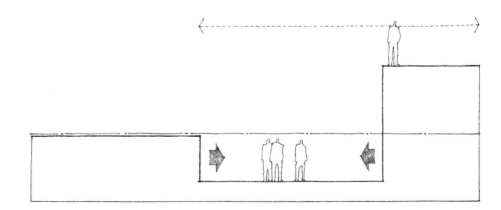

**Theater at Epidauros**, *Greece, c. 350 B.C., Polycleitos*

Depressed areas in the topography of a site can serve as stages for outdoor arenas and amphitheaters. The natural change in level benefits both the sightlines and the acoustical quality of these spaces.

**Underground village near Loyang, China**

**Lower Plaza, Rockefeller Center**, New York City, 1930,
Wallace K. Harrison & Max Abramovitz.
Rockefeller Center's lower plaza, an outdoor cafe in the summertime
and a skating rink in the winter, can be viewed from the upper plaza while
shops open onto it at the lower level.

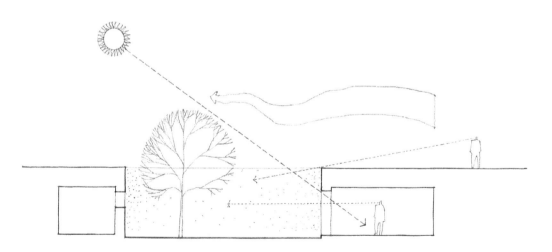

The ground plane can be lowered to define sheltered outdoor
spaces for underground buildings. A sunken courtyard, while
protected from surface-level wind and noise by the mass
surrounding it, remains a source of air, light, and views for the
underground spaces opening onto it.

In both of these examples, Alvar Aalto has defined a reading area within a larger library space by dropping its floor plane below the main level of the library. He then uses the vertical bounding surfaces of the reading area for additional book storage.

**Library, Wolfsburg Cultural Center**, Essen, Germany, 1962, Alvar Aalto

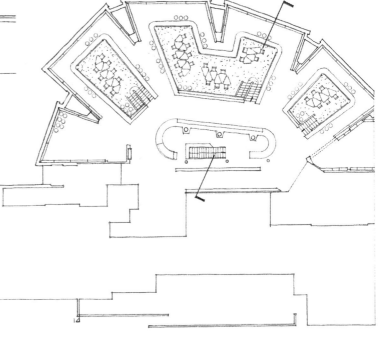

**Partial Plan, Library in Rovaniemi,** Finland, 1965–68, Alvar Aalto

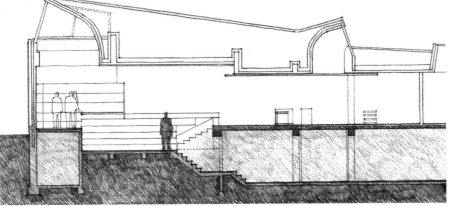

**Partial Section**
through the main reading room

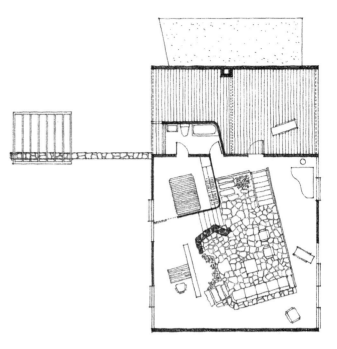

**House on the Massachusetts Coast**, 1948, Hugh Stubbins

An area within a large room can be sunken to reduce the scale of the room and define a more intimate space within it. A sunken area can also serve as a transitional space between two floors of a building.

**View of the lowered living level**

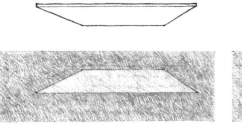

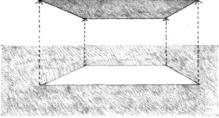

Similar to the manner in which a shade tree offers a sense of enclosure beneath its umbrella structure, an overhead plane defines a field of space between itself and the ground plane. Since the edges of the overhead plane establish the boundaries of this field, its shape, size, and height above the ground plane determines the formal qualities of the space.

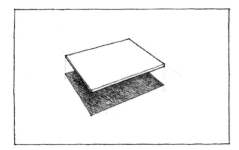

While the previous manipulations of the ground or floor plane defined fields of space whose upper limits were established by their context, an overhead plane has the ability to define a discrete volume of space virtually by itself.

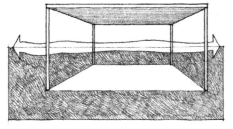

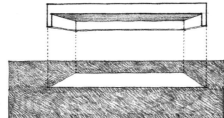

If vertical linear elements such as columns or posts are used to support the overhead plane, they will aid in visually establishing the limits of the defined space without disrupting the flow of space through the field.

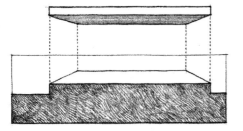

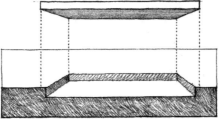

Similarly, if the edges of the overhead plane are turned downward, or if the base plane beneath it is articulated by a change in level, the boundaries of the defined volume of space will be visually reinforced.

Moving the roof of a house in Guinea

The major overhead element of a building is its roof plane. It not only shelters the interior spaces of a building from sun, rain, and snow, but also has a major impact on the overall form of a building and the shaping of its spaces. The form of the roof plane, in turn, is determined by the material, geometry, and proportions of its structural system and the manner in which it transfers its loads across space to its supports.

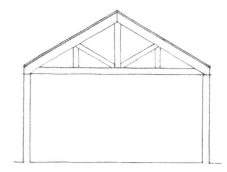

Wood Truss

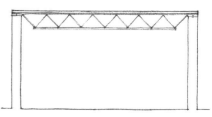

Steel Joist

Masonry Vault

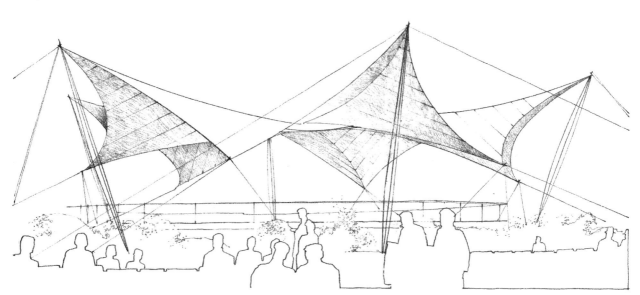

Tensile Structure, National Garden Show, Cologne, Germany, 1957, Frei Otto and Peter Stromeyer

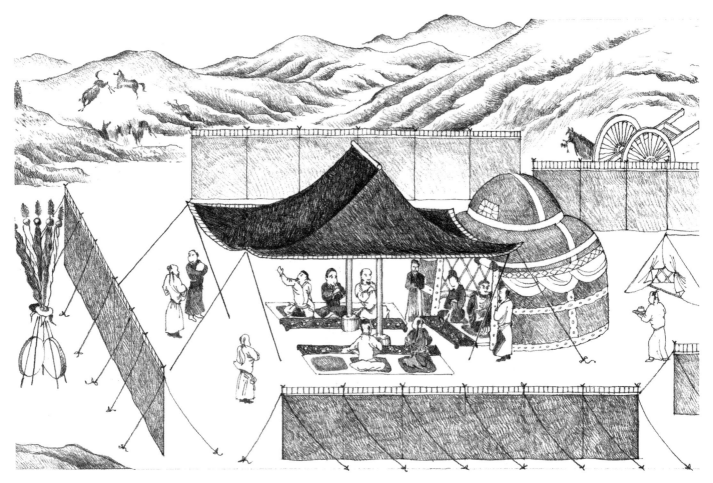

Chinese painting illustrating the use of a pavilion structure to define a shaded resting place within an encampment.

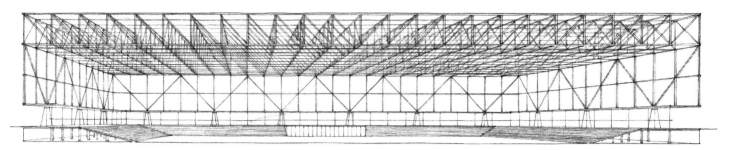

The roof plane can visually express how its pattern of structural members resolves forces and transfers loads to a system of supports.

**Convention Hall for Chicago (Project)**, 1953, Mies van der Rohe

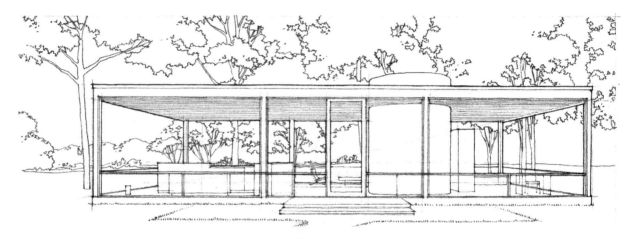

**Glass House**, New Canaan, Connecticut, 1949, Philip Johnson

The roof plane can be the major space-defining element of a building and visually organize a series of forms and spaces beneath its sheltering canopy.

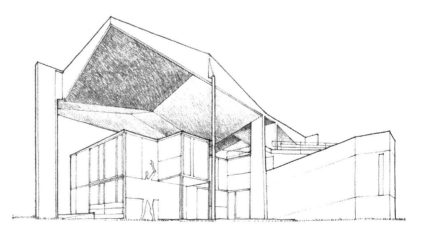

**Centre Le Corbusier**, Zurich, 1963–67, Le Corbusier

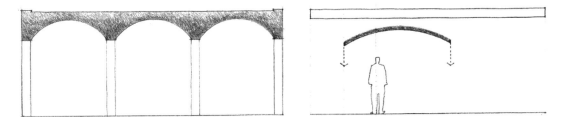

The ceiling plane of an interior space can reflect the form of the structural system supporting the overhead floor or roof plane. Since it need not resist any weathering forces nor carry any major loads, the ceiling plane can also be detached from the floor or roof plane and become a visually active element in a space.

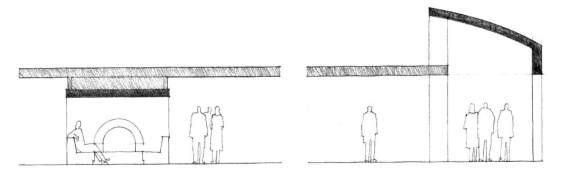

As in the case of the base plane, the ceiling plane can be manipulated to define and articulate zones of space within a room. It can be lowered or elevated to alter the scale of a space, define a path of movement through it, or allow natural light to enter it from above.

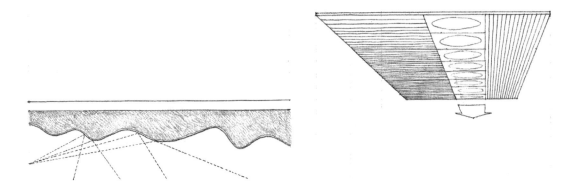

The form, color, texture, and pattern of the ceiling plane can be manipulated as well to improve the quality of light or sound within a space or give it a directional quality or orientation.

**Side Chapels in the Cistercian Monastery of La Tourette**,
near Lyons, France, 1956–59, Le Corbusier

Well-defined negative areas or voids within an overhead plane,
such as for skylights, can be seen as positive shapes that
establish the presence of spatial fields below their openings.

**Interior of Church, Parish Center**, Wolfsburg, Germany,
1960–62, Alvar Aalto

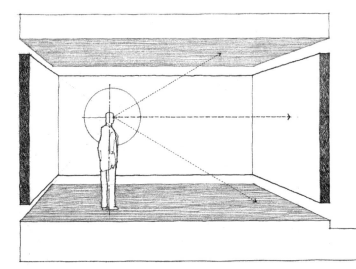

In the previous section of this chapter, horizontal planes defined fields of space in which the vertical boundaries were implied rather than explicitly described. The following section discusses the critical role vertical elements of form play in firmly establishing the visual limits of a spatial field.

Vertical forms have a greater presence in our visual field than horizontal planes and are therefore more instrumental in defining a discrete volume of space and providing a sense of enclosure and privacy for those within it. In addition, they serve to separate one space from another and establish a common boundary between the interior and exterior environments.

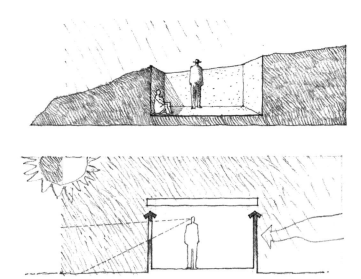

Vertical elements of form also play important roles in the construction of architectural forms and spaces. They serve as structural supports for floor and roof planes. They provide shelter and protection from the climatic elements and aid in controlling the flow of air, heat, and sound into and through the interior spaces of a building.

## Vertical Linear Elements

Vertical linear elements define the perpendicular edges of a volume of space.

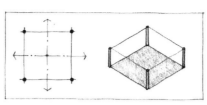 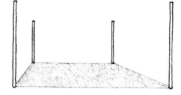

## Single Vertical Plane

A single vertical plane articulates the space on which it fronts.

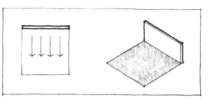 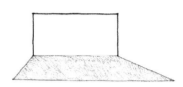

## L-shaped Plane

An L-shaped configuration of vertical planes generates a field of space from its corner outward along a diagonal axis.

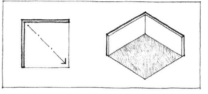 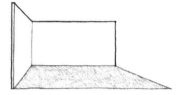

## Parallel Planes

Two parallel vertical planes define a volume of space between them that is oriented axially toward both open ends of the configuration.

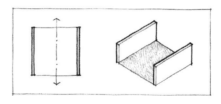 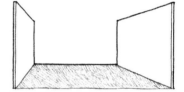

## U-shaped Plane

A U-shaped configuration of vertical planes defines a volume of space that is oriented primarily toward the open end of the configuration.

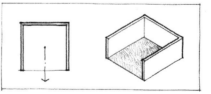 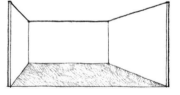

## Four Planes: Closure

Four vertical planes establish the boundaries of an introverted space and influence the field of space around the enclosure.

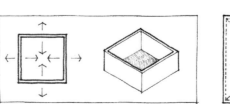 

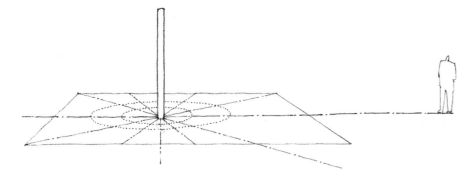

A vertical linear element, such as a column, obelisk, or tower, establishes a point on the ground plane and makes it visible in space. Standing upright and alone, a slender linear element is nondirectional except for the path that would lead us to its position in space. Any number of horizontal axes can be made to pass through it.

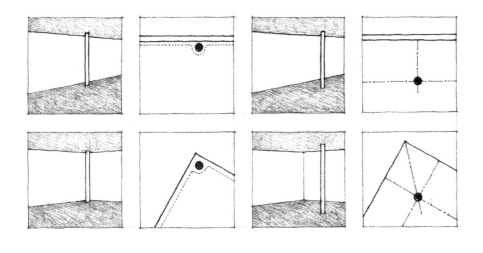

When located within a defined volume of space, a column will generate a spatial field about itself and interact with the spatial enclosure. A column attached to a wall buttresses the plane and articulates its surface. At the corner of a space, a column punctuates the meeting of two wall planes. Standing free within a space, a column defines zones of space within the enclosure.

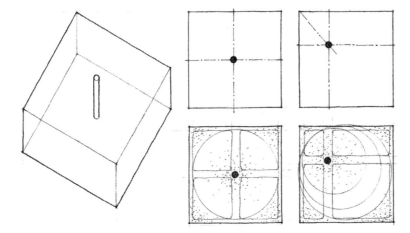

When centered in a space, a column will assert itself as the center of the field and define equivalent zones of space between itself and the surrounding wall planes. When offset, the column will define hierarchical zones of space differentiated by size, form, and location.

No volume of space can be established without the definition of its edges and corners. Linear elements serve this purpose in marking the limits of spaces that require visual and spatial continuity with their surroundings.

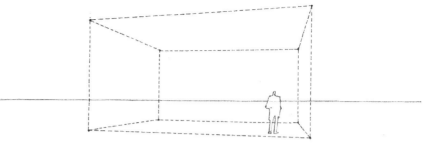

Two columns establish a transparent spatial membrane by the visual tension between their shafts. Three or more columns can be arranged to define the corners of a volume of space. This space does not require a larger spatial context for its definition, but relates freely to it.

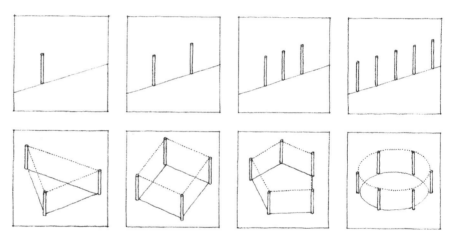

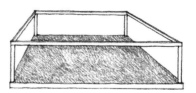

The edges of the volume of space can be visually reinforced by articulating its base plane and establishing its upper limits with beams spanning between the columns or with an overhead plane. A repetitive series of column elements along its perimeter would further strengthen the definition of the volume.

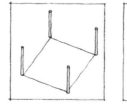
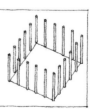
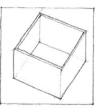

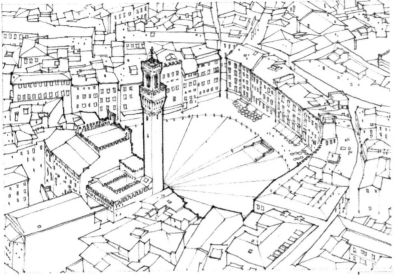

**Piazza del Campo**, Siena, Italy

Vertical linear elements can terminate an axis, mark the center of an urban space, or provide a focus for an urban space along its edge.

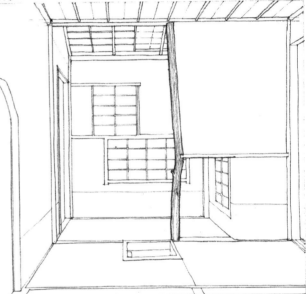

**Shokin-Tei Pavilion**, **Katsura Palace**, Kyoto, Japan, 17th century.
In the example above, the tokobashira, often a tree trunk in natural form, is a symbolic element that marks one edge of the tokonoma in a Japanese tearoom.

**Piazza of St. Peter**, Rome, 1655—67, Giovanni Bernini

**Taj Mahal, Tomb of Muntaz Mahal**, wife of Shah Jahan, Agra, India, 1630–53

A bosket or grove of trees defining a shady place in a garden or park.

In these examples, various forms of minarets mark the corners of a platform and establish a field of space—a three-dimensional framework—for the Mogul mausoleum structures.

From an analysis of Islamic Indian Architecture by Andras Volwahsen

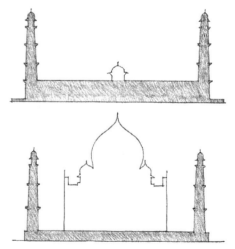

**Tomb of Jahangir**, near Lahore

**Tomb of Muntaz Mahal**, Agra

**Tomb of I'timad-ud-daula**, Agra

**Tetrastyle Atrium**, **House of the Silver Wedding**, Pompeii,
2nd century B.C.

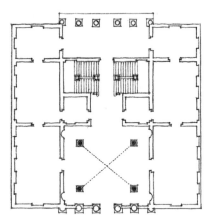

**Palazzo Antonini**, Udine, Italy, 1556,
Andrea Palladio

Four columns can establish the corners of a discrete volume of space within a larger room or setting. Supporting a canopy, the columns form an aedicule, a diminutive pavilion that serves as a shrine or the symbolic center of a space.

Traditional Roman houses typically were organized about an atrium open to the sky and surrounded by a roof structure supported at the corners by four columns. Vitruvius termed this a tetrastyle atrium.

During the Renaissance, Andrea Palladio incorporated the tetrastyle theme in the vestibules and halls of a number of villas and palazzi. The four columns not only supported the vaulted ceiling and the floor above but also adjusted the dimensions of the rooms to Palladian proportions.

In the Sea Ranch condominium units, four posts along with a sunken floor and an overhead plane define an intimate aedicular space within a larger room.

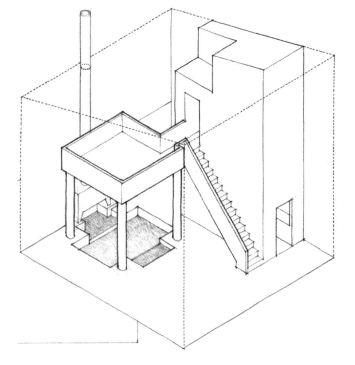

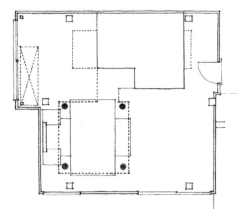

**Condominium Unit No. 5, Sea Ranch**, California, 1966, MLTW

**Cloister and Salle des Chevaliers,**
Mont S. Michel, France, 1203–28

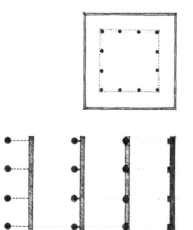

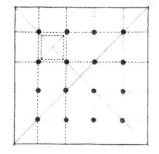

A regularly-spaced series of columns or similar vertical elements form a colonnade. This archetypal element in the vocabulary of architectural design effectively defines an edge of a spatial volume while permitting visual and spatial continuity to exist between the space and its surroundings. A row of columns can also engage a wall and become a pilastrade that supports the wall, articulates its surface, and tempers the scale, rhythm, and proportioning of its bays.

A grid of columns within a large room or hall not only serves to support the floor or roof plane above. The orderly rows of columns also punctuate the spatial volume, mark off modular zones within the spatial field, and establish a measurable rhythm and scale which make the spatial dimensions comprehensible.

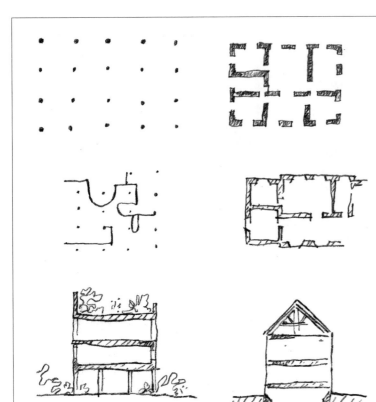

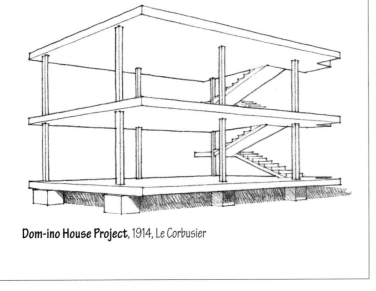

Sketches for *The Five Points of the New Architecture*, 1926, Le Corbusier

**Dom-ino House Project**, 1914, Le Corbusier

In 1926, Le Corbusier stated what he believed to be the "Five Points of the New Architecture." His observations were to a great extent the result of the development of reinforced concrete construction that began in the late nineteenth century. This type of construction, in particular the use of concrete columns to support floor and roof slabs, afforded new possibilities for the definition and enclosure of spaces within a building.

Concrete slabs could cantilever beyond their column supports and enable the "free facade" of the building to be "light membranes" of "screen walls and windows." Within the building, a "free plan" was possible since the enclosure and layout of spaces were not determined or restricted by the pattern of heavy load-bearing walls. Interior spaces could be defined with non-load-bearing partitions, and their layout could respond freely to programmatic requirements.

On the facing page, two contrasting examples of the use of a column grid are illustrated:

1. A column grid establishes a fixed, neutral field of space in which interior spaces are freely formed and distributed.
2. A grid of columns or posts corresponds closely to the layout of the interior spaces; there is a close fit between structure and space.

1. Millowners' Association Building,
   Ahmedabad, India, 1954, Le Corbusier

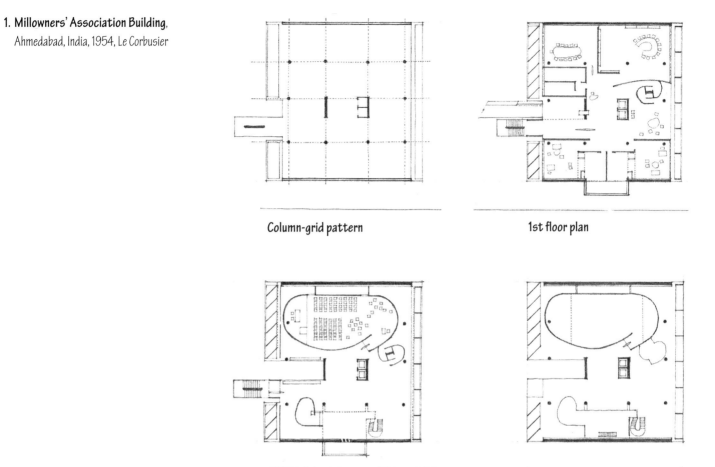

Column-grid pattern

1st floor plan

2nd floor plan

3rd floor plan

2. Traditional Japanese Residence

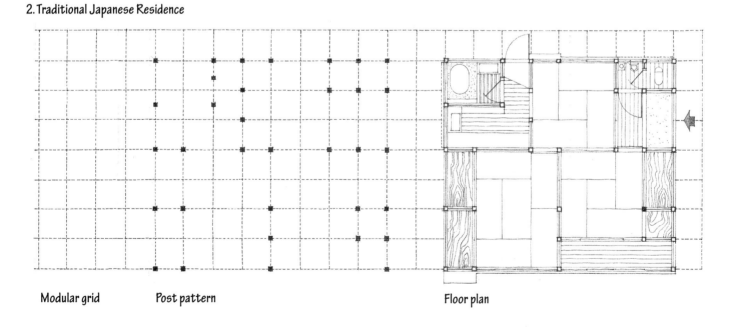

Modular grid          Post pattern                              Floor plan

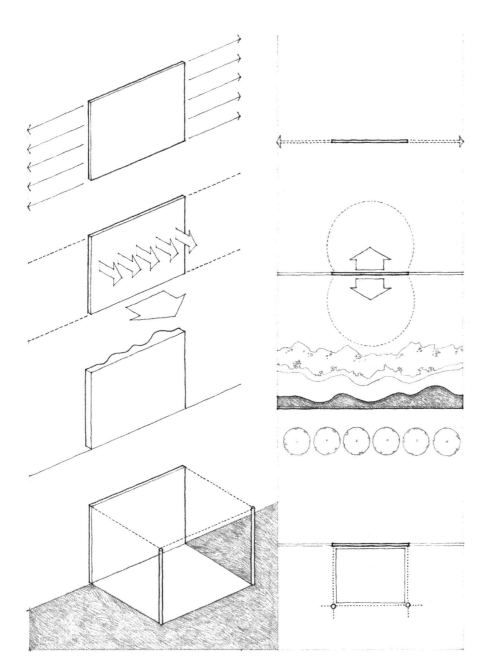

A single vertical plane, standing alone in space, has visual qualities uniquely different from those of a freestanding column. A round column has no preferred direction except for its vertical axis. A square column has two equivalent sets of faces and therefore two identical axes. A rectangular column also has two axes, but they differ in their effect. As the rectangular column becomes more like a wall, it can appear to be merely a fragment of an infinitely larger or longer plane, slicing through and dividing a volume of space.

A vertical plane has frontal qualities. Its two surfaces or faces front on and establish the edges of two separate and distinct spatial fields.

These two faces of a plane can be equivalent and front similar spaces. Or they can be differentiated in form, color, or texture, in order to respond to or articulate different spatial conditions. A vertical plane can therefore have either two fronts or a front and a back.

The field of space on which a single vertical plane fronts is not well-defined. The plane by itself can establish only a single edge of the field. To define a three-dimensional volume of space, the plane must interact with other elements of form.

The height of a vertical plane relative to our body height and eye level is the critical factor that affects the ability of the plane to visually describe space. When two-feet high, a plane defines the edge of a spatial field but provides little or no sense of enclosure. When waist-high, it begins to provide a sense of enclosure while allowing for visual continuity with the adjoining space. When it approaches our eye level in height, it begins to separate one space from another. Above our height, a plane interrupts the visual and spatial continuity between two fields and provides a strong sense of enclosure.

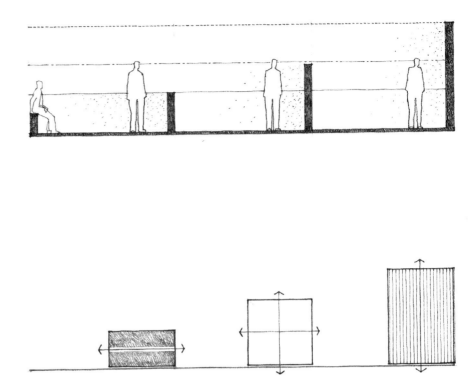

The surface color, texture, and pattern of a plane affect our perception of its visual weight, scale, and proportion.

When related to a defined volume of space, a vertical plane can be the primary face of the space and give it a specific orientation. It can front the space and define a plane of entry into it. It can be a freestanding element within a space and divide the volume into two separate but related areas.

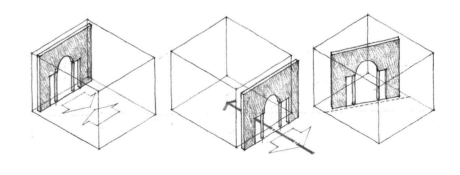

S. Agostino, Rome, 1479–83, Giacomo da Pietrasanta

Arch of Septimius Severus, Rome, A.D. 203

A single vertical plane can define the principal facade of a building fronting a public space, establish a gateway through which one passes, as well as articulate spatial zones within a larger volume.

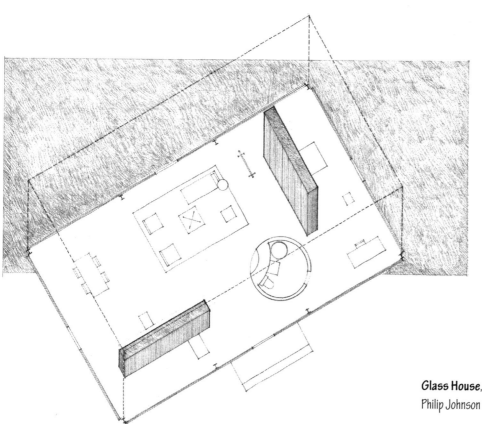

Glass House, New Canaan, Connecticut, 1949, Philip Johnson

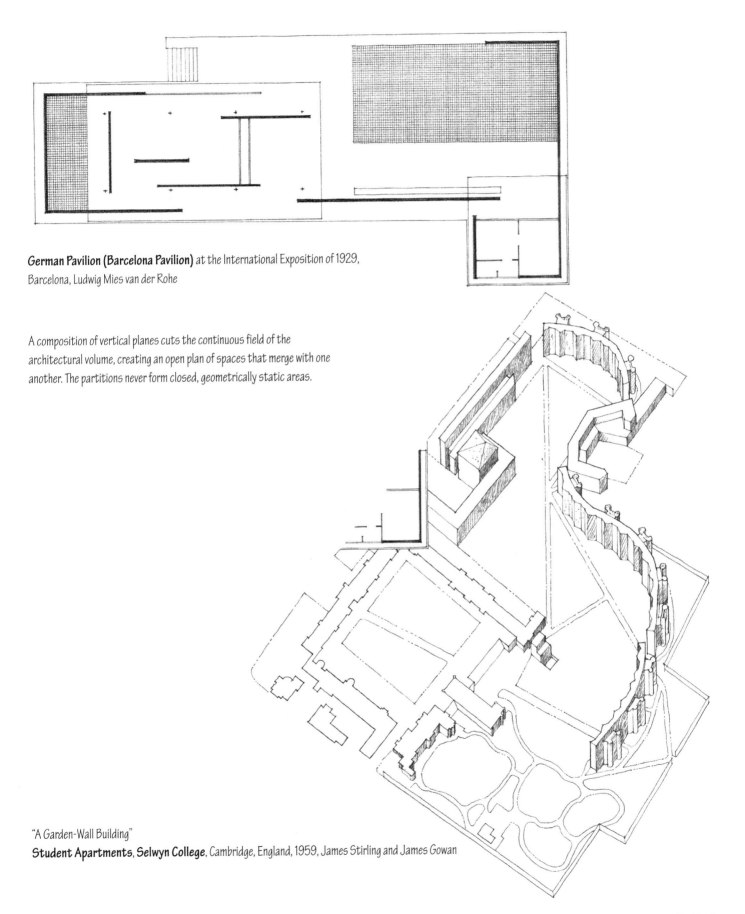

**German Pavilion (Barcelona Pavilion)** at the International Exposition of 1929, Barcelona, Ludwig Mies van der Rohe

A composition of vertical planes cuts the continuous field of the architectural volume, creating an open plan of spaces that merge with one another. The partitions never form closed, geometrically static areas.

"A Garden-Wall Building"
**Student Apartments, Selwyn College**, Cambridge, England, 1959, James Stirling and James Gowan

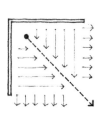
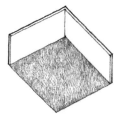
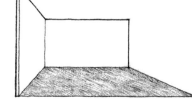

An L-shaped configuration of vertical planes defines a field of space along a diagonal from its corner outward. While this field is strongly defined and enclosed at the corner of the configuration, it dissipates rapidly as it moves away from the corner. The introverted field at the interior corner becomes extroverted along its outer edges.

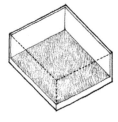

While two edges of the field are clearly defined by the two planes of the configuration, its other edges remain ambiguous unless further articulated by additional vertical elements, manipulations of the base plane, or an overhead plane.

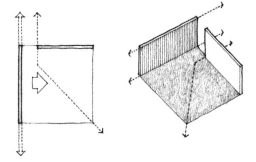

If a void is introduced to one side of the corner of the configuration, the definition of the field will be weakened. The two planes will be isolated from each other and one will appear to slide by and visually dominate the other.

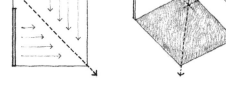

If neither plane extends to the corner, the field will become more dynamic and organize itself along the diagonal of the configuration.

A building form can have an L-shaped configuration and be subject to the following readings. One of the arms of the configuration can be a linear form that incorporates the corner within its boundaries while the other arm is seen as an appendage to it. Or the corner can be articulated as an independent element that joins two linear forms together.

A building can have an L-shaped configuration to establish a corner of its site, enclose a field of outdoor space to which its interior spaces relate, or shelter a portion of outdoor space from undesirable conditions around it.

L-shaped configurations of planes are stable and self-supporting and can stand alone in space. Because they are open-ended, they are flexible space-defining elements. They can be used in combination with one another or with other elements of form to define a rich variety of spaces.

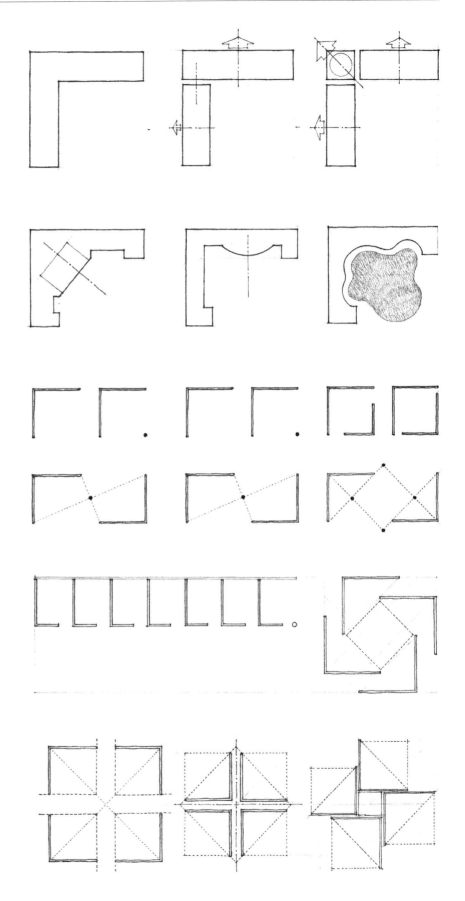

**Vegetation Forming L-shaped Windscreens**, Shimane Prefecture, Japan

The sheltering aspect of an L-shaped configuration is expressed well in this example where Japanese farmers coaxed pine trees to grow into tall, thick, L-shaped hedges to shield their houses and land from winter winds and snowstorms.

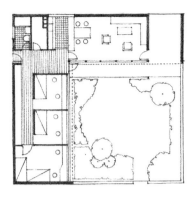

**Basic Housing Unit**

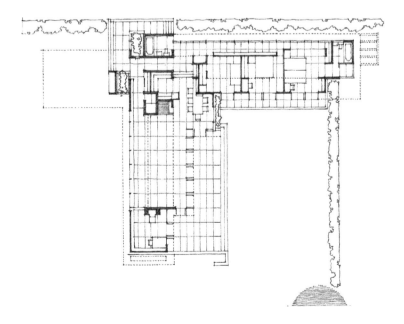

**Kingo Housing Estate** near Elsinore, Denmark
1958–63, Jorn Utzon

Site Plan

A common theme found in examples of residential architecture is an L-shaped configuration of rooms enclosing an outdoor living space. Typically, one wing contains the communal living spaces while the other contains private, individual spaces. The service and utility spaces usually occupy a corner position or are strung along the backside of one of the wings.

The advantage of this type of layout is its provision of a private courtyard, sheltered by the building form and to which interior spaces can be directly related. In the Kingo Housing estate, a fairly high density is achieved with this type of unit, each with its own private outdoor space.

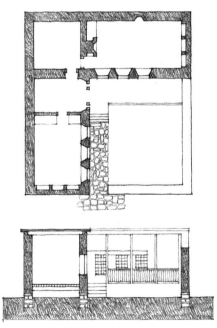

**Traditional House in Konya, Turkey**

**Rosenbaum House,** Florence, Alabama, 1939, Frank Lloyd Wright

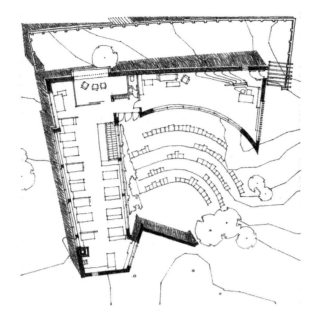

**Architect's Studio, Helsinki**, 1955–56, Alvar Aalto

Similar to the residential examples on the preceding page, these buildings use their L-shaped forms as sheltering or enclosing elements. The History Faculty Building at Cambridge uses a seven-story, L-shaped block to functionally and symbolically enclose a large, roof-lit library which is the most important space in the building.

The outdoor space enclosed by the architect's studio in Helsinki is used as an amphitheater for lectures and social occasions. It is not a passive space whose form is determined by the building that encloses it. Rather, it asserts its positive form and pressures the form of its enclosure.

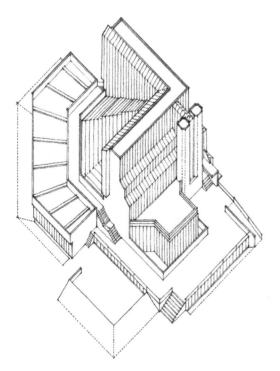

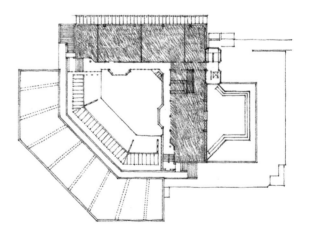

**History Faculty Building, Cambridge University**, England, 1964–67, James Stirling

**Berlin Building Exposition House**, 1931, Mies van der Rohe

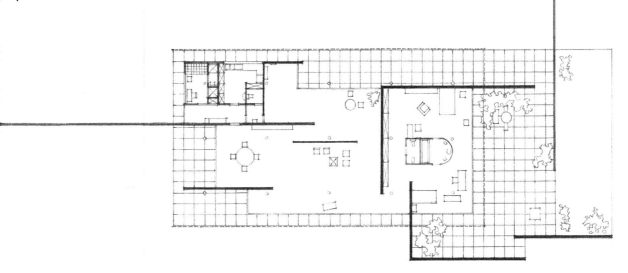

**Suntop Homes**, Four-family Housing Units,
Ardmore, Pennsylvania, 1939, Frank Lloyd Wright

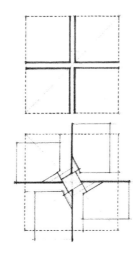

**Diagram, St. Mark's Tower**,
New York City, 1929, Frank Lloyd Wright

In these examples, L-shaped walls separate the units of a quadruplex housing
organization and define zones within a building as well as spaces within a room.

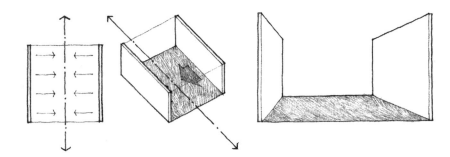

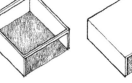

A pair of parallel vertical planes defines a field of space between them. The open ends of the field, established by the vertical edges of the planes, give the space a strong directional quality. Its primary orientation is along the axis about which the planes are symmetrical. Since the parallel planes do not meet to form corners and fully enclose the field, the space is extroverted in nature.

The definition of the spatial field along the open ends of the configuration can be visually reinforced by manipulating the base plane or adding overhead elements to the composition.

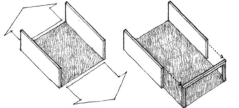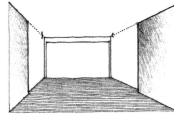

The spatial field can be expanded by extending the base plane beyond the open ends of the configuration. This expanded field can, in turn, be terminated by a vertical plane whose width and height is equal to that of the field.

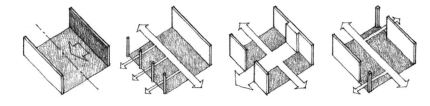

If one of the parallel planes is differentiated from the other by a change in form, color, or texture, a secondary axis, perpendicular to the flow of the space, will be established within the field. Openings in one or both of the planes can also introduce secondary axes to the field and modulate the directional quality of the space.

Various elements in architecture can be seen as parallel planes that define a field of space:

- a pair of parallel interior walls within a building
- a street space formed by the facades of two facing buildings
- a colonnaded arbor or pergola
- a promenade or allée bordered by rows of trees or hedges
- a natural topographical form in the landscape

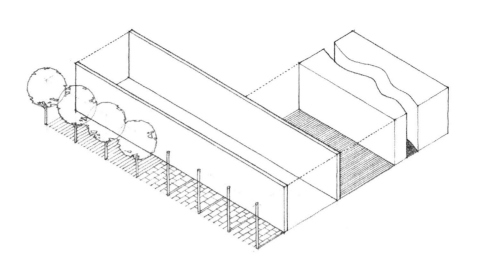

The image of parallel vertical planes is often associated with the bearing-wall structural system, wherein a floor or roof structure spans the spaces between two or more parallel load-bearing walls.

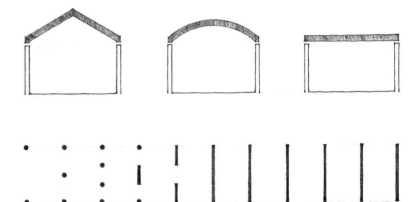

Sets of parallel vertical planes can be transformed into a wide variety of configurations. Their spatial fields can be related to one another either through the open ends of their configurations or through openings in the planes themselves.

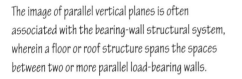

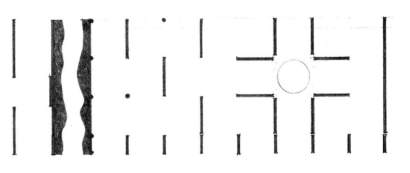

Nave of the basilican church, **S. Apollinare in Classe**, Ravenna, Italy, 534–39

**Champ de Mars**, Paris

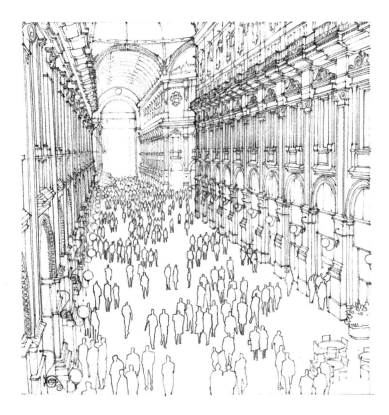

**Galleria Vittorio Emanuelle**, Milan, Italy, 1865–77, G. Mengoni

The directional quality and flow of the space defined by parallel planes are naturally manifested in spaces used for circulation and movement, such as the streets and boulevards of towns and cities. These linear spaces can be defined by the facades of the buildings fronting them, as well as by the more permeable planes established by colonnades, arcades, or rows of trees.

**House in Old Westbury**, New York, 1969–71, Richard Meier

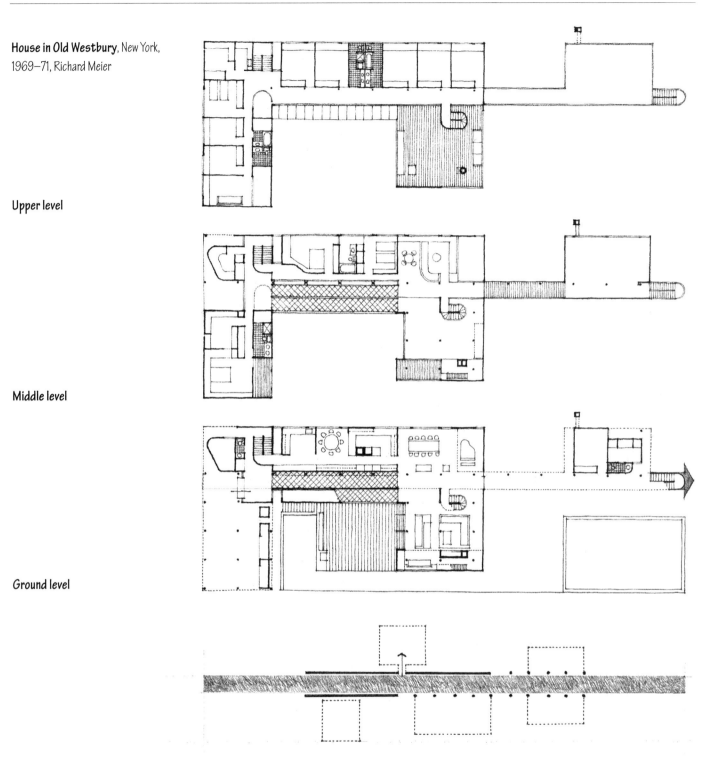

Upper level

Middle level

Ground level

The flow of the space defined by parallel planes corresponds naturally to the paths of movement within a building, along its corridors, halls, and galleries.

The parallel planes that define a circulation space can be solid and opaque to provide privacy for the spaces along the circulation path. The planes can also be established by a row of columns so that the circulation path, open on one or both of its sides, becomes part of the spaces it passes through.

**Sarabhai House**, Ahmedabad, India, 1955, Le Corbusier

The parallel vertical planes of a bearing-wall structural system can be the generating force behind the form and organization of a building. Their repetitive pattern can be modified by varying their length or by introducing voids within the planes to accommodate the dimensional requirements of larger spaces. These voids can also define circulation paths and establish visual relationships perpendicular to the wall planes.

The slots of space defined by parallel wall planes can also be modulated by altering the spacing and configuration of the planes.

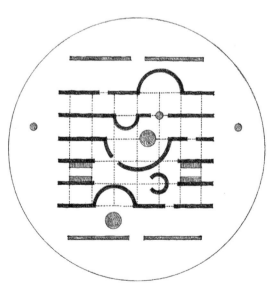

**Arnheim Pavilion**, The Netherlands, 1966, Aldo van Eyck

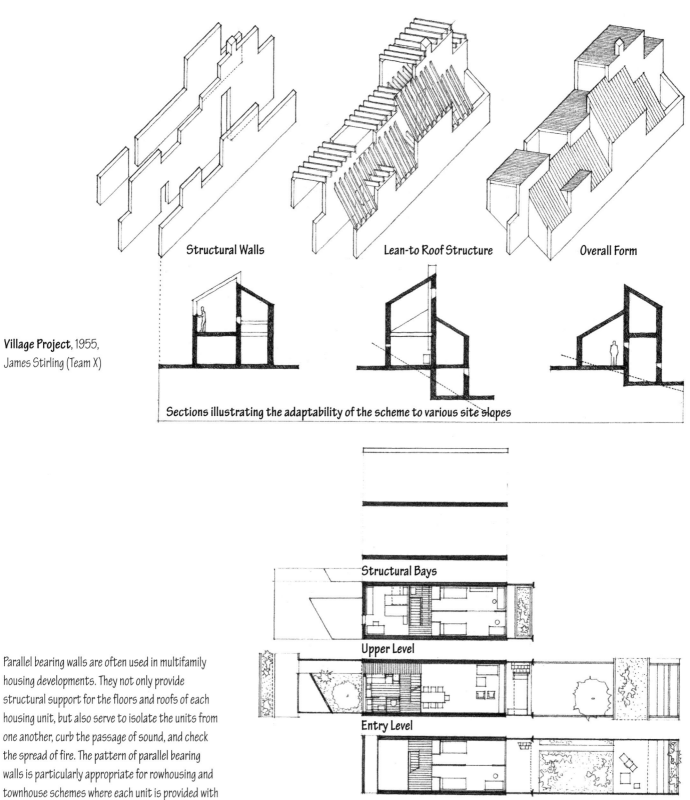

Structural Walls    Lean-to Roof Structure    Overall Form

**Village Project**, 1955,
James Stirling (Team X)

Sections illustrating the adaptability of the scheme to various site slopes

Structural Bays

Upper Level

Entry Level

Ground Level

Parallel bearing walls are often used in multifamily housing developments. They not only provide structural support for the floors and roofs of each housing unit, but also serve to isolate the units from one another, curb the passage of sound, and check the spread of fire. The pattern of parallel bearing walls is particularly appropriate for rowhousing and townhouse schemes where each unit is provided with two orientations.

**Siedlung Halen**, near Bern, Switzerland, 1961, Atelier 5

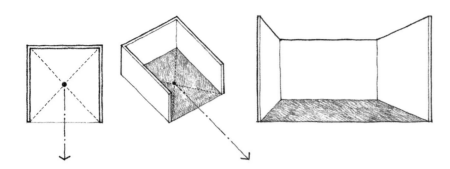

A U-shaped configuration of vertical planes defines a field of space that has an inward focus as well as an outward orientation. At the closed end of the configuration, the field is well defined. Toward the open end of the configuration, the field becomes extroverted in nature.

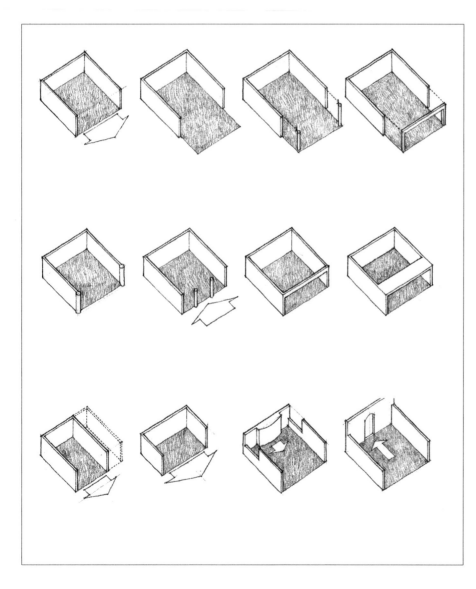

The open end is the primary aspect of the configuration by virtue of its uniqueness relative to the other three planes. It allows the field to have visual and spatial continuity with the adjoining space. The extension of the spatial field into the adjoining space can be visually reinforced by continuing the base plane beyond the open end of the configuration.

If the plane of the opening is further defined with columns or overhead elements, the definition of the original field will be reinforced and continuity with the adjoining space will be interrupted.

If the configuration of planes is rectangular and oblong in form, the open end can be along its narrow or wide side. In either case, the open end will remain the primary face of the spatial field, and the plane opposite the open end will be the principal element among the three planes of the configuration.

If openings are introduced at the corners of the configuration, secondary zones will be created within a multidirectional and dynamic field.

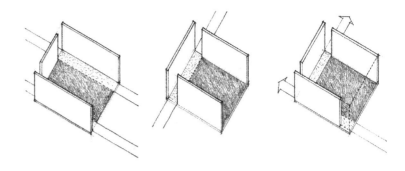

If the field is entered through the open end of the configuration, the rear plane, or a form placed in front of it, will terminate our view of the space. If the field is entered through an opening in one of the planes, the view of what lies beyond the open end will draw our attention and terminate the sequence.

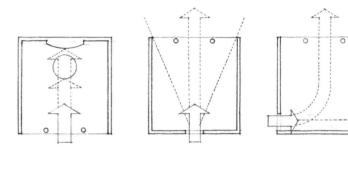

If the end of a long, narrow field is open, the space will encourage movement and induce a progression or sequence of events. If the field is square, or nearly square, the space will be static and have the character of a place to be in, rather than a space to move through. If the side of a long, narrow field is open, the space will be susceptible to a subdivision into a number of zones.

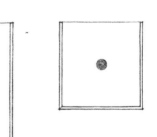

U-shaped configurations of building forms and organizations have the inherent ability to capture and define outdoor space. Their composition can be seen to consist essentially of linear forms. The corners of the configuration can be articulated as independent elements or can be incorporated into the body of the linear forms.

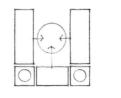

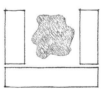

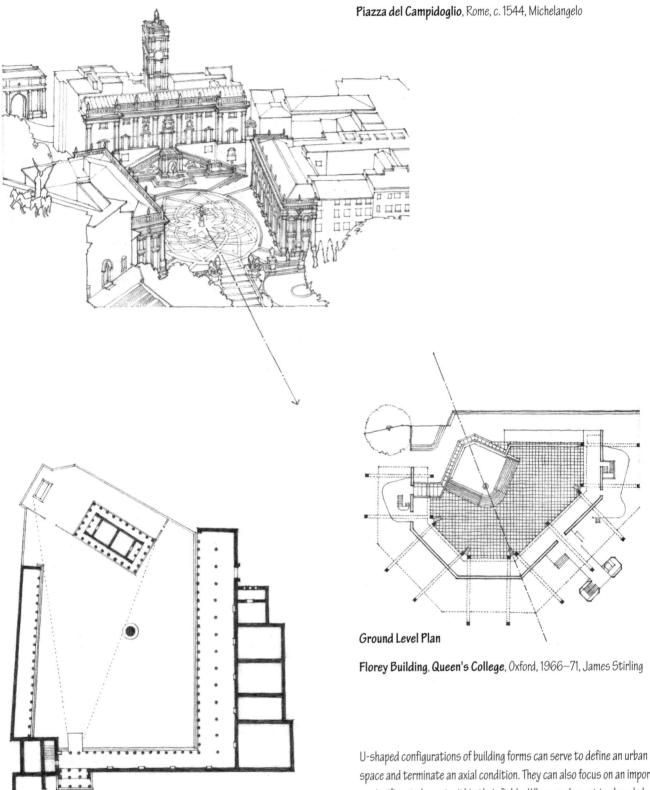

**Piazza del Campidoglio**, Rome, c. 1544, Michelangelo

**Sacred Precinct of Athena**, Pergamon, Asia Minor, 4th century B.C.

**Ground Level Plan**

**Florey Building, Queen's College**, Oxford, 1966–71, James Stirling

U-shaped configurations of building forms can serve to define an urban space and terminate an axial condition. They can also focus on an important or significant element within their fields. When an element is placed along the open end of its field, it gives the field a point of focus as well as a greater sense of closure.

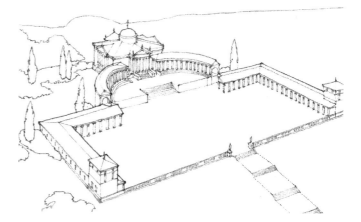

**Villa Trissino at Meledo**, From *The Four Books on Architecture*, Andrea Palladio

A U-shaped building form can serve as a container and can organize within its field a cluster of forms and spaces.

The U-shaped organization can also define a forecourt for the approach to a building as well as form an entrance recessed within the building volume.

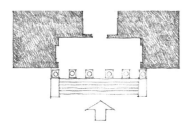

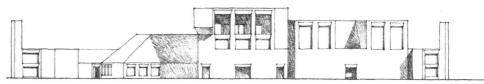

**Front Elevation**

**Convent for the Dominican Sisters**, project, Media, Pennsylvania, 1965–68, Louis Kahn.
The cells form an enclave for a village of community rooms.

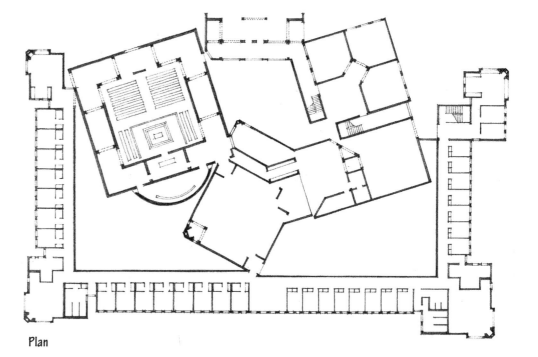

Plan

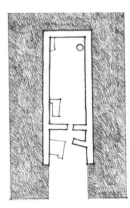

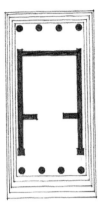

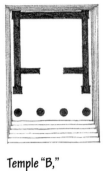

**Temple of Nemesis,**
Rhamnus

**Temple "B,"**
Selinus

**Early Megaron Space**
Principal room or hall of an
early Anatolian or Aegean
house

**Plans of Greek Temples**

**Temple on the Ilissus,**
Athens

U-shaped enclosures of interior space have a specific orientation toward their open ends. These U-shaped enclosures can group themselves around a central space to form an introverted organization.

The Hotel for Students at Otaniemi, by Alvar Aalto, demonstrates the use of U-shaped enclosures to define the basic unit of space in double-loaded schemes for dormitories, apartment, and hotels. These units are extroverted. They turn their back on the corridor and orient themselves to the exterior environment.

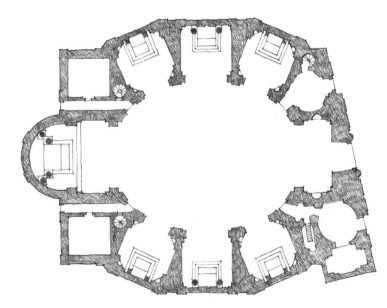

**Sketch of an Oval Church by Borromini,** Genesis of San Carlo Alle Quattro Fontane

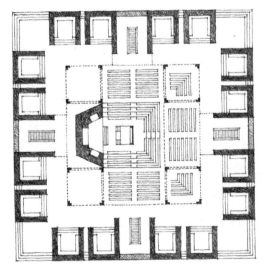

**Hurva Synagogue (project),** Jerusalem, 1968, Louis Kahn

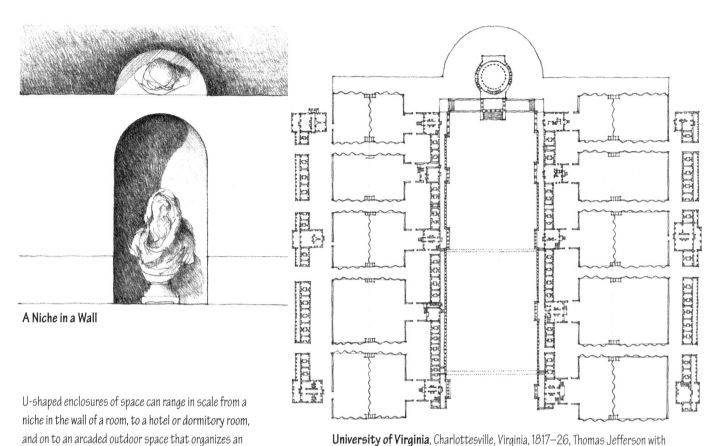

**A Niche in a Wall**

U-shaped enclosures of space can range in scale from a niche in the wall of a room, to a hotel or dormitory room, and on to an arcaded outdoor space that organizes an entire complex of buildings.

**University of Virginia**, Charlottesville, Virginia, 1817–26, Thomas Jefferson with Thornton and Latrobe

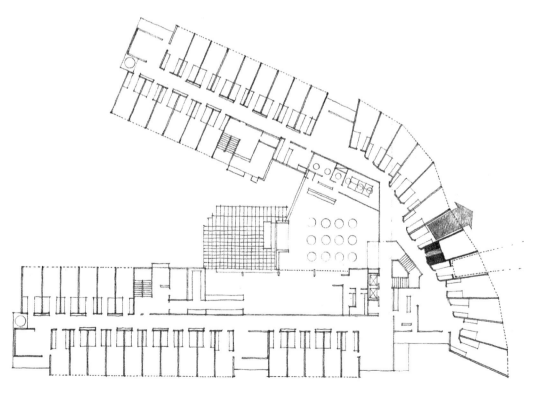

**Hotel for Students at Otaniemi**, Finland, 1962–66, Alvar Aalto

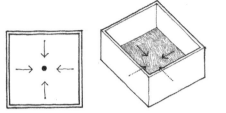

Four vertical planes encompassing a field of space is probably the most typical, and certainly the strongest, type of spatial definition in architecture. Since the field is completely enclosed, its space is naturally introverted. To achieve visual dominance within a space or become its primary face, one of the enclosing planes can be differentiated from the others by its size, form, surface articulation, or by the nature of the openings within it.

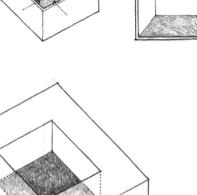

Well-defined, enclosed fields of space can be found in architecture at various scales, from a large urban square, to a courtyard or atrium space, to a single hall or room within a building complex. The examples on this and the following pages illustrate enclosed spatial fields in both urban and building-scale situations.

Historically, four planes have often been used to define a visual and spatial field for a sacred or significant building that stands as an object within the enclosure. The enclosing planes may be ramparts, walls, or fences that isolate the field and exclude surrounding elements from the precinct.

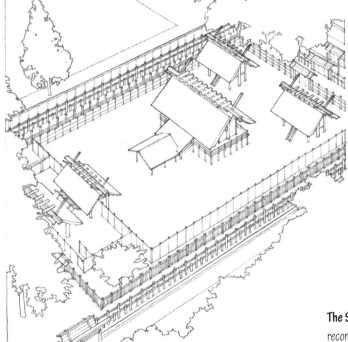

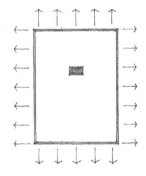

**The Sacred Enclosure, Ise Shrine**, Mie Prefecture, Japan, reconstructed every 20 years since A.D. 690.

In an urban context, a defined field of space can organize a series of buildings along its perimeter. The enclosure may consist of arcades or gallery spaces that promote the inclusion of surrounding buildings into their domain and activate the space they define.

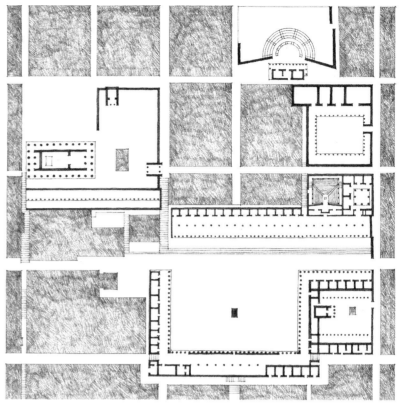

**Plan of the Agora at Priene and its surroundings**, 4th century B.C.

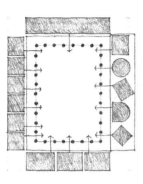

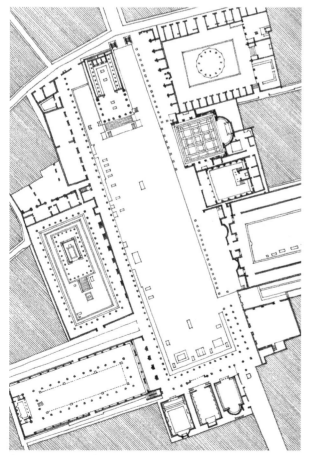

**Forum at Pompeii**, 2nd century B.C.

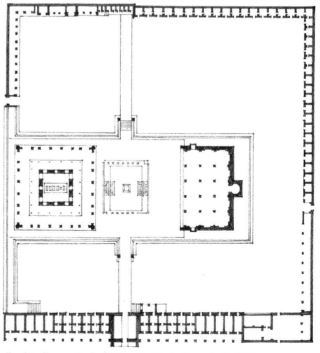

**Ibrahim Rauza**, Tomb of Sultan Ibrahim II, Bijapur, India, 1615

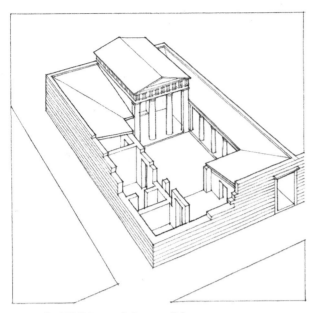

House No. 33, Priene, c. 3rd century B.C.

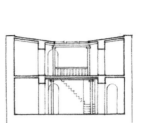

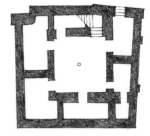

House, Ur of the Chaldees, c. 2000 B.C.

The examples on these two pages illustrate the use of enclosed volumes of space as ordering elements about which the spaces of a building can be clustered and organized. These organizing spaces can generally be characterized by their centrality, their clarity of definition, their regularity of form, and their dominating size. They are manifested here in the atrium spaces of houses, the arcaded cortile of an Italian palazzo, the enclosure of a Greek shrine, the courtyard of a Finnish town hall, and the cloister of a monastery.

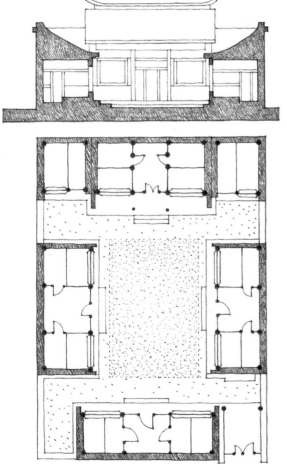

Chinese Patio House

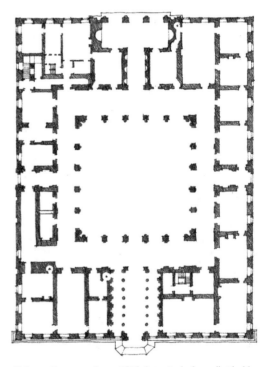

Palazzo Farnese, Rome, 1515, Antonio da Sangallo the Younger

*Enclosure of the Shrine of Apollo Delphinios*, Miletus, c. 2nd century B.C.

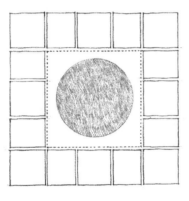

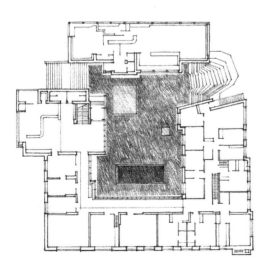

**Town Hall**, **Säynätsalo**, Finland, 1950–52, Alvar Aalto

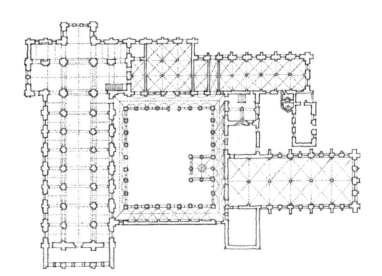

**Fontenay Abbey**, Burgundy, France, c. 1139

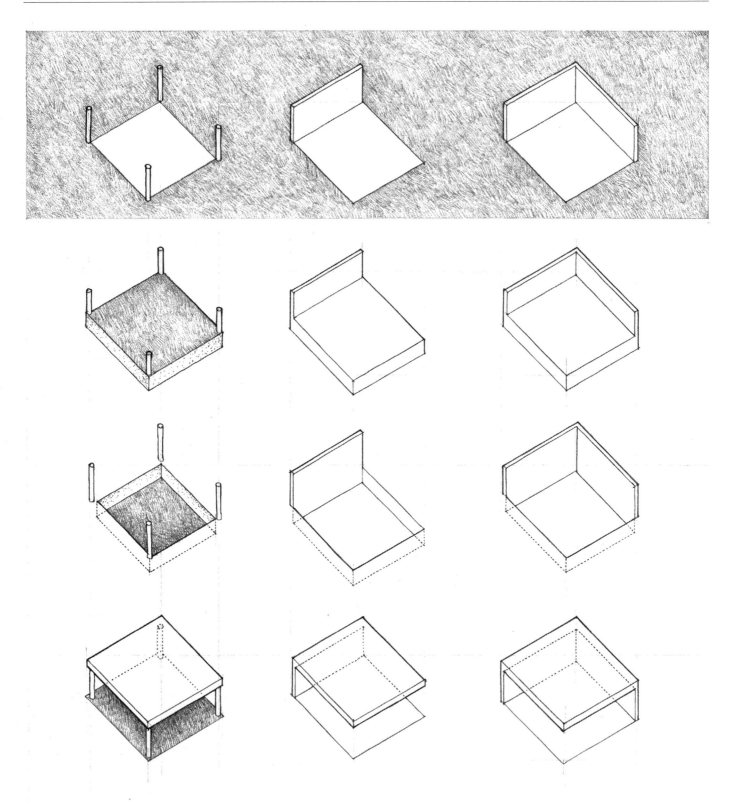

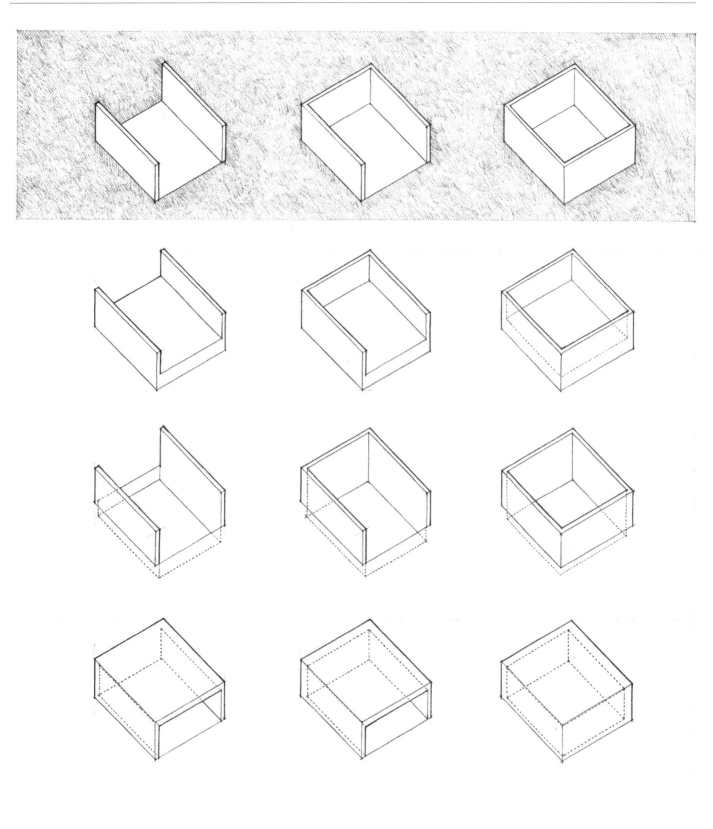

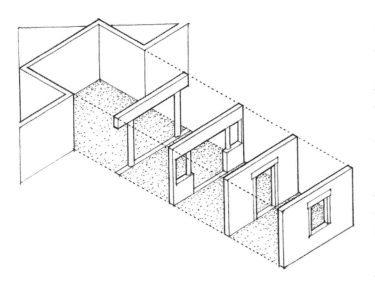

No spatial or visual continuity is possible with adjacent spaces without openings in the enclosing planes of a spatial field. Doors offer entry into a room and determine the patterns of movement and use within it. Windows allow light to penetrate the space and illuminate the surfaces of a room, offer views from the room to the exterior, establish visual relationships between the room and adjacent spaces, and provide for the natural ventilation of the space.

While these openings provide continuity with adjacent spaces, they can, depending on their size, number, and location, begin to weaken the enclosure of the space. These openings also affect the orientation and flow of the space, its quality of light, its outlook and views, and the pattern of use and movement within it.

The following section of this chapter focuses on enclosed spaces at the scale of a room, where the nature of the openings within the room's enclosure is a major factor in determining the quality of its space.

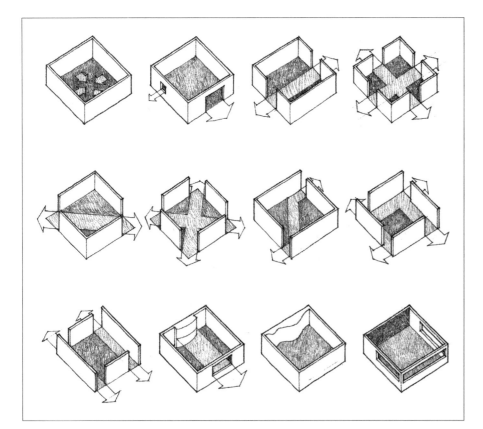

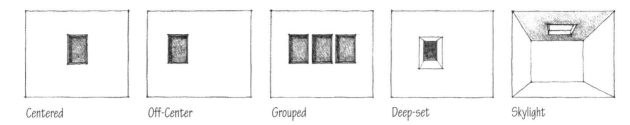

Centered    Off-Center    Grouped    Deep-set    Skylight

**Within Planes**    An opening can be located wholly within a wall or ceiling plane and be surrounded on all sides by the surface of the plane.

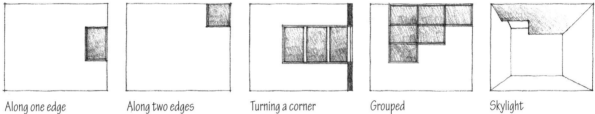

Along one edge    Along two edges    Turning a corner    Grouped    Skylight

**At Corners**    An opening can be located along one edge or at a corner of a wall or ceiling plane. In either case, the opening will be at a corner of a space.

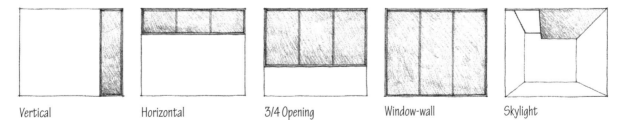

Vertical    Horizontal    3/4 Opening    Window-wall    Skylight

**Between Planes**    An opening can extend vertically between the floor and ceiling planes or horizontally between two wall planes. It can grow in size to occupy an entire wall of a space.

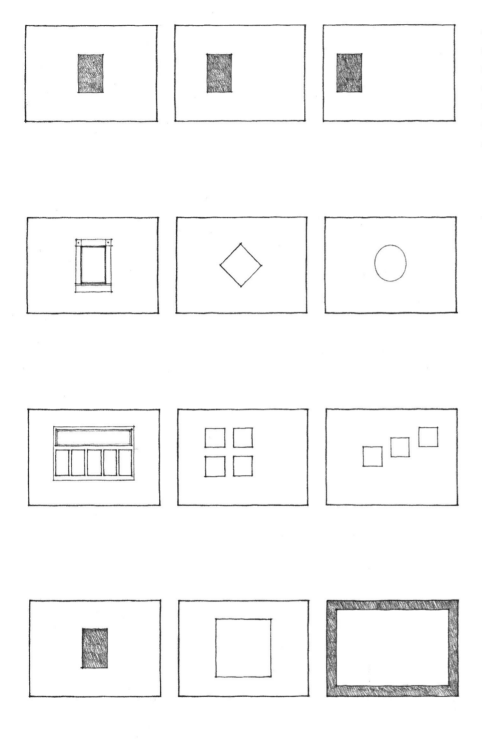

An opening located wholly within a wall or ceiling plane often appears as a bright figure on a contrasting field or background. If centered within the plane, the opening will appear stable and visually organize the surface around it. Moving the opening off-center will create a degree of visual tension between the opening and the edges of the plane toward which it is moved.

The shape of the opening, if similar to the shape of the plane in which it is located, will create a redundant compositional pattern. The shape or orientation of the opening may contrast with the enclosing plane to emphasize its individuality as a figure. The singularity of the opening may be visually reinforced with a heavy frame or articulated trimwork.

Multiple openings may be clustered to form a unified composition within a plane, or be staggered or dispersed to create visual movement along the surface of the plane.

As an opening within a plane increases in size, it will at some point cease to be a figure within an enclosing field and become instead a positive element in itself, a transparent plane bounded by a heavy frame.

Openings within planes naturally appear brighter than their adjacent surfaces. If the contrast in brightness along the edges of the openings becomes excessive, the surfaces can be illuminated by a second light source from within the space, or a deep-set opening can be formed to create illuminated surfaces between the opening and the surrounding plane.

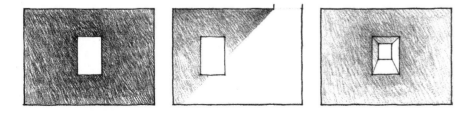

**Chapel Space**, **Notre Dame Du Haut**, Ronchamp, France, 1950–55, Le Corbusier

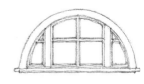

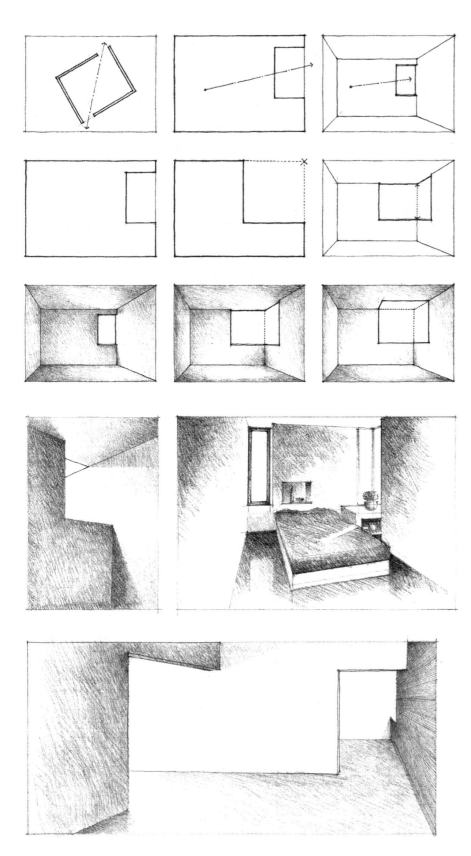

Openings that are located at corners give a space and the planes in which they are located a diagonal orientation. This directional effect may be desirable for compositional reasons, or the corner opening may be established to capture a desirable view or brighten a dark corner of a space.

A corner opening visually erodes the edges of the plane in which it is located and articulates the edge of the plane adjacent and perpendicular to it. The larger the opening, the weaker will be the definition of the corner. If the opening were to turn the corner, the angle of the space would be implied rather than real and the spatial field would extend beyond its enclosing planes.

If openings are introduced between the enclosing planes at all four corners of a space, the individual identity of the planes will be reinforced and diagonal or pinwheel patterns of space, use, and movement will be encouraged.

The light that enters a space through a corner opening washes the surface of the plane adjacent and perpendicular to the opening. This illuminated surface itself becomes a source of light and enhances the brightness of the space. The level of illumination can be enhanced further by turning the corner with the opening or adding a skylight above the opening.

Studio, **Amédée Ozenfant House**, Paris, 1922–23, Le Corbusier

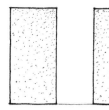
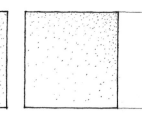
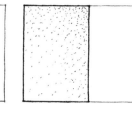

A vertical opening that extends from the floor to the ceiling plane of a space visually separates and articulates the edges of the adjacent wall planes.

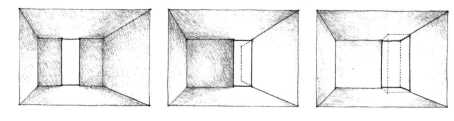

If located at a corner, the vertical opening will erode the definition of the space and allow it to extend beyond the corner to the adjacent space. It will also allow incoming light to wash the surface of the wall plane perpendicular to it and articulate the primacy of that plane in the space. If allowed to turn the corner, the vertical opening will further erode the definition of the space, allow it to interlock with adjacent spaces, and emphasize the individuality of the enclosing planes.

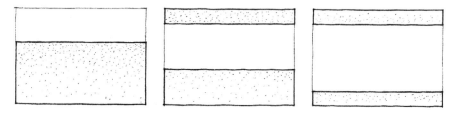

A horizontal opening that extends across a wall plane will separate it into a number of horizontal layers. If the opening is not very deep, it will not erode the integrity of the wall plane. If, however, its depth increases to the point where it is greater than the bands above and below it, then the opening will become a positive element bounded at its top and bottom by heavy frames.

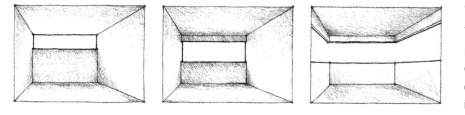

Turning a corner with a horizontal opening reinforces the horizontal layering of a space and broadens the panoramic view from within the space. If the opening continues around the space, it will visually lift the ceiling plane from the wall planes, isolate it, and give it a feeling of lightness.

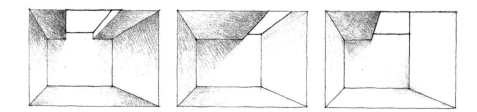

Locating a linear skylight along the edge where a wall and ceiling plane meet allows incoming light to wash the surface of the wall, illuminate it, and enhance the brightness of the space. The form of the skylight can be manipulated to capture direct sunlight, indirect daylight, or a combination of both.

**Living Room, Samuel Freeman House,**
Los Angeles, California, 1924, Frank Lloyd Wright

Window-walls offer more expansive views and permit a greater amount of daylight to penetrate a space than any of the previous examples of openings. If they are oriented to capture direct sunlight, sun-shading devices may be necessary to reduce glare and excessive heat gain within the space.

While a window-wall weakens the vertical boundaries of a space, it creates the potential for visually expanding the space beyond its physical boundaries.

**Living Room, Villa Mairea,** Noormarkku, Finland, 1938–39, Alvar Aalto

Combining a window-wall with a large skylight overhead creates a sun room or greenhouse space. The boundaries between inside and outside, defined by the linear members of a frame, become obscure and tenuous.

The basic patterns of linear and planar elements which define discrete volumes of space, and the varieties of openings that serve to connect these spatial volumes to one other and their context are presented on pages 156–57 and 159. The qualities of an architectural space, however, are much richer than what the diagrams are able to portray. The spatial qualities of form, proportion, scale, texture, light, and sound ultimately depend on the properties of the enclosure of a space. Our perception of these qualities is often a response to the combined effects of the properties encountered and is conditioned by culture, prior experiences, and personal interest or inclination.

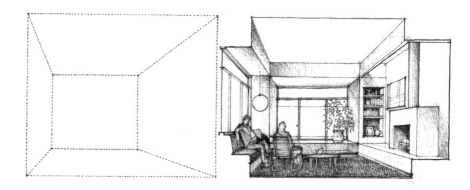

| Properties of Enclosure | Qualities of Space |
|---|---|
| • Shape | • Form |
| • Surface | • Color |
| • Edges | • Texture |
| | • Pattern |
| | • Sound |
| • Dimensions | • Proportion |
| | • Scale |
| • Configuration | • Definition |
| • Openings | • Degree of Enclosure |
| | • Light |
| | • View |

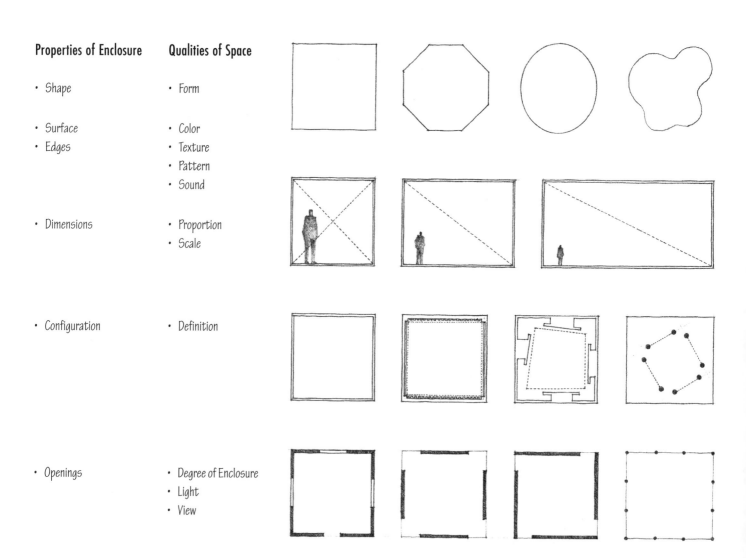

**Bay Window of the Living Room, Hill House**, Helensburgh, Scotland, 1902–03, Charles Rennie Mackintosh

Chapter 2 discusses the impact of shape, surface, and edges on our perception of form. Chapter 6 presents the issues of dimensions, proportion, and scale. While the first part of this chapter outlines how basic configurations of linear and planar elements define volumes of space, this concluding section describes how the size, shape, and location of openings or voids within the enclosing forms of a space influence the following qualities of a room:

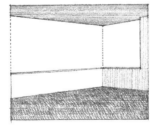
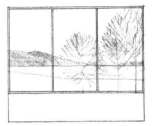

- **degree of enclosure** . . . . the form of the space
- **view** . . . . . . . . . . . . . . . . . . the focus of the space
- **light** . . . . . . . . . . . . . . . . . . the illumination of its surfaces and forms

The degree of enclosure of a space, as determined by the configuration of its defining elements and the pattern of its openings, has a significant impact on our perception of its form and orientation. From within a space, we see only the surface of a wall. It is this thin layer of material that forms the vertical boundary of the space. The actual thickness of a wall plane can be revealed only along the edges of door and window openings.

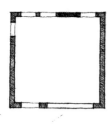

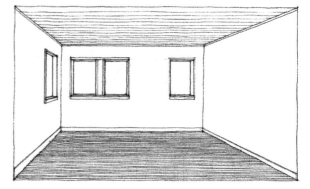

Openings lying wholly within the enclosing planes of a space do not weaken the edge definition nor the sense of closure of the space. The form of the space remains intact and perceptible.

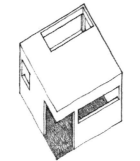
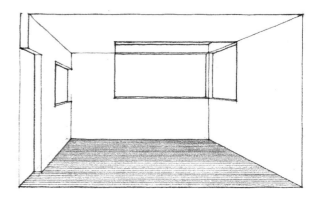

Openings located along the edges of the enclosing planes of a space visually weaken the corner boundaries of the volume. While these openings erode the overall form of a space, they also promote its visual continuity and interaction with adjacent spaces.

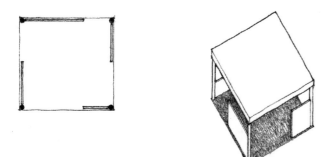
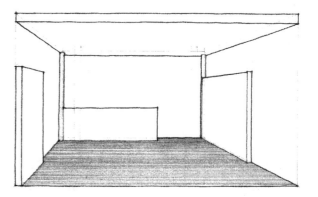

Openings between the enclosing planes of a space visually isolate the planes and articulate their individuality. As these openings increase in number and size, the space loses its sense of enclosure, becomes more diffuse, and begins to merge with adjacent spaces. The visual emphasis is on the enclosing planes rather than the volume of space defined by the planes.

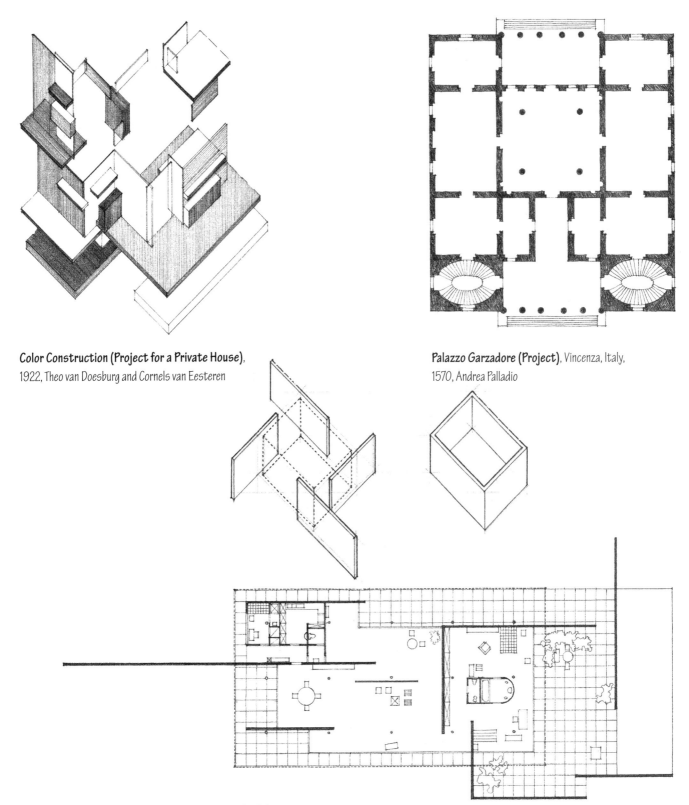

**Color Construction (Project for a Private House)**, 1922, Theo van Doesburg and Cornels van Eesteren

**Palazzo Garzadore (Project)**, Vincenza, Italy, 1570, Andrea Palladio

**House, Berlin Building Exposition**, 1931, Mies van der Rohe

"Architecture is the masterly, correct and magnificent play of
masses brought together in light. Our eyes are made to see forms in light;
light and shade reveal these forms . . ."
Le Corbusier: *Towards a New Architecture*

**Notre Dame Du Haut**, Ronchamp, France, 1950–55, Le Corbusier

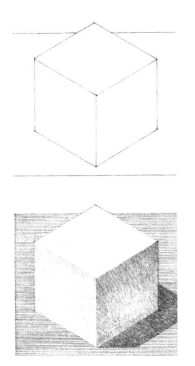

**Kaufmann House (Falling Water)**, *Second-story Bedroom, Connellsville, Pennsylvania,1936—37, Frank Lloyd Wright*

The sun is the rich source of natural light for the illumination of forms and spaces in architecture. While the sun's radiation is intense, the quality of its light, manifested in the form of direct sunlight or diffuse daylight, varies with the time of day, from season to season, and from place to place. As the luminous energy of the sun is dispersed by clouds, haze, and precipitation, it transmits the changing colors of the sky and the weather to the forms and surfaces it illuminates.

Penetrating a space through windows in a wall plane, or through skylights in the overhead roof plane, the radiant energy of the sun falls upon the surfaces within the room, enlivens their colors, and reveals their textures. With the shifting patterns of light, shade, and shadows that it creates, the sun animates the space of the room, and articulates the forms within it. By its intensity and dispersion within the room, the luminous energy of the sun can clarify the form of the space or distort it. The color and brilliance of sunlight can create a festive atmosphere within the room or a more diffuse daylight can instill within it a somber mood.

Since the intensity and direction of the light the sun radiates is fairly predictable, its visual impact on the surfaces, forms, and space of a room can be predicated on the size, location, and orientation of windows and skylights within the enclosure.

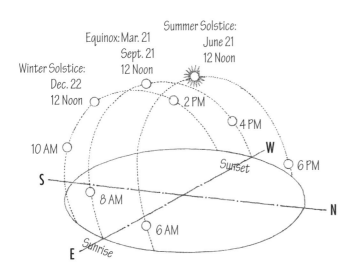

**Sun-Path Diagram for the Northern Hemisphere**

The size of a window or skylight controls the amount of daylight a room receives. The size of an opening in a wall or roof plane, however, is also regulated by factors other than light, such as the materials and construction of the wall or roof plane; requirements for views, visual privacy, and ventilation; the desired degree of enclosure for the space; and the effect of openings on the exterior form of a building. The location and orientation of a window or skylight, therefore, can be more important than its size in determining the quality of daylight a room receives.

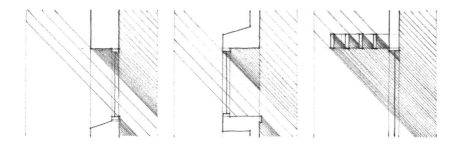

An opening can be oriented to receive direct sunlight during certain portions of the day. Direct sunlight provides a high degree of illumination that is especially intense during mid-day hours. It creates sharp patterns of light and dark on the surfaces of a room and crisply articulates the forms within the space. Possible detrimental effects of direct sunlight, such as glare and excessive heat gain, can be controlled by shading devices built into the form of the opening or provided by the foliage of nearby trees or adjacent structures.

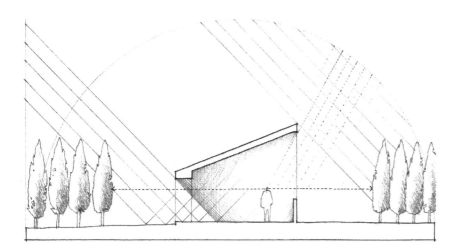

An opening can also be oriented away from direct sunlight and receive instead the diffuse, ambient light from the sky vault overhead. The sky vault is a beneficial source of daylight since it remains fairly constant, even on cloudy days, and can help to soften the harshness of direct sunlight and balance the light level within a space.

The location of an opening affects the manner in which natural light enters a room and illuminates its forms and surfaces. When located entirely within a wall plane, an opening can appear as a bright spot of light on a darker surface. This condition can induce glare if an excessive degree of contrast exists between the brightness of the opening and the darker surface surrounding it. The uncomfortable or debilitating glare caused by excessive brightness ratios between adjacent surfaces or areas in a room can be ameliorated by allowing daylight to enter the space from at least two directions.

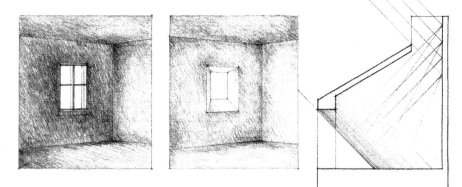

When an opening is located along the edge of a wall or at the corner of a room, the daylight entering through it will wash the surface of the wall adjacent and perpendicular to the plane of the opening. This illuminated surface itself becomes a source of light and enhances the light level within the space.

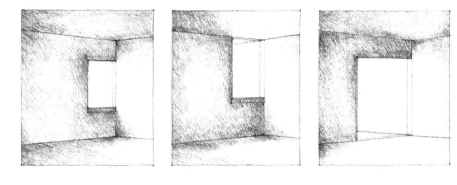

Additional factors influence the quality of light within a room. The shape and articulation of an opening is reflected in the shadow pattern cast by sunlight on the forms and surfaces of the room. The color and texture of these forms and surfaces, in turn, affect their reflectivity and the ambient light level within the space.

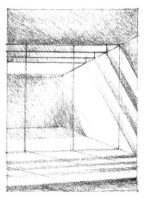

Another quality of space that must be considered in establishing openings in the enclosure of a room is its focus and orientation. While some rooms have an internal focus, such as a fireplace, others have an outward orientation given to them by a view to the outdoors or an adjacent space. Window and skylight openings provide this view and establish a visual relationship between a room and its surroundings. The size and location of these openings determine, of course, the nature of the outlook as well as the degree of visual privacy for an interior space.

A small opening tends to frame a view so that we see it as a painting on a wall. A long, narrow opening gives only a hint of what lies beyond the room. A large opening opens a room up to a broad vista. The large scene can dominate a space or serve as a backdrop for the activities within it. A large bay window projects a person into a scene.

A window can be located in the corner of a room to give the space a diagonal orientation. It can be located in such a way that a view can be seen from only one position in the room. It can be oriented upward to offer a view of treetops and the sky. A group of windows can be sequenced to fragment a scene and encourage movement within a space.

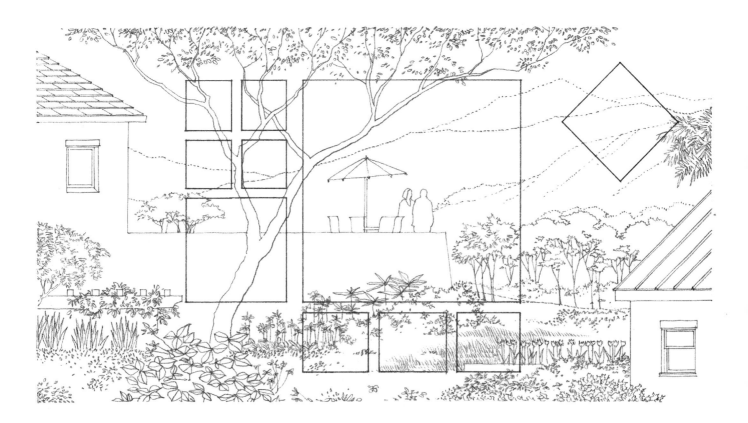

**Interior of Horyu-Ji Temple**, Nara, Japan, A.D. 607

**Vista**, based on a sketch by Le Corbusier for the design of the
Ministry of National Education and Public Health in Rio de Janeiro, 1936

Interior openings providing views from one space to another.

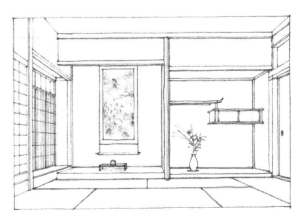

**Tokonoma**, an internal focus in a Traditional Japanese House

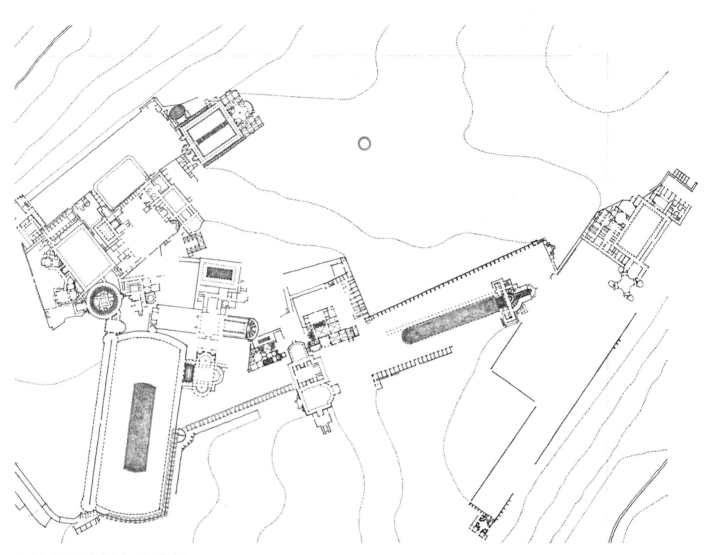

**Hadrian's Villa**, Tivoli, Italy, A.D. 118–125

# 4
# Organization

"... A good house is a single thing, as well as a collection of many, and to make it requires a conceptual leap from the individual components to a vision of the whole. The choices . . . represent ways of assembling the parts.

... the basic parts of a house can be put together to make more than just basic parts: They can also make space, pattern, and outside domains. They dramatize the most elementary act which architecture has to perform. To make one plus one equal more than two, you must in doing any one thing you think important (making rooms, putting them together, or fitting them to the land) do something else that you think important as well (make spaces to live, establish a meaningful pattern inside, or claim other realms outside)."

Charles Moore, Gerald Allen, Donlyn Lyndon
*The Place of Houses*
1974

The last chapter laid out how various configurations of form could be manipulated to define a solitary field or volume of space, and how their patterns of solids and voids affected the visual qualities of the defined space. Few buildings, however, consist of a solitary space. They are normally composed of a number of spaces which are related to one another by function, proximity, or a path of movement. This chapter lays out for study and discussion the basic ways the spaces of a building can be related to one another and organized into coherent patterns of form and space.

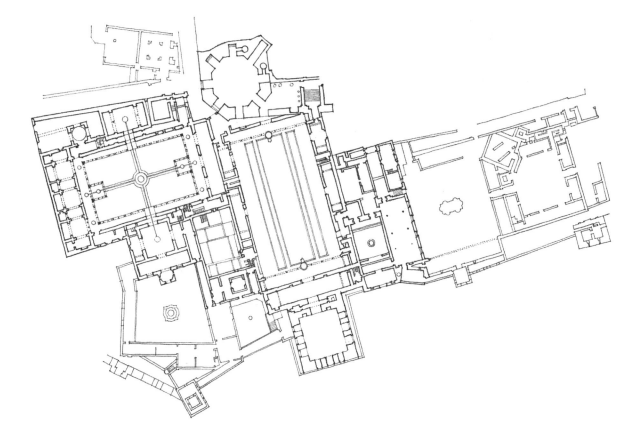

**Alhambra**, Palace and Citadel of the Moorish kings, Granada, Spain, 1248–1354

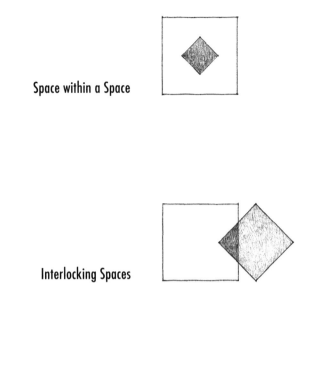

Space within a Space

Interlocking Spaces

Adjacent Spaces

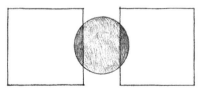

Spaces Linked by a Common Space

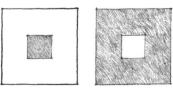
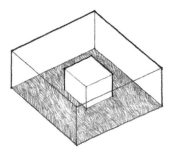

A large space can envelop and contain a smaller space within its volume. Visual and spatial continuity between the two spaces can be easily accommodated, but the smaller, contained space depends on the larger, enveloping space for its relationship to the exterior environment.

In this type of spatial relationship, the larger, enveloping space serves as a three-dimensional field for the smaller space contained within it. For this concept to be perceived, a clear differentiation in size is necessary between the two spaces. If the contained space were to increase in size, the larger space would begin to lose its impact as an enveloping form. If the contained space continued to grow, the residual space around it would become too compressed to serve as an enveloping space. It would become instead merely a thin layer or skin around the contained space. The original notion would be destroyed.

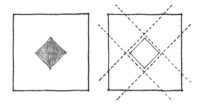
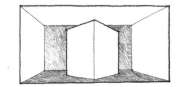

To endow itself with a higher attention-value, the contained space may share the form of the enveloping shape, but be oriented in a different manner. This would create a secondary grid and a set of dynamic, residual spaces within the larger space.

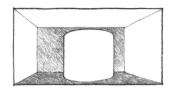

The contained space may also differ in form from the enveloping space in order to strengthen its image as a freestanding volume. This contrast in form may indicate a functional difference between the two spaces or the symbolic importance of the contained space.

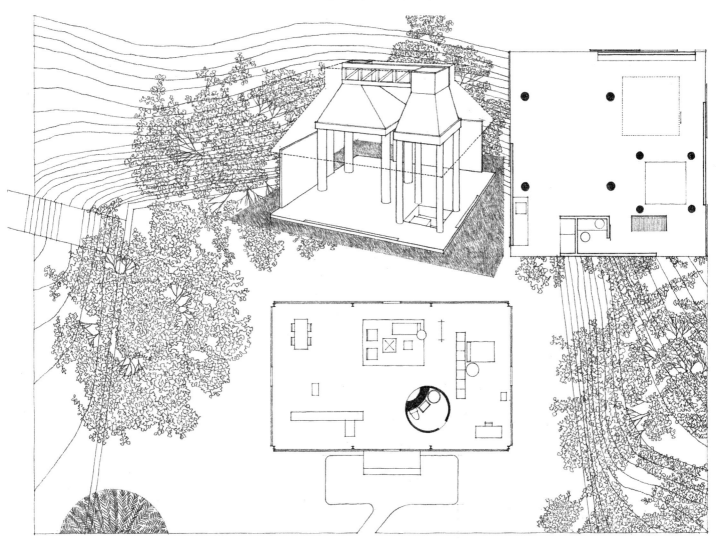

**Moore House**, Orinda, California, 1961, Charles Moore

**Glass House**, New Canaan, Connecticut, 1949, Philip Johnson

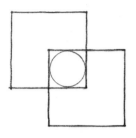
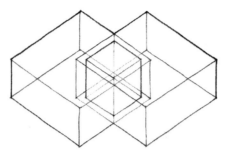

An interlocking spatial relationship results from the overlapping of two spatial fields and the emergence of a zone of shared space. When two spaces interlock their volumes in this manner, each retains its identity and definition as a space. But the resulting configuration of the two interlocking spaces is subject to a number of interpretations.

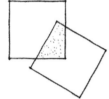
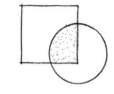

The interlocking portion of the two volumes can be shared equally by each space.

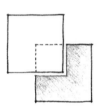
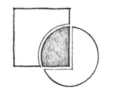

The interlocking portion can merge with one of the spaces and become an integral part of its volume.

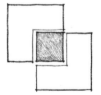
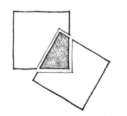

The interlocking portion can develop its own integrity as a space that serves to link the two original spaces.

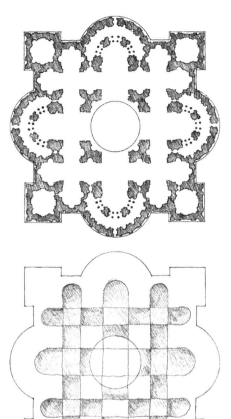

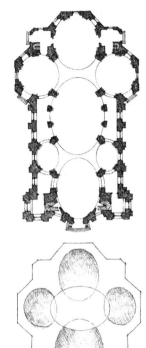

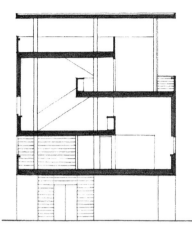

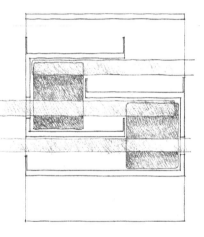

**Plan for St. Peter** (Second Version), Rome, 1506–1520, Donato Bramante & Baldassare Peruzzi

**Pilgrimage Church**, Vierzehnheiligen, Germany, 1744–72, Balthasar Neumann

**Villa at Carthage**, Tunisia, 1928, Le Corbusier

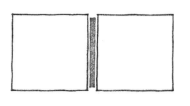
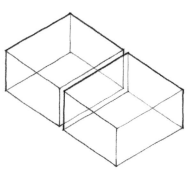

Adjacency is the most common type of spatial relationship. It allows each space to be clearly defined and to respond, each in its own way, to specific functional or symbolic requirements. The degree of visual and spatial continuity that occurs between two adjacent spaces depends on the nature of the plane that both separates and binds them together.

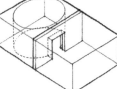
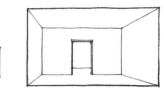

The separating plane may:

- limit visual and physical access between two adjacent spaces, reinforce the individuality of each space, and accommodate their differences.

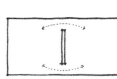
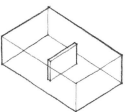
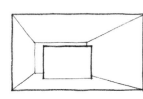

- appear as a freestanding plane in a single volume of space.

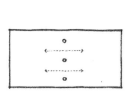
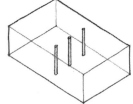
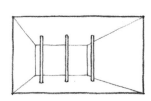

- be defined with a row of columns that allows a high degree of visual and spatial continuity between the two spaces.

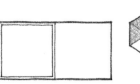
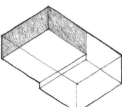
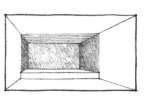

- be merely implied with a change in level or a contrast in surface material or texture between the two spaces. This and the preceding two cases can also be read as single volumes of space which are divided into two related zones.

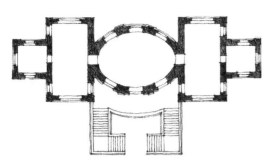

**Pavilion Design,** 17th century, Fischer von Erlach

The spaces in these two buildings are individualistic in size, shape, and form. The walls that enclose them adapt their forms to accommodate the differences between adjacent spaces.

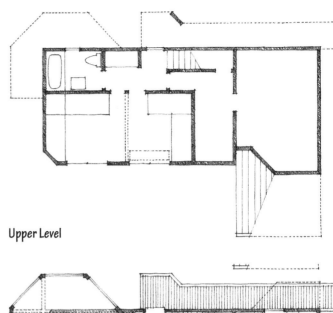

**Upper Level**

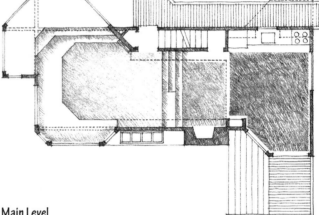

**Main Level**

Three spaces—the living, fireplace, and dining areas—are defined by changes in floor level, ceiling height, and quality of light and view, rather than by wall planes.

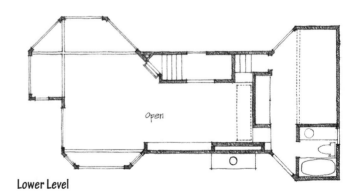

**Lower Level**

**Chiswick House,** Chiswick, England, 1729, Lord Burlington & William Kent

**Lawrence House,** Sea Ranch, California, 1966, Moore-Turnbull/MLTW

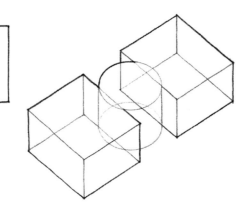

Two spaces which are separated by distance can be linked or related to each other by a third, intermediate, space. The visual and spatial relationship between the two spaces depends on the nature of the third space with which they share a common bond.

The intermediate space can differ in form and orientation from the two spaces to express its linking function.

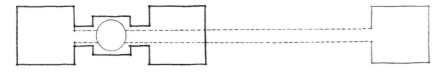

The two spaces, as well as the intermediate space, can be equivalent in size and shape and form a linear sequence of spaces.

The intermediate space can itself become linear in form to link two spaces which are distant from each other, or join a whole series of spaces which have no direct relationship to one another.

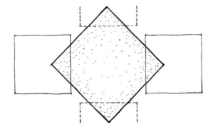

The intermediate space can, if large enough, become the dominant space in the relationship, and be capable of organizing a number of spaces about itself.

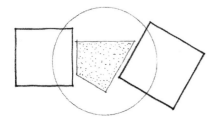

The form of the intermediate space can be residual in nature and be determined solely by the forms and orientations of the two spaces being linked.

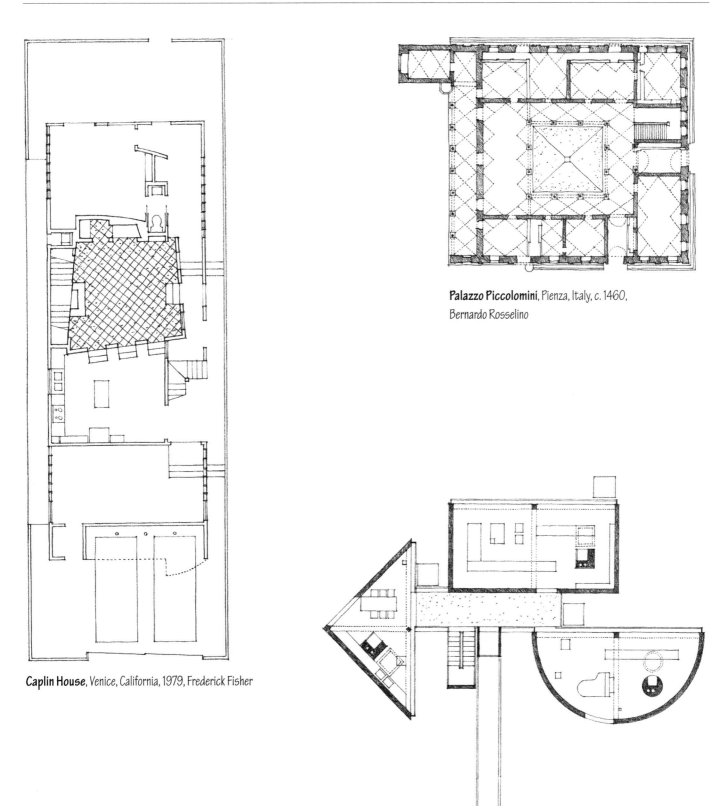

**Palazzo Piccolomini**, Pienza, Italy, c. 1460,
Bernardo Rosselino

**Caplin House**, Venice, California, 1979, Frederick Fisher

**One-half House** (Project), 1966, John Hejduk

*Compositions of Nine Squares:*
A Bauhaus Study

The following section lays out the basic ways we can arrange and organize the spaces of a building. In a typical building program, there are usually requirements for various kinds of spaces. There may be requirements for spaces that:

- have specific functions or require specific forms
- are flexible in use and can be freely manipulated
- are singular and unique in their function or significance to the building organization
- have similar functions and can be grouped into a functional cluster or repeated in a linear sequence
- require exterior exposure for light, ventilation, outlook, or access to outdoor spaces
- must be segregated for privacy
- must be easily accessible

The manner in which these spaces are arranged can clarify their relative importance and functional or symbolic role in the organization of a building. The decision as to what type of organization to use in a specific situation will depend on:

- demands of the building program, such as functional proximities, dimensional requirements, hierarchical classification of spaces, and requirements for access, light, or view
- exterior conditions of the site that might limit the organization's form or growth, or that might encourage the organization to address certain features of its site and turn away from others

Each type of spatial organization is introduced by a section that discusses the formal characteristics, spatial relationships, and contextual responses of the category. A range of examples then illustrates the basic points made in the introduction. Each of the examples should be studied in terms of:

- What kinds of spaces are accommodated and where? How are they defined?
- What kinds of relationships are established among the spaces, one to another, and to the exterior environment?
- Where can the organization be entered and what configuration does the path of circulation have?
- What is the exterior form of the organization and how might it respond to its context?

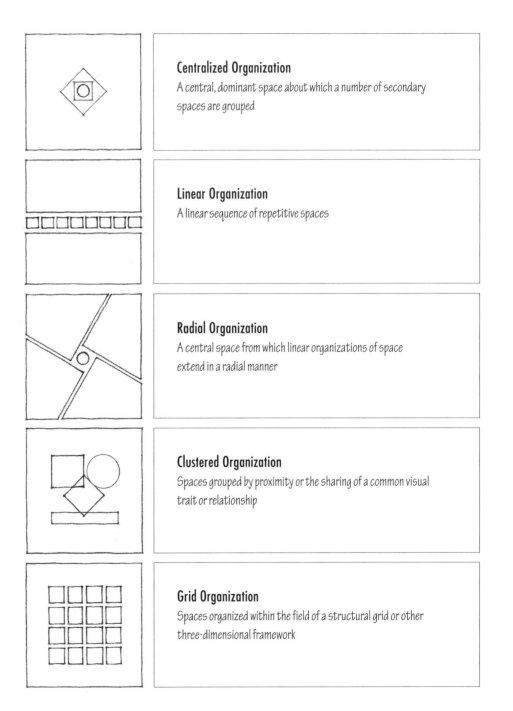

**Centralized Organization**
A central, dominant space about which a number of secondary spaces are grouped

**Linear Organization**
A linear sequence of repetitive spaces

**Radial Organization**
A central space from which linear organizations of space extend in a radial manner

**Clustered Organization**
Spaces grouped by proximity or the sharing of a common visual trait or relationship

**Grid Organization**
Spaces organized within the field of a structural grid or other three-dimensional framework

A centralized organization is a stable, concentrated composition that consists of a number of secondary spaces grouped around a large, dominant, central space.

The central, unifying space of the organization is generally regular in form and large enough in size to gather a number of secondary spaces about its perimeter.

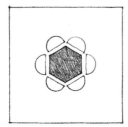 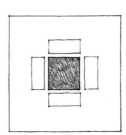 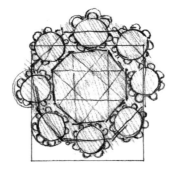

**Ideal Church** by Da Vinci

The secondary spaces of the organization may be equivalent to one another in function, form, and size, and create an overall configuration that is geometrically regular and symmetrical about two or more axes.

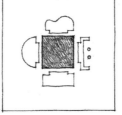 

**San Lorenzo Maggiore**

The secondary spaces may differ from one another in form or size in order to respond to individual requirements of function, express their relative importance, or acknowledge their surroundings. This differentiation among the secondary spaces also allows the form of a centralized organization to respond to the environmental conditions of its site.

Since the form of a centralized organization is inherently non-directional, conditions of approach and entry must be specified by the site and the articulation of one of the secondary spaces as an entrance or gateway.

The pattern of circulation and movement within a centralized organization may be radial, loop, or spiral in form. In almost every case, however, the pattern will terminate in or around the central space.

Centralized organizations whose forms are relatively compact and geometrically regular can be used to:

• establish points or places in space
• terminate axial conditions
• serve as an object-form within a defined field
  or volume of space

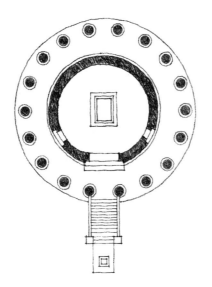

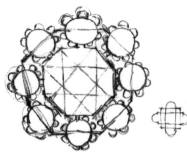

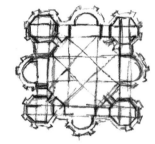

These drawings are based on Leonardo da Vinci's sketches of ideal church plans. c. 1490

**Centralized Plans**, 1547, Sebastiano Serlio

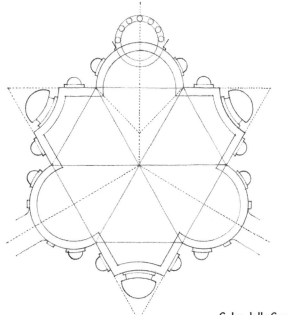

**S. Ivo della Sapienze**, Rome, 1642–50, Francesco Borromini

Plan for St. Peter's (First Version), Rome, c. 1503, Donato Bramante

Palazzo Farnese, Caprarola, 1547–49, Giacomo da Vignola

**National Assembly Building**, Capitol Complex at Dacca, Bangladesh, begun 1962, Louis Kahn

**Villa Capra (The Rotunda)**, Vicenza, Italy, 1552–67, Andrea Palladio

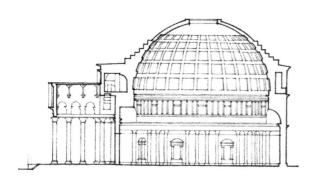

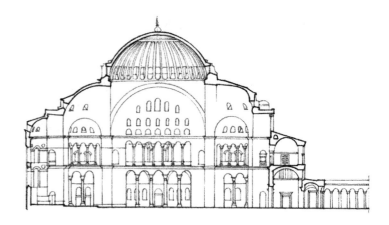

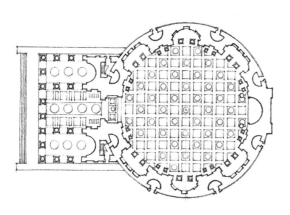

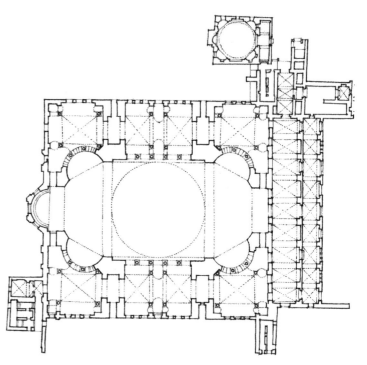

**The Pantheon**, Rome, A.D. 120-124. Portico from temple of 25 B.C.

**Hagia Sophia**, Constantinople (Istanbul), A.D. 532–37,
Anthemius of Tralles and Isidorus of Miletus

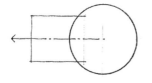

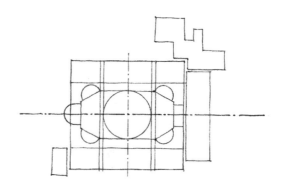

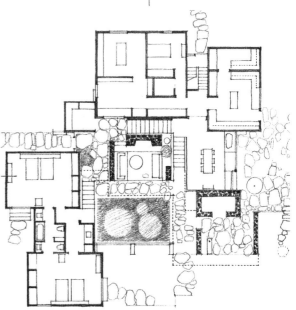

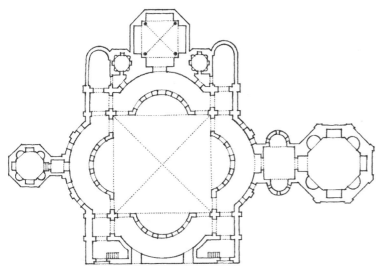

**San Lorenzo Maggiore**, Milan, Italy, c. A.D. 480

**Greenhouse House**, Connecticut, 1973–75, John M. Johansen

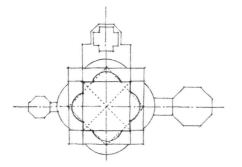

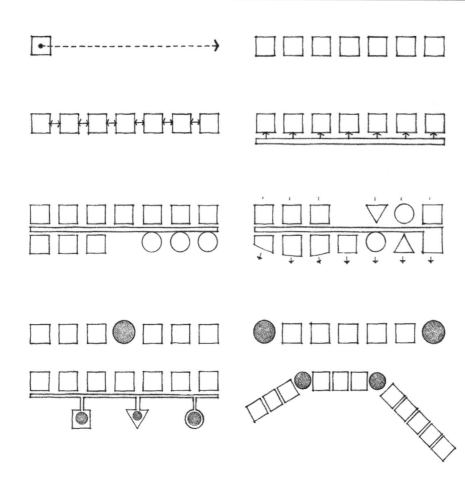

A linear organization consists essentially of a series of spaces. These spaces can either be directly related to one another or be linked through a separate and distinct linear space.

A linear organization usually consists of repetitive spaces which are alike in size, form, and function. It may also consist of a single linear space that organizes along its length a series of spaces that differ in size, form, or function. In both cases, each space along the sequence has an exterior exposure.

Spaces that are functionally or symbolically important to the organization can occur anywhere along the linear sequence and have their importance articulated by their size and form. Their significance can also be emphasized by their location:

- at the end of the linear sequence
- offset from the linear organization
- at pivotal points of a segmented linear form

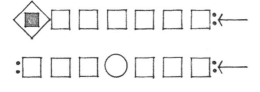

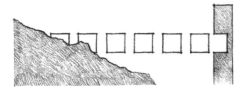

Because of their characteristic length, linear organizations express a direction and signify movement, extension, and growth. To limit their growth, linear organizations can be terminated by a dominant space or form, by an elaborate or articulated entrance, or by merging with another building form or the topography of its site.

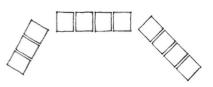

The form of a linear organization is inherently flexible and can respond readily to various conditions of its site. It can adapt to changes in topography, maneuver around a body of water or a stand of trees, or turn to orient spaces to capture sunlight and views. It can be straight, segmented, or curvilinear. It can run horizontally across its site, diagonally up a slope, or stand vertically as a tower.

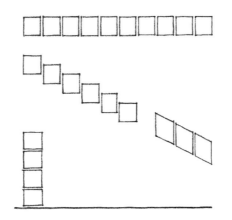

The form of a linear organization can relate to other forms in its context by:

- linking and organizing them along its length
- serving as a wall or barrier to separate them into different fields
- surrounding and enclosing them within a field of space

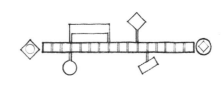

Curved and segmented forms of linear organizations enclose a field of exterior space on their concave sides and orient their spaces toward the center of the field. On their convex sides, these forms appear to front space and exclude it from their fields.

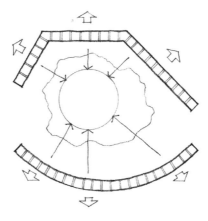

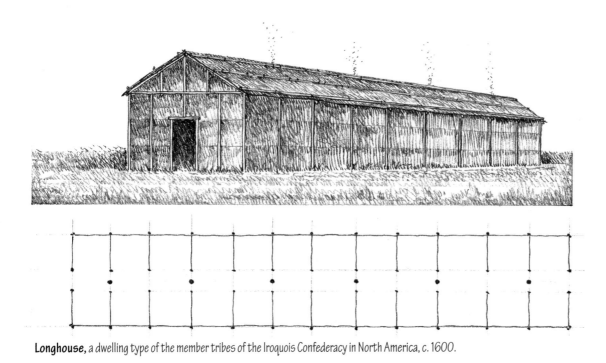

**Longhouse,** a dwelling type of the member tribes of the Iroquois Confederacy in North America, c. 1600.

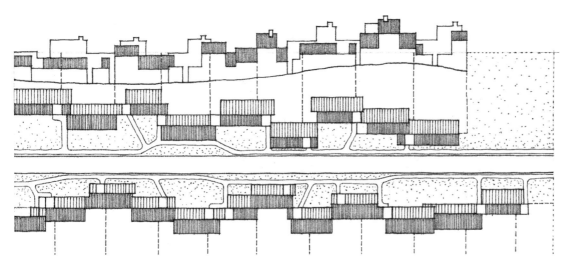

**Terraced Housing Fronting a Village Street, Village Project,** 1955, James Stirling (Team X)

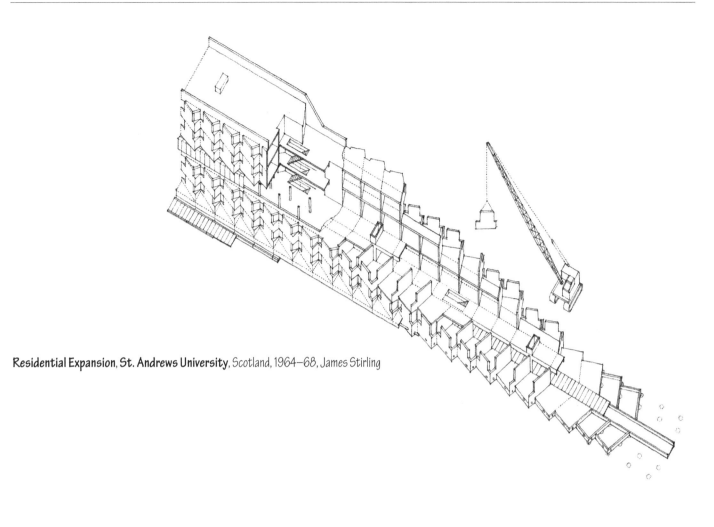

**Residential Expansion, St. Andrews University**, Scotland, 1964–68, James Stirling

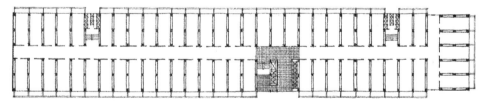

**Typical Apartment Floor, Unité d'Habitation**, Marseilles, 1946–52, Le Corbusier

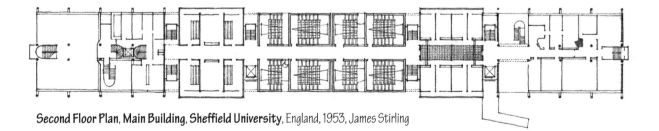

**Second Floor Plan, Main Building, Sheffield University**, England, 1953, James Stirling

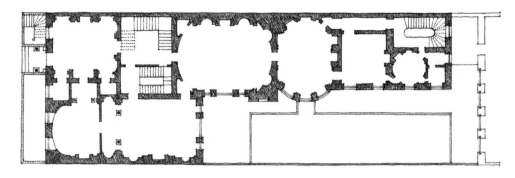

**Lord Derby's House**, London, 1777,
Robert Adam

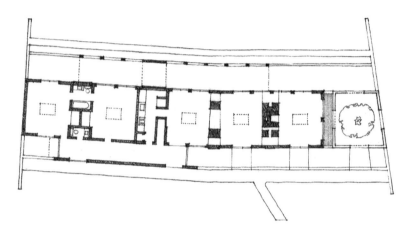

**Pearson House** (Project), 1957,
Robert Venturi

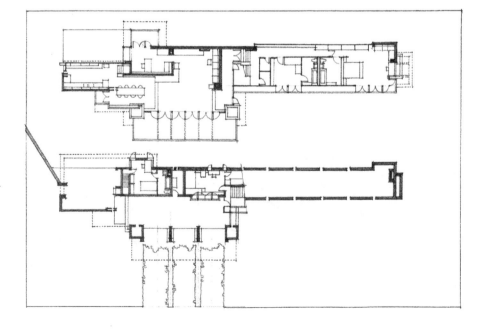

**Lloyd Lewis House**, Libertyville, Illinois,
1940, Frank Lloyd Wright

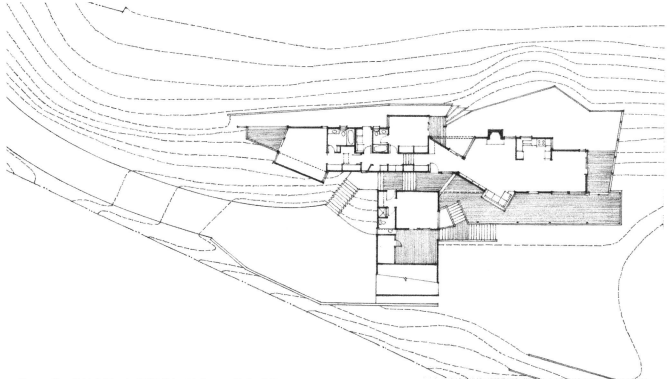

**Romano House**, Kentfield, California, 1970, Esherick Homsey Dodge & Davis

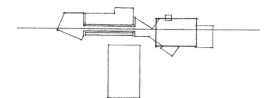

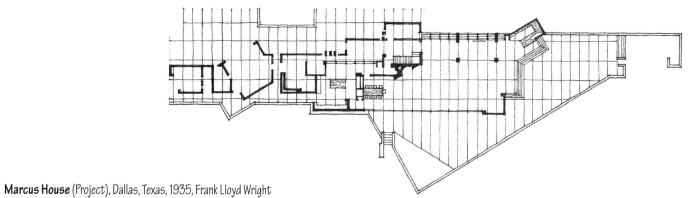

**Marcus House** (Project), Dallas, Texas, 1935, Frank Lloyd Wright

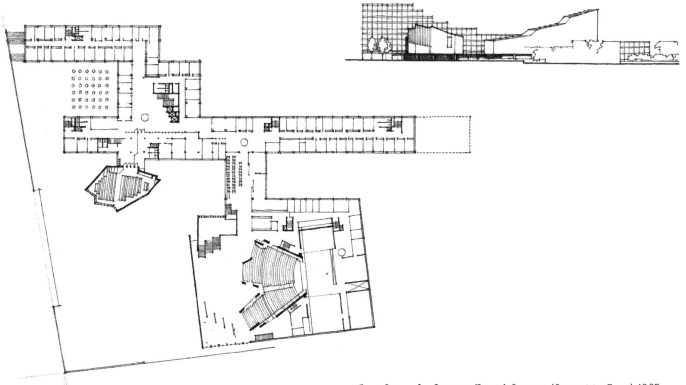

**Town Center for Castrop-Rauxel**, Germany, (Competition Entry), 1965, Alvar Aalto

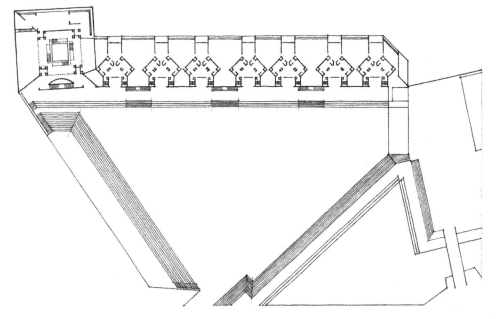

**Interama, Project for an Inter-American Community**, Florida, 1964–67, Louis Kahn

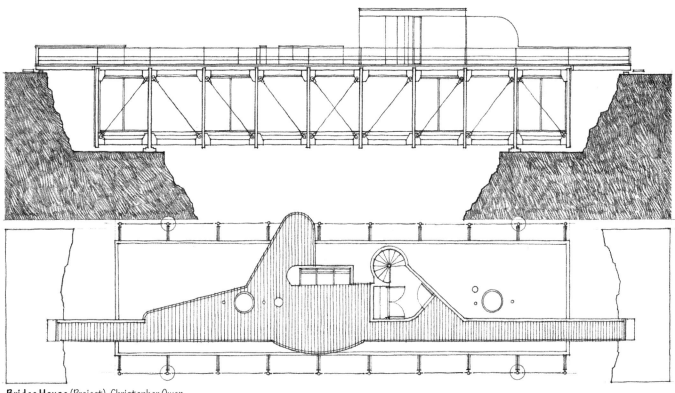

**Bridge House** (Project), Christopher Owen

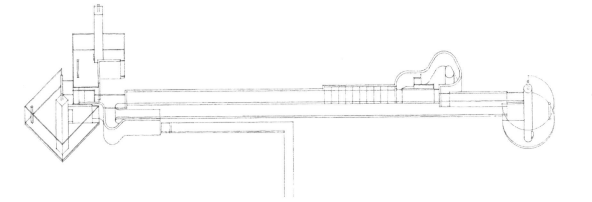

**House 10** (Project), 1966, John Hejduk

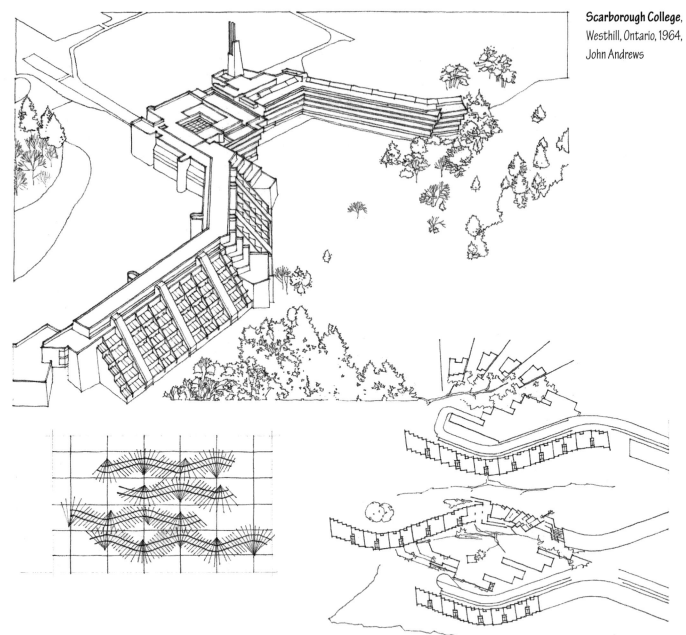

**Housing Development**, Pavia, Italy, 1966, Alvar Aalto

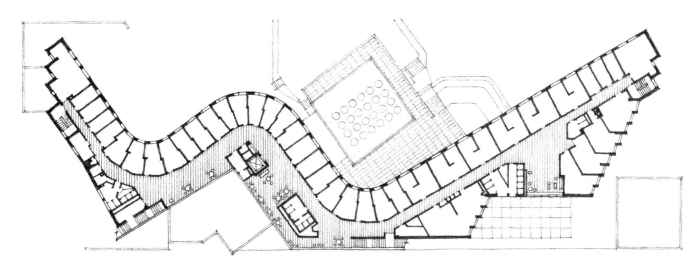

**Typical Upper-floor Plan**, **Baker House**, Massachusetts Institute of Technology,
Cambridge, Massachusetts, 1948, Alvar Aalto

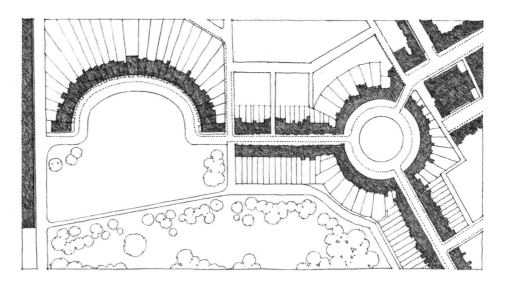

**Plan for the Circus** (1754, John Wood, Sr.) and
the **Royal Crescent** (1767–75, John Wood) at
Bath, England

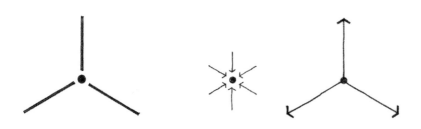

A radial organization of space combines elements of both centralized and linear organizations. It consists of a dominant central space from which a number of linear organizations extend in a radial manner. Whereas a centralized organization is an introverted scheme that focuses inward on its central space, a radial organization is an extroverted plan that reaches out to its context. With its linear arms, it can extend and attach itself to specific elements or features of its site.

As with centralized organizations, the central space of a radial organization is generally regular in form. The linear arms, for which the central space is the hub, may be similar to one another in form and length and maintain the regularity of the organization's overall form.

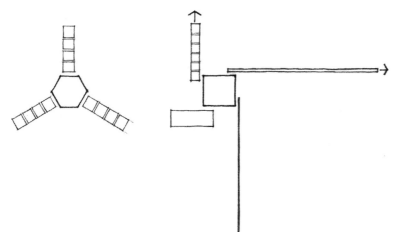

The radiating arms may also differ from one another in order to respond to individual requirements of function and context.

A specific variation of a radial organization is the pinwheel pattern wherein the linear arms of the organization extend from the sides of a square or rectangular central space. This arrangement results in a dynamic pattern that visually suggests a rotational movement about the central space.

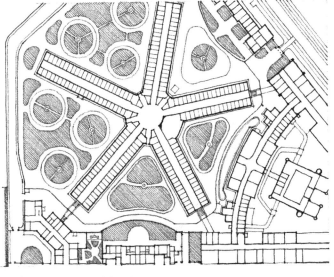

**Moabit Prison**, Berlin, 1869–79, Herrman

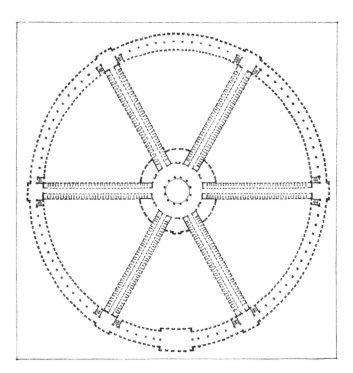

**Hôtel Dieu (**Hospital), 1774, Antoine Petit

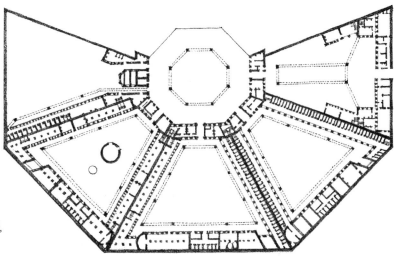

**Maison de Force** (Prison), Ackerghem near Ghent, Belgium, 1772–75, Malfaison and Kluchman

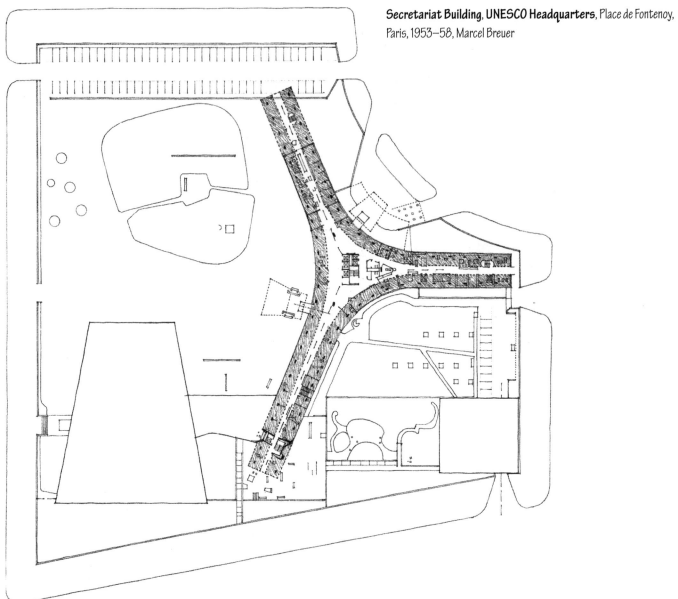

**Secretariat Building, UNESCO Headquarters**, Place de Fontenoy, Paris, 1953–58, Marcel Breuer

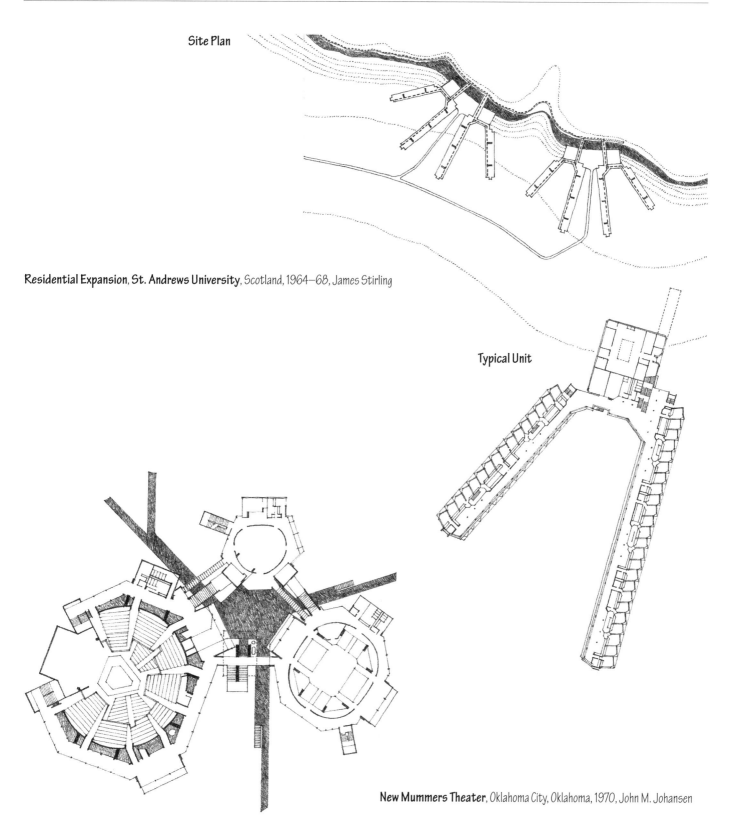

Site Plan

**Residential Expansion, St. Andrews University**, *Scotland, 1964–68, James Stirling*

Typical Unit

**New Mummers Theater**, *Oklahoma City, Oklahoma, 1970, John M. Johansen*

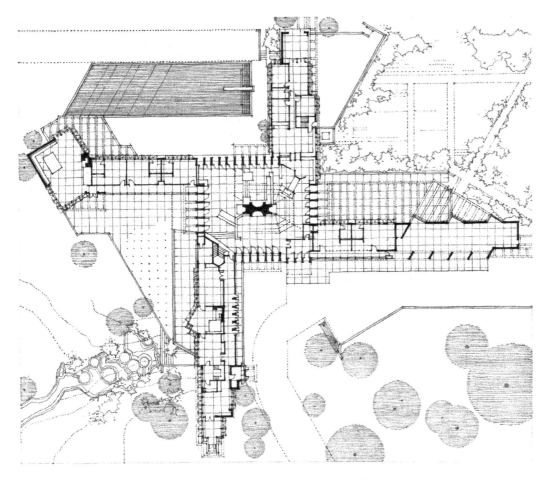

**Herbert F. Johnson House** (Wingspread), Wind Point, Wisconsin, 1937, Frank Lloyd Wright

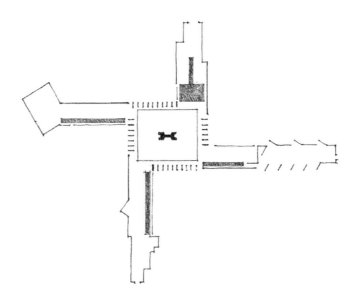

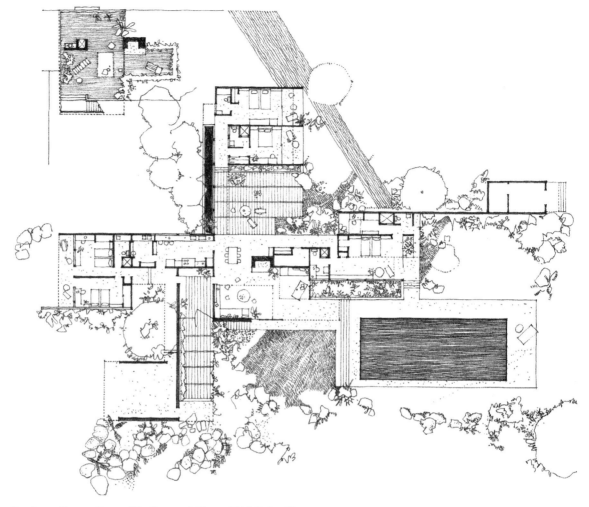

**Kaufmann Desert House**, Palm Springs, California, 1946, Richard Neutra

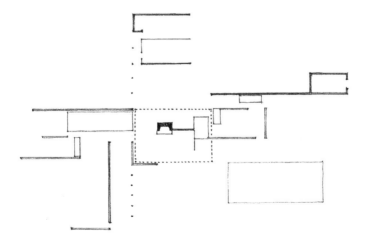

# CLUSTERED ORGANIZATIONS

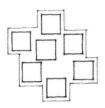

Repetitive spaces

Sharing a common
shape

Organized by an axis

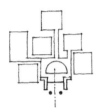

Clustered about an entry

Grouped along a path

A loop path

Centralized pattern

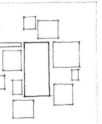

Clustered pattern

Contained within a space

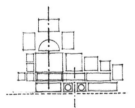

Axial conditions

Axial condition

Symmetrical condition

A clustered organization relies on physical proximity to relate its spaces to one another. It often consists of repetitive, cellular spaces that have similar functions and share a common visual trait such as shape or orientation. A clustered organization can also accept within its composition spaces that are dissimilar in size, form, and function, but related to one another by proximity or a visual ordering device such as symmetry or an axis. Because its pattern does not originate from a rigid geometrical concept, the form of a clustered organization is flexible and can accept growth and change readily without affecting its character.

Clustered spaces can be organized about a point of entry into a building or along the path of movement through it. The spaces can also be clustered about a large defined field or volume of space. This pattern is similar to that of a centralized organization, but it lacks the latter's compactness and geometrical regularity. The spaces of a clustered organization can also be contained within a defined field or volume of space.

Since there is no inherent place of importance within the pattern of a clustered organization, the significance of a space must be articulated by its size, form, or orientation within the pattern.

Symmetry or an axial condition can be used to strengthen and unify portions of a clustered organization and help articulate the importance of a space or group of spaces within the organization.

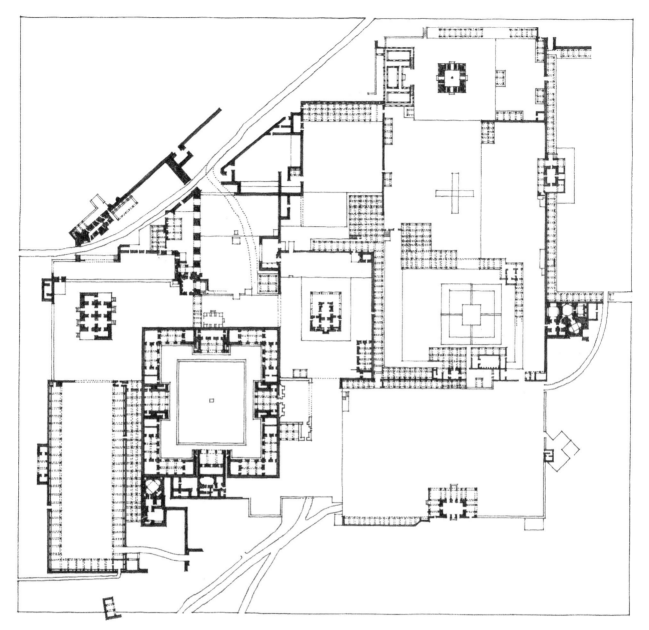

**Fatehpur Sikri**, *Palace Complex of Akbar the Great Mogul Emperor of India, 1569–74*

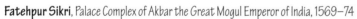

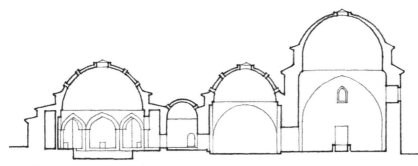

Section

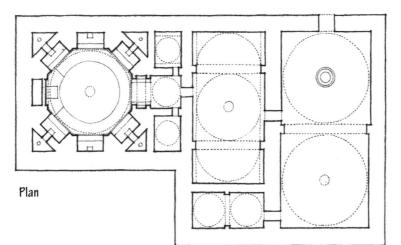

Plan

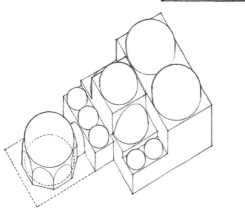

Axonometric

**Yeni-Kaplica (Thermal Bath)**, Bursa, Turkey

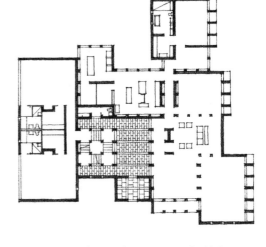

**Morris House (Project)**, Mount Kisco, New York, 1958, Louis Kahn

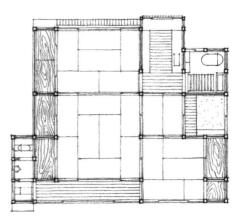

**Traditional Japanese House**

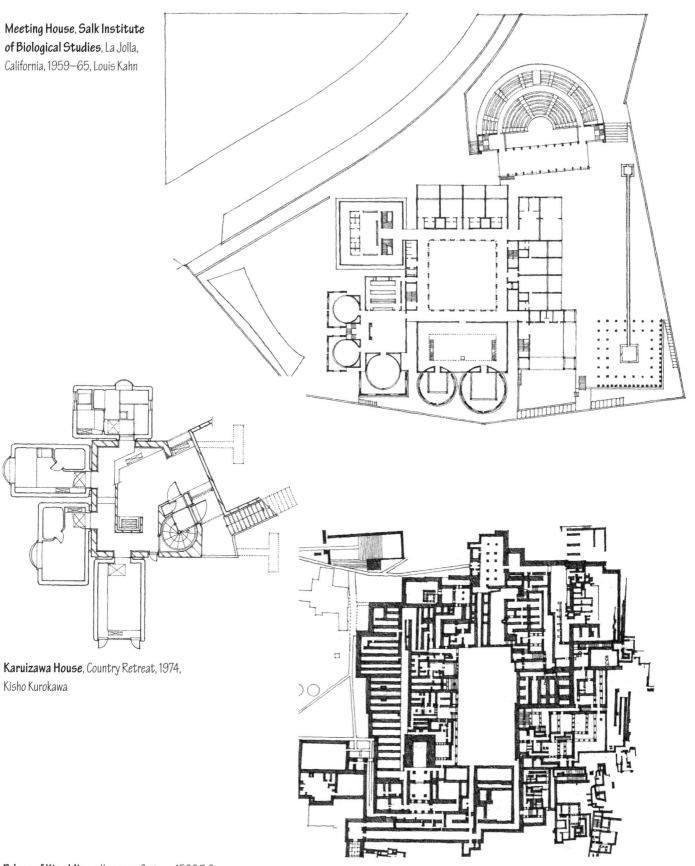

**Meeting House, Salk Institute of Biological Studies**, La Jolla, California, 1959–65, Louis Kahn

**Karuizawa House**, Country Retreat, 1974, Kisho Kurokawa

**Palace of King Minos**, Knossos, Crete, c. 1500 B.C.

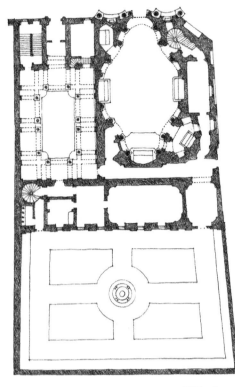

S. Carlo alle Quattro Fontane, Rome, 1633–41,
Francesco Borromini

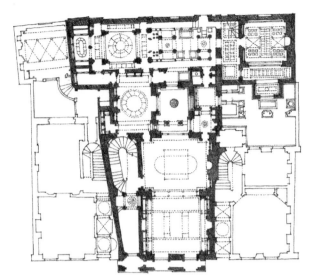

Soane House, London, England, 1812–34, Sir John Soane

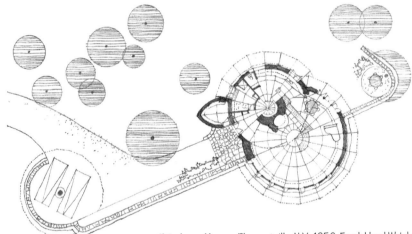

Friedman House, Pleasantville, N.Y., 1950, Frank Lloyd Wright

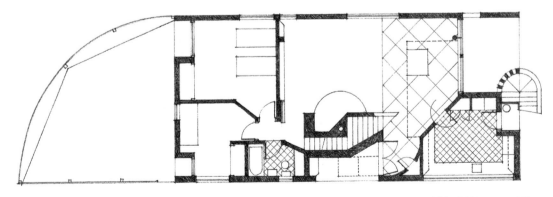

House for Mrs. Robert Venturi, Chestnut Hill, Pennsylvania, 1962–64, Venturi and Short

**Kaufmann House (Falling Water)**, Connellsville, Pennsylvania, 1936–37, Frank Lloyd Wright

**Mercer's Castle (Fonthill)**, Doylestown, Pennsylvania, 1908–10, Henry Mercer

**Wyntoon**, Country Estate for the Hearst Family in northern California,1903, Bernard Maybeck

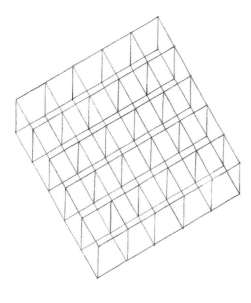

A grid organization consists of forms and spaces whose positions in space and relationships with one another are regulated by a three-dimensional grid pattern or field.

 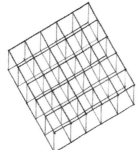 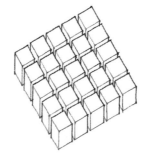

A grid is created by two, usually perpendicular, sets of parallel lines which establish a regular pattern of points at their intersections. Projected into the third dimension, the grid pattern is transformed into a set of repetitive, modular units of space.

The organizing power of a grid results from the regularity and continuity of its pattern that pervades the elements it organizes. Its pattern establishes a stable set or field of reference points and lines in space with which the spaces of a grid organization, although dissimilar in size, form, or function, can share a common relationship.

A grid is established in architecture most often by a skeletal structural system of columns and beams. Within the field of this grid, spaces can occur as isolated events or as repetitions of the grid module. Regardless of their disposition within the field, these spaces, if seen as positive forms, will create a second set of negative spaces.

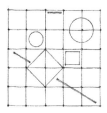 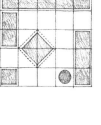 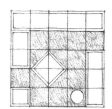

Since a three-dimensional grid consists of repetitive, modular units of space, it can be subtracted from, added to, or layered, and still maintain its identity as a grid with the ability to organize spaces. These formal manipulations can be used to adapt a grid form to its site, to define an entrance or outdoor space, or to allow for its growth and expansion.

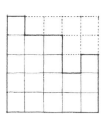 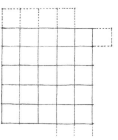 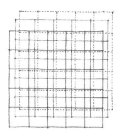

To accommodate the specific dimensional requirements of its spaces or to articulate zones of space for circulation or service, a grid can be made irregular in one or two directions. This dimensional transformation would create a hierarchical set of modules differentiated by size, proportion, and location.

A grid can also undergo other transformations. Portions of the grid can slide to alter the visual and spatial continuity across its field. A grid pattern can be interrupted to define a major space or accommodate a natural feature of its site. A portion of the grid can be dislocated and rotated about a point in the basic pattern. Across its field, a grid can transform its image from a pattern of points to lines, to planes, and finally, to volumes.

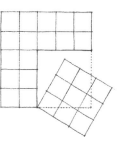 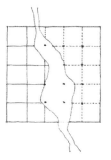

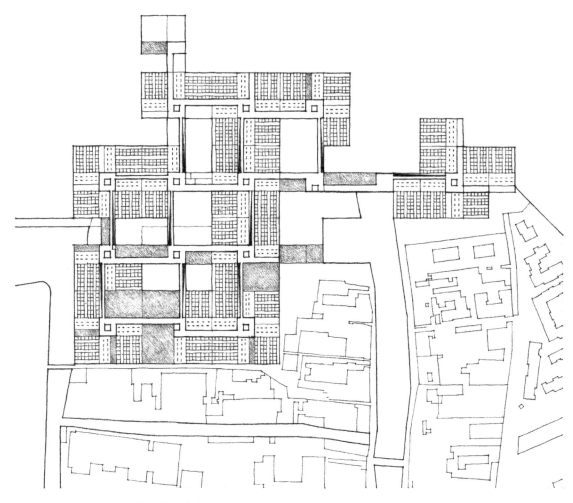

**Hospital Project**, Venice, 1964–66, Le Corbusier

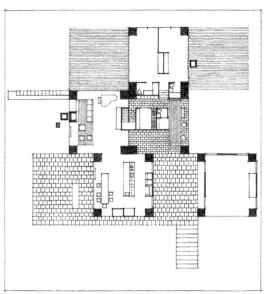

**Adler House** (Project), Philadelphia, Pennsylvania, 1954, Louis Kahn

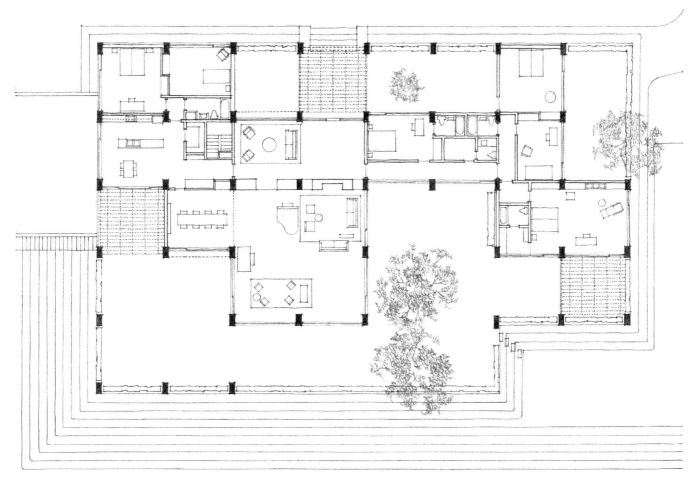

**Eric Boissonas House I**, New Canaan, Connecticut, 1956, Philip Johnson

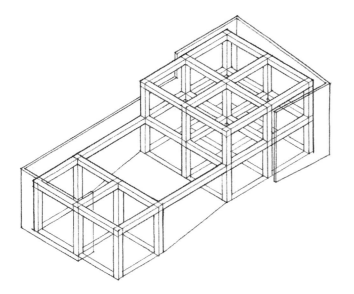

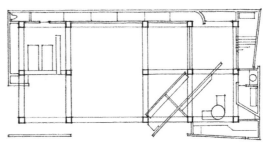

**Manabe Residence**, Tezukayama, Osaka, Japan, 1976–77, Tadao Ando

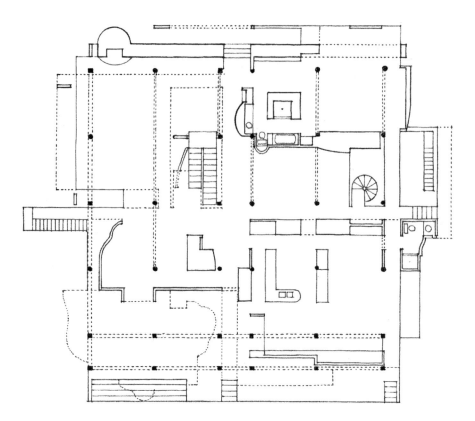

**Snyderman House**, Fort Wayne, Indiana, 1972, Michael Graves

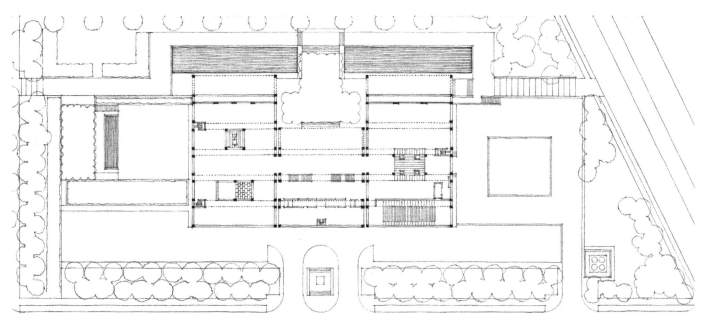

**Kimball Art Museum**, Forth Worth, Texas, 1967–72, Louis Kahn

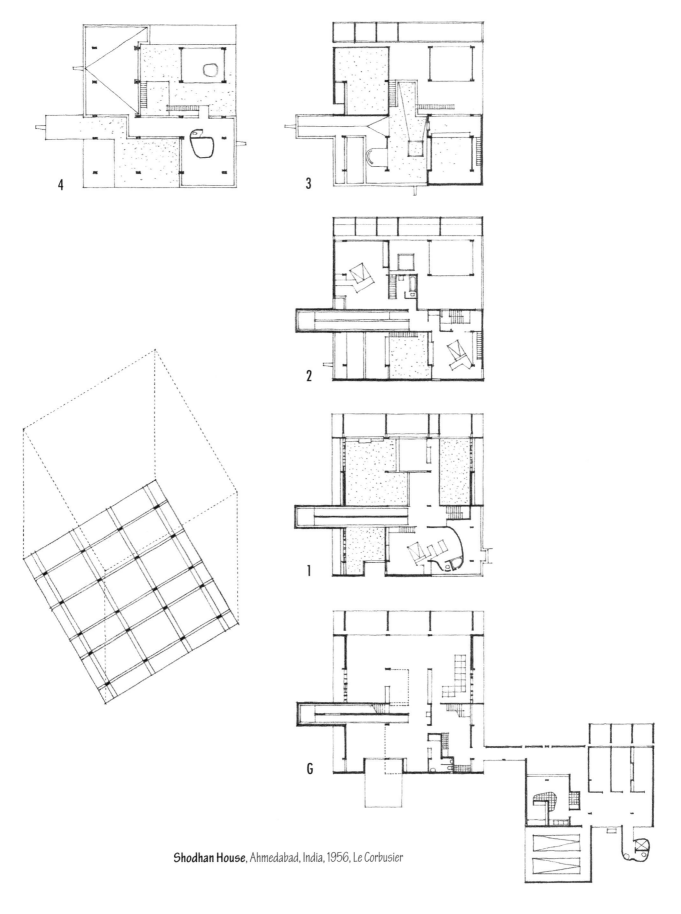

**Shodhan House**, Ahmedabad, India, 1956, Le Corbusier

**Great Temple of Rameses II**, Abu Simbel, 1301–1235 B.C.

Plan

# 5
# Circulation

" . . . we have been observing that the human body, which is our most
fundamental three-dimensional possession, has not itself been a central
concern in the understanding of architectural form; that architecture, to
the extent that it is considered an art, is characterized in its design stages
as an abstract visual art and not as a body-centered art . . . We believe that
the most essential and memorable sense of three-dimensionality originates
in the body experience and that this sense may constitute a basis for
understanding spatial feeling in our experience of buildings.

. . . The interplay between the world of our bodies and the world of our
dwelling places is always in flux. We make places that are an expression of
our haptic experiences even as these experience are generated by the places
we have already created. Whether we are conscious or innocent of this
process, our bodies and our movement are in constant dialogue with our
buildings."

Charles Moore and Robert Yudell
*Body, Memory, and Architecture*
1977

The path of our movement can be conceived as the perceptual thread that links the spaces of a building, or any series of interior or exterior spaces, together.

Since we move in **Time**
    through a **Sequence**
        of **Spaces**,
we experience a space in relation to where we've been and where we anticipate going. This chapter presents the principal components of a building's circulation system as positive elements that affect our perception of the forms and spaces of the building.

**Skylighted Concourse, Olivetti Headquarters,**
Milton Keynes, 1971, James Stirling & Michael Wilford

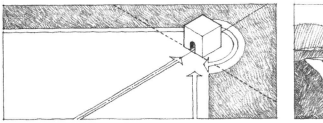

**Approach**
• The Distant View

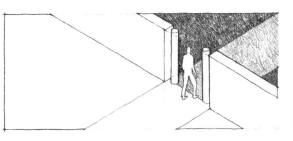
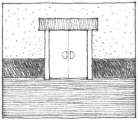

**Entrance**
• From Outside to Inside

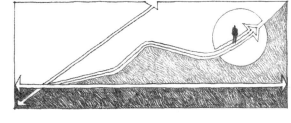
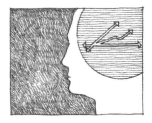

**Configuration of the Path**
• The Sequence of Spaces

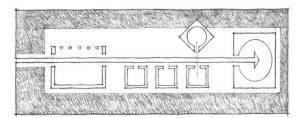
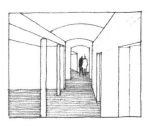

**Path-space Relationships**
• Edges, Nodes, and Terminations of the Path

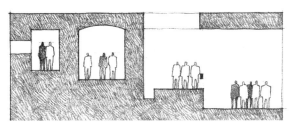
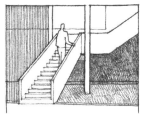

**Form of the Circulation Space**
• Corridors, Halls, Galleries, Stairways and Rooms

Approach to **Notre Dame Du Haut**, Ronchamp, France, 1950–55, Le Corbusier

Prior to actually passing into the interior of a building, we approach its entrance along a path. This is the first phase of the circulation system, during which we are prepared to see, experience, and use the spaces within a building.

The approach to a building and its entrance may vary in duration from a few paces through a compressed space to a lengthy and circuitous route. It may be perpendicular to the primary facade of a building or be oblique to it. The nature of the approach may contrast with what is confronted at its termination, or it may be continued on into the building's interior sequence of spaces, obscuring the distinction between inside and outside.

## Frontal

A frontal approach leads directly to the entrance of a building along a straight, axial path. The visual goal that terminates the approach is clear; it may be the entire front facade of a building or an elaborated entrance within the plane.

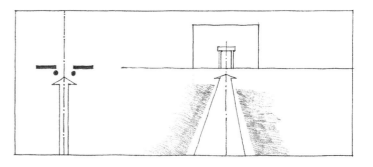

## Oblique

An oblique approach enhances the effect of perspective on the front facade and form of a building. The path can be redirected one or more times to delay and prolong the sequence of the approach. If a building is approached at an extreme angle, its entrance can project beyond its facade to be more clearly visible.

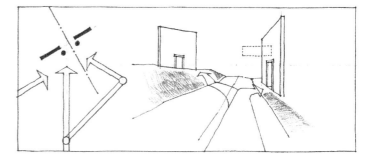

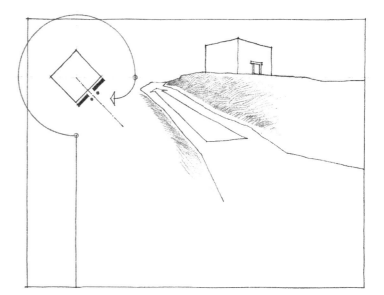

## Spiral

A spiral path prolongs the sequence of the approach and emphasizes the three-dimensional form of a building as we move around its perimeter. The building entrance might be viewed intermittently during the approach to clarify its position or it may be hidden until the point of arrival.

**Villa Barbaro**, Maser, Italy, 1560—68, Andrea Palladio

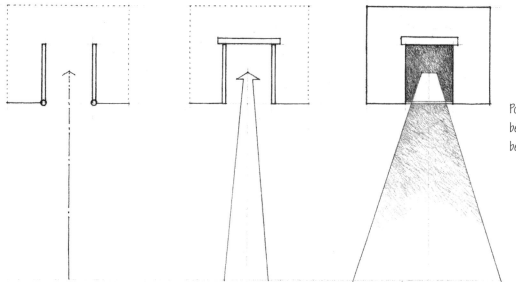

Portals and gateways have traditionally been means of orienting us to the path beyond and welcoming our entry.

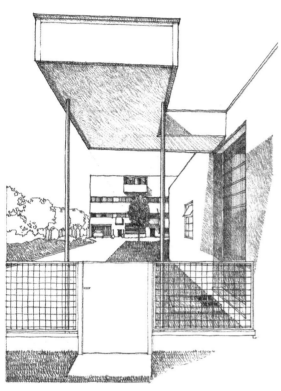

**Villa Garches**, Vaucresson, France, 1926–27, Le Corbusier

**Qian Men**, Link between the Forbidden City to the north and the Outer City to the south in Peking (Beijing), China, 15th century

**Catholic Church**, Taos, New Mexico, 17th century

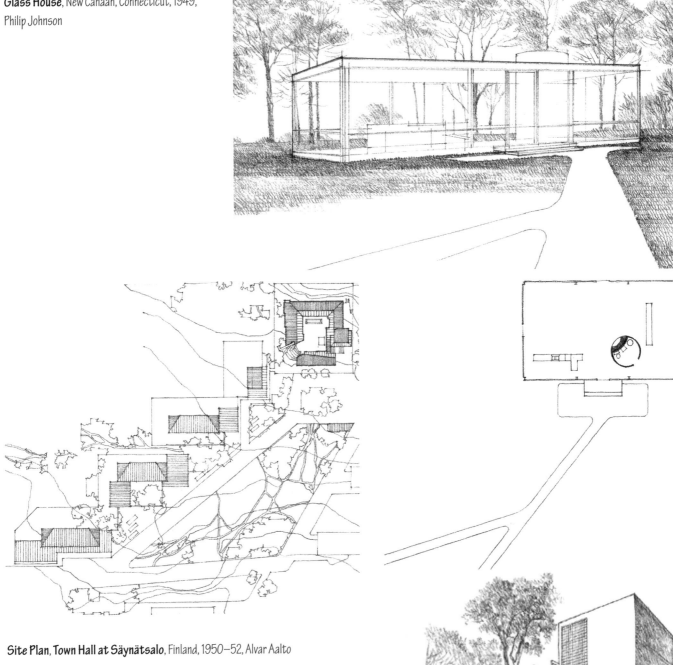

**Glass House**, New Canaan, Connecticut, 1949,
Philip Johnson

**Site Plan, Town Hall at Säynätsalo**, Finland, 1950–52, Alvar Aalto

Ramp Into and Through Building, **Carpenter Center for the Visual Arts**, Harvard University,
Cambridge, Massachusetts, 1961–64, Le Corbusier

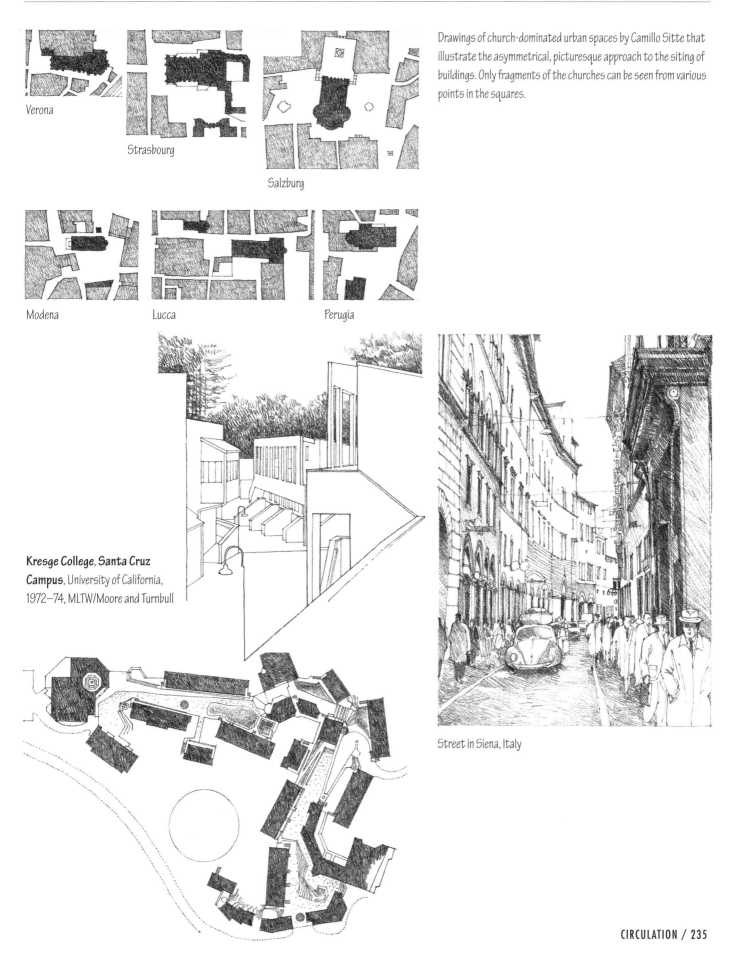

Verona

Strasbourg

Salzburg

Modena

Lucca

Perugia

Drawings of church-dominated urban spaces by Camillo Sitte that illustrate the asymmetrical, picturesque approach to the siting of buildings. Only fragments of the churches can be seen from various points in the squares.

**Kresge College, Santa Cruz Campus**, University of California, 1972–74, MLTW/Moore and Turnbull

Street in Siena, Italy

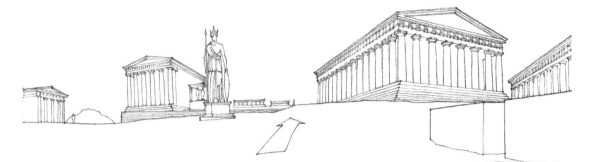

View looking east from the Propylaea

**Aerial view of the Acropolis,** Athens, Greece.
Dotted line indicates the path through the Propylaea to the
east end of the Parthenon.

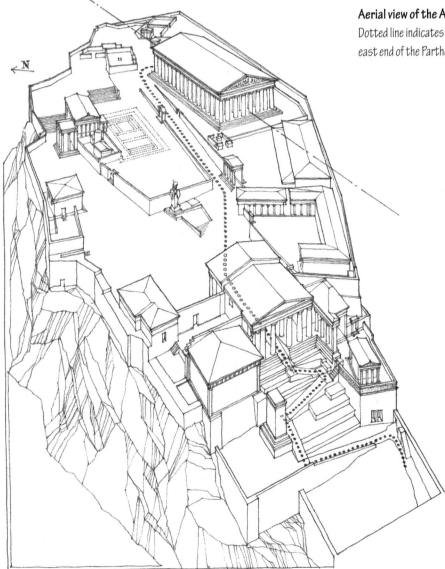

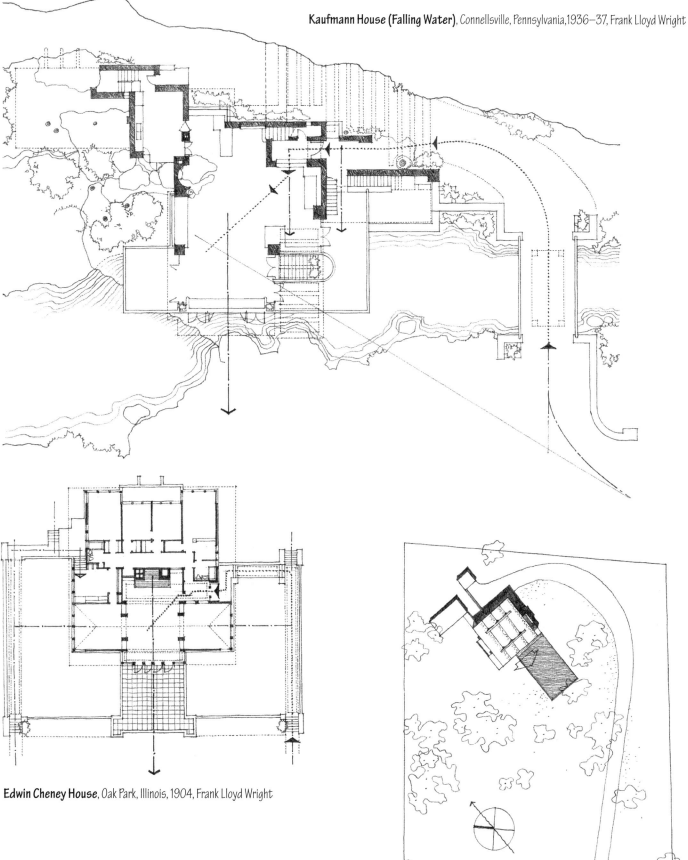

**Kaufmann House (Falling Water)**, Connellsville, Pennsylvania, 1936–37, Frank Lloyd Wright

**Edwin Cheney House**, Oak Park, Illinois, 1904, Frank Lloyd Wright

**Villa Hutheesing** (Project), Ahmedabad, India, 1952, Le Corbusier

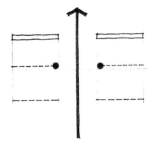 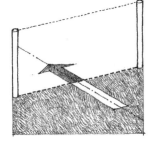 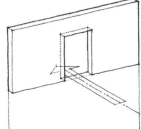

Entering a building, a room within a building, or a defined field of exterior space, involves the act of penetrating a vertical plane that distinguishes one space from another and separates "here" from "there."

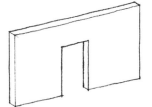 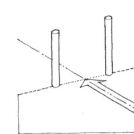 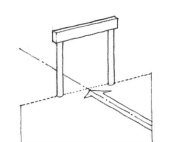

The act of entering can be signified in more subtle ways than punching a hole in a wall. It may be a passage through an implied plane established by two pillars or an overhead beam. In situations where greater visual and spatial continuity between two spaces is desired, even a change in level can establish a threshold and mark the passage from one place to another.

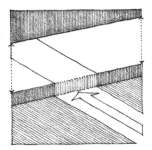 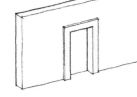 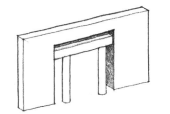

In the normal situation where a wall is used to define and enclose a space or series of spaces, an entrance is accommodated by an opening in the plane of the wall. The form of the opening, however, can range from a simple hole in the wall to an elaborate, articulated gateway.

 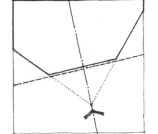

Regardless of the form of the space being entered or the form of its enclosure, the entrance into the space is best signified by establishing a real or implied plane perpendicular to the path of the approach.

Entrances may be grouped formally into the following categories: flush, projected, and recessed. A flush entrance maintains the continuity of the surface of a wall and can be, if desired, deliberately obscured. A projected entrance forms a transitional space, announces its function to the approach, and provides overhead shelter. A recessed entrance also provides shelter and receives a portion of exterior space into the realm of the building.

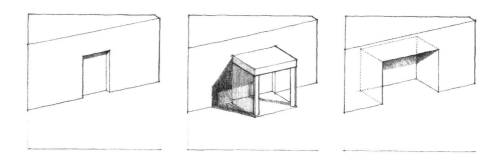

In each of the above categories, the form of the entrance can be similar to, and serve as a preview of, the form of the space being entered. Or it can contrast with the form of the space to reinforce its boundaries and emphasize its character as a place.

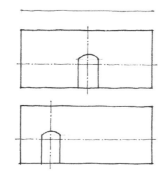
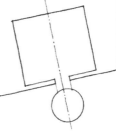
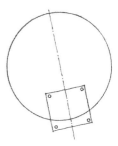

In terms of location, an entrance can be centered within the frontal plane of a building or be placed off-center to create a condition of local symmetry about its opening. The location of an entrance relative to the form of the space being entered will determine the configuration of the path and the pattern of the activities within the space.

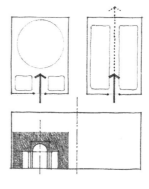
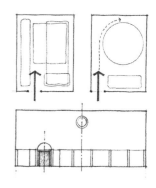

The notion of an entrance can be visually reinforced by:

- making the opening lower, wider, or narrower than anticipated
- making the entrance deep or circuitous
- articulating the opening with ornamentation or decorative embellishment

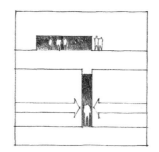
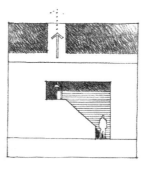

**Palazzo Zuccari**, Rome, c. 1592, Federico Zuccari

**Piazza San Marco**, Venice. View of the sea framed by the Doge's Palace on the left and Scamozzi's Library on the right. The entrance to the piazza from the sea is marked by two granite columns, the Lion's Column (1189) and the Column of St. Theodore (1329).

**O-torii, first gate to the Toshogu Shrine**, Nikko, Tochigi Prefecture, Japan, 1636

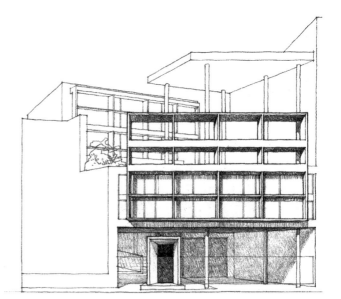

**Dr. Currutchet's House**, La Plata, Argentina, 1949, Le Corbusier
A portal marks the entrance for pedestrians within a larger opening that includes space for a carport.

**Von Sternberg House**, Los Angeles, California, 1936, Richard Neutra
A curving drive leads to an entranceway for automobiles while the front door
to the interior of this residence is in an entry court beyond.

**S. Giorgio Maggiore**, Venice, 1566–1610, Andrea Palladio.
Facade completed by Vicenzo Scamozzi.
The entrance facade operates at two scales: that of the
building as a whole facing a public space and another at the
size of a person entering the church.

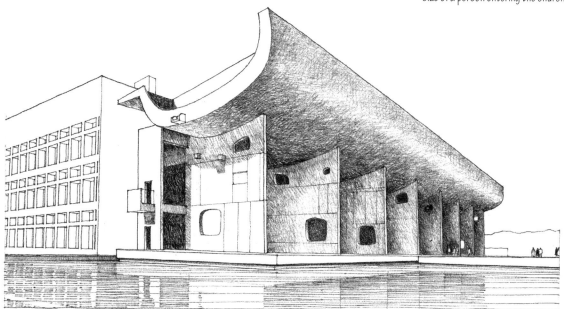

**Legislative Assembly Building, Chandigarh**, Capitol Complex of Punjab, India, 1956–59, Le Corbusier.
The entrance colonnade is scaled to the public nature of the building.

**Katsura Palace,** Kyoto, Japan, 17th century.
While the fence separates, the gateway and the stepping stones provide continuity
between the Imperial Carriage Stop and the Gepparo (Moon-Wave Pavilion) beyond.

**Morris Gift Shop**, San Francisco, California, 1948–49,
Frank Lloyd Wright

**Merchants' National Bank**, Grinnell, Iowa, 1914, Louis Sullivan

Elaborated openings within vertical planes mark the entrances to these two buildings.

**Entrance Pylons, Temple of Horus at Edfu**, 257–37 B.C.

A vertical break or separation in the facade defines the entrances to these buildings.

**House for Mrs. Robert Venturi**, Chestnut Hill, Pennsylvania, 1962–64, Venturi and Short

**John F. Kennedy Memorial**, Dallas, Texas, 1970, Philip Johnson

**Entrance to the Administration Building**, **Johnson Wax Co.**, Racine, Wisconsin, 1936–39, Frank Lloyd Wright

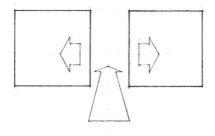

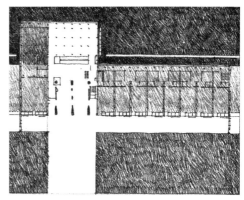

**The High Court**, **Chandigarh**, Capitol Complex of Punjab, India, 1956, Le Corbusier

**Plan Diagram**

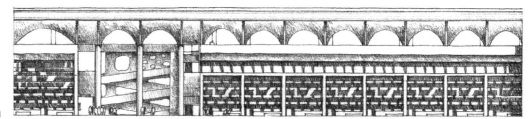

**North Elevation**

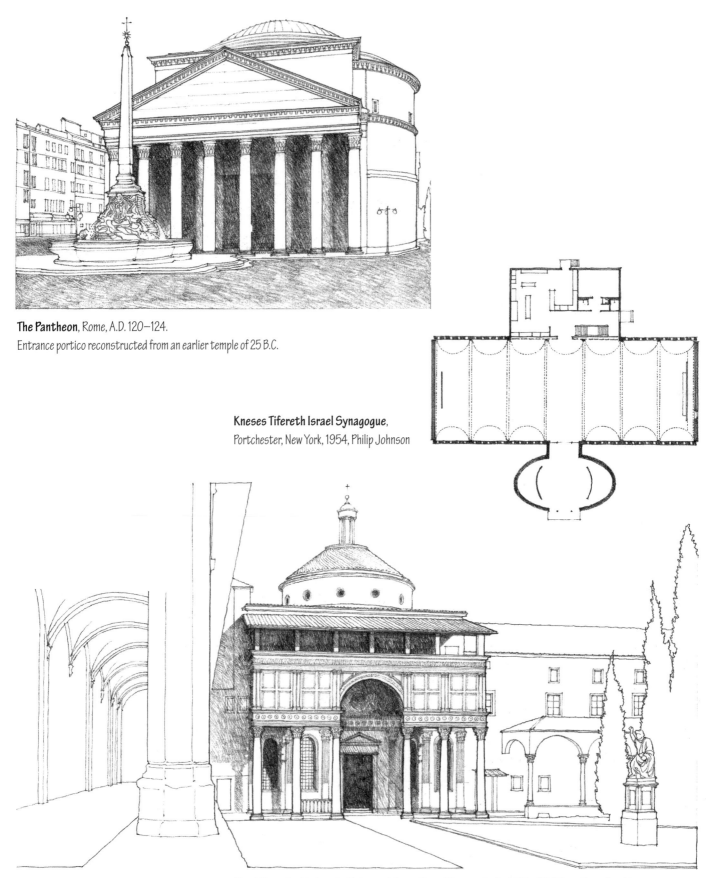

**The Pantheon**, Rome, A.D. 120–124.
Entrance portico reconstructed from an earlier temple of 25 B.C.

**Kneses Tifereth Israel Synagogue**,
Portchester, New York, 1954, Philip Johnson

**Pazzi Chapel**, added to the Cloister of Santa Croce, Florence, Italy, 1429–46, Filippo Brunelleschi

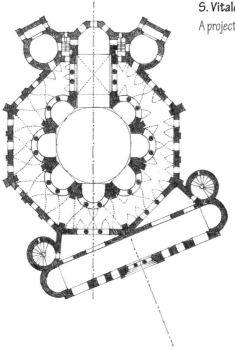

**S. Vitale**, Ravenna, Italy, A.D. 526–46
A projected entry space can reorient the principle axis of a building organization to that of the exterior space it fronts.

Porches, porticos, and marquees project from the main mass of a building to provide shelter, welcome, and announce the point of entry.

**The Oriental Theater**, Milwaukee, Wisconsin, 1927, Dick and Bauer

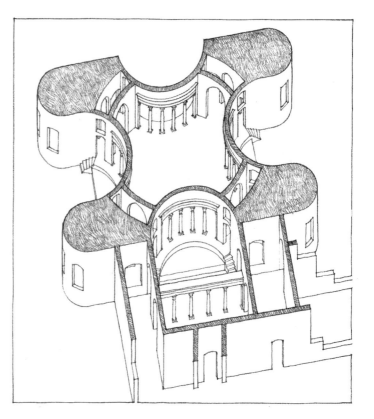

**Pavilion of the Academia, Hadrian's Villa**, Tivoli, Italy, A.D. 118–125
(after a drawing by Heine Kahler)

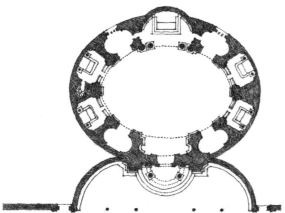

**S. Andrea del Quirinale**, Rome, 1670, Giovanni Bernini

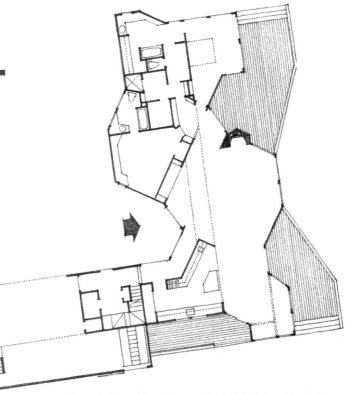

**Gagarin House**, Peru, Vermont, 1968, MLTW/Moore-Turnbull

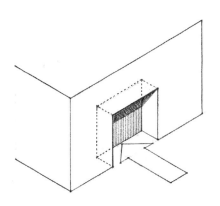

Examples of spaces recessed to receive those entering a building.

**S. Andrea**, **Mantua**, Italy 1472–94, Leon Battista Alberti

**East Building**, **National Gallery of Art**,
Washington, D.C., 1978, I.M. Pei and Partners

Steps and ramps introduce a vertical dimension and add a temporal quality to the act of entering a building.

**Rowhouses** in Galena, Illinois

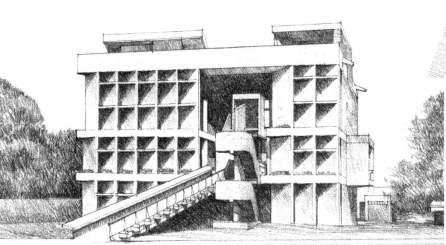

**Millowners Association Building**, Ahmedabad, India, 1954, Le Corbusier

**Taliesin West**, near Phoenix, Arizona, 1938, Frank Lloyd Wright

A Stele and Tortoise Guarding the **Tomb of Emperor Wan Li** (1563-1620), northwest of Peking (Beijing), China

**Interior Doorway** by Francesco Borromini

Entrances that pierce thick walls create transitional spaces through which one passes in moving from one place to another.

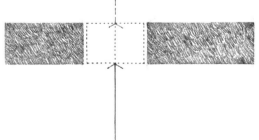

**Santa Barbara Courthouse**, California, 1929, William Mooser. The main entrance frames a view to the garden and hills beyond.

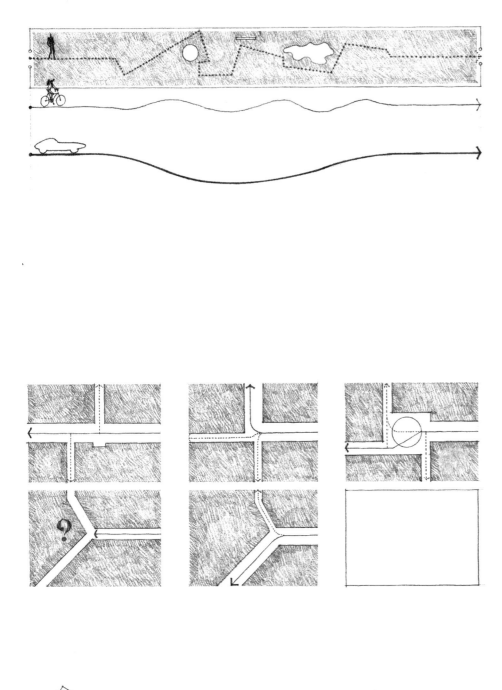

All paths of movement, whether of people, cars, goods, or services, are linear in nature. And all paths have a starting point, from which we are taken through a sequence of spaces to our destination. The contour of a path depends on our mode of transportation. While we as pedestrians can turn, pause, stop, and rest at will, a bicycle has less freedom, and a car even less, in changing its pace and direction abruptly. Interestingly though, while a wheeled vehicle may require a path with smooth contours that reflect its turning radius, the width of the path can be tailored tightly to its dimensions. Pedestrians, on the other hand, although able to tolerate abrupt changes in direction, require a greater volume of space than their bodily dimensions and greater freedom of choice along a path.

The intersection or crossing of paths is always a point of decision-making for the person approaching it. The continuity and scale of each path at an intersection can help us distinguish between major routes leading to major spaces and secondary paths leading to lesser spaces. When the paths at a crossing are equivalent to each another, sufficient space should be provided to allow people to pause and orient themselves. The form and scale of entrances and paths should also convey the functional and symbolic distinction between public prom-enades, private halls, and service corridors.

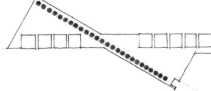

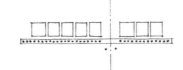

The nature of the configuration of a path both influences and is influenced by the organiza-tional pattern of the spaces it links. The configuration of a path may reinforce a spatial organization by paralleling its pattern. Or the configuration may contrast with the form of the spatial organization and serve as a visual counterpoint to it. Once we are able to map out in our minds the overall configuration of the paths in a building, our orientation within the building and our understanding of its spatial layout will be made clear.

## 1. Linear

All paths are linear. A straight path, however, can be the primary organizing element for a series of spaces. In addition, it can be curvilinear or segmented, intersect other paths, have branches, or form a loop.

## 2. Radial

A radial configuration has linear paths extending from or terminating at a central, common point.

## 3. Spiral

A spiral configuration is a single, continuous path that originates from a central point, revolves around it, and becomes increasingly distant from it.

## 4. Grid

A grid configuration consists of two sets of parallel paths that intersect at regular intervals and create square or rectangular fields of space.

## 5. Network

A network configuration consists of paths that connect established points in space.

## 6. Composite

In reality, a building normally employs a combination of the preceding patterns. Important points in any pattern are centers of activity, entrances to rooms and halls, and places for vertical circulation provided by stairways, ramps, and elevators. These nodes punctuate the paths of movement through a building and provide opportunities for pause, rest, and reorientation. To avoid the creation of a disorienting maze, a hierarchical order among the paths and nodes of a building should be established by differentiating their scale, form, length, and placement.

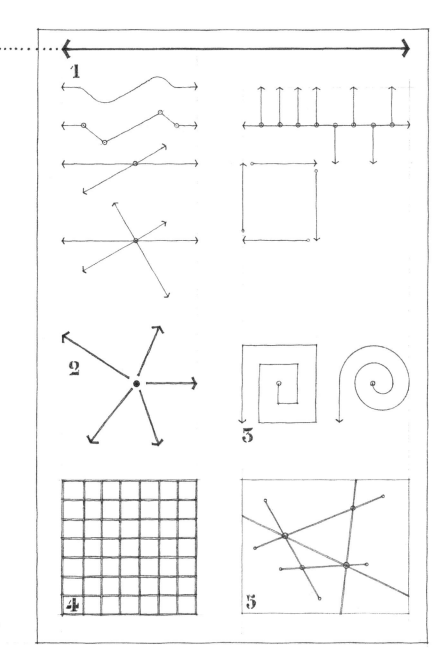

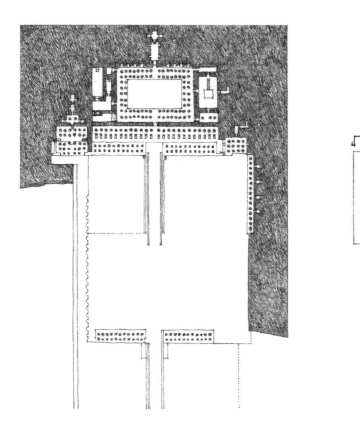

**Mortuary Temple of Queen Hatshepsut**, Dêr el-Bahari,
Thebes, 1511–1480 B.C., Senmut

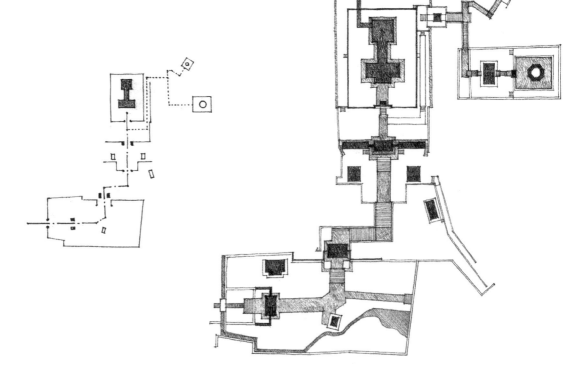

Plan of Taiyu-In Precinct of the **Toshogu Shrine**, Nikko, Tochigi Prefecture, Japan, 1636

Ground Level Plan

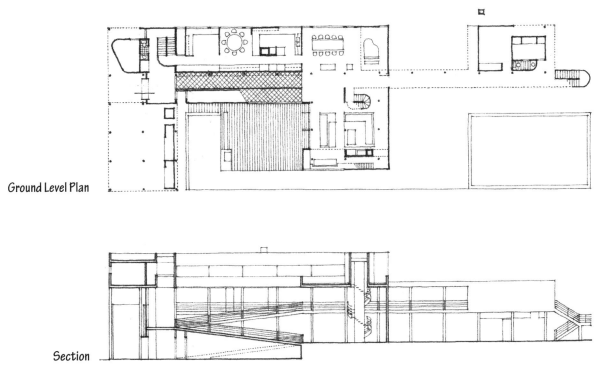

Section

**House in Old Westbury**, New York, 1969–71, Richard Meier

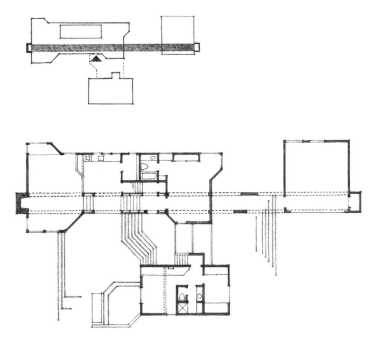

**First Floor Plan**, **Hines House**, Sea Ranch, California, 1966, MLTW/Moore and Turnbull

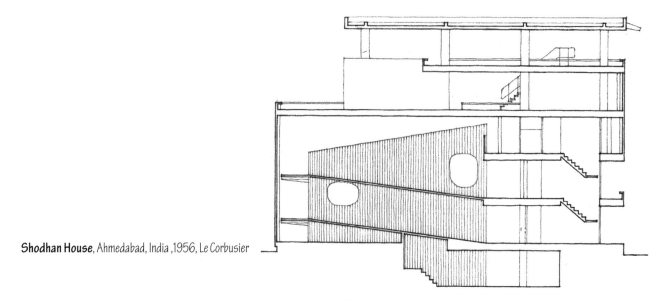

**Shodhan House**, Ahmedabad, India ,1956, Le Corbusier

### Section through ramp and stair

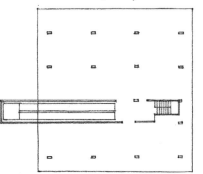

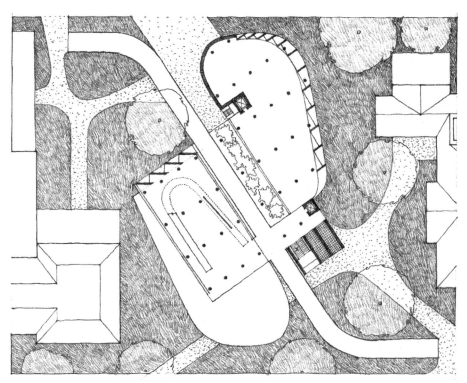

**Carpenter Center for the Visual Arts**,
Harvard University, Cambridge, Massachusetts,
1961–64, Le Corbusier

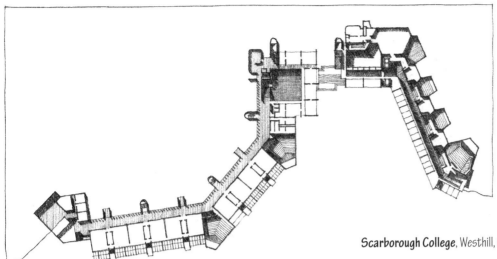

**Scarborough College**, Westhill, Ontario, 1964, John Andrews

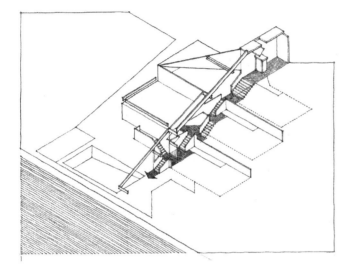

**Bookstaver House**, Westminster, Vermont, 1972, Peter L. Gluck

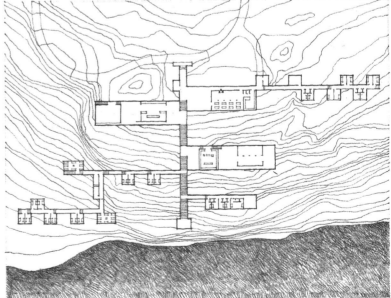

**Haystack Mountain School of Arts and Crafts**,
Deer Isle, Maine, 1960, Edward Larrabee Barnes

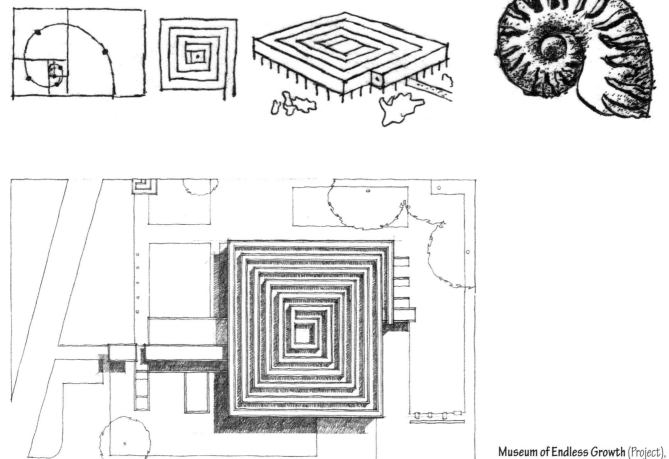

Museum of Endless Growth (Project),
Philippeville, Algeria, 1939, Le Corbusier

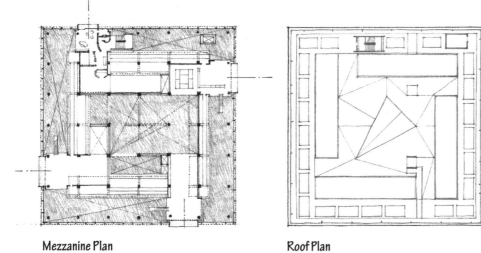

Mezzanine Plan

Roof Plan

Museum of Western Art, Tokyo, 1957–59,
Le Corbusier

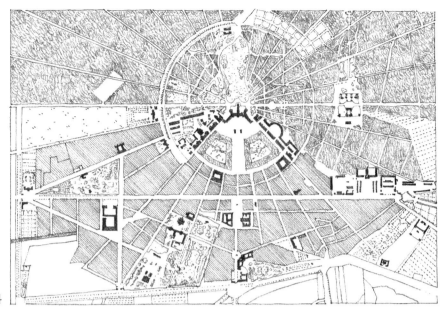

**Karlsruhe**, Germany, 1834

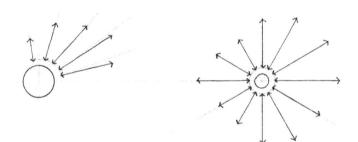

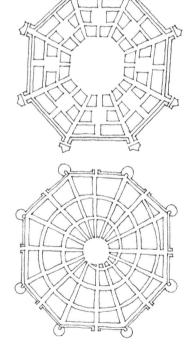

City on a Plain

City on a Hill

**Plans of Ideal Cities**, 1451–1464,
Francesco di Giorgi Martini

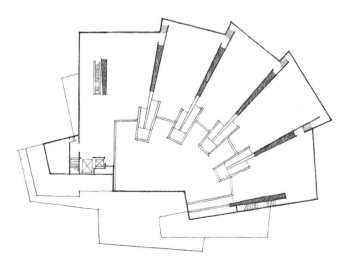

**University Art Museum**, University of California–Berkeley, 1971,
Mario J. Ciampi and Associates

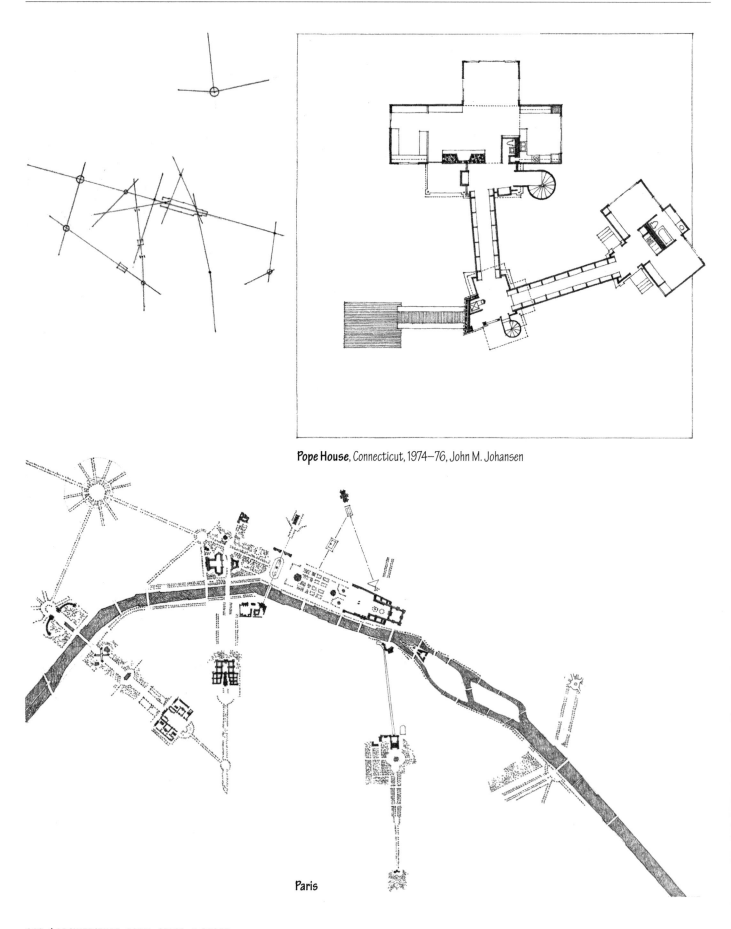

**Pope House**, Connecticut, 1974–76, John M. Johansen

Paris

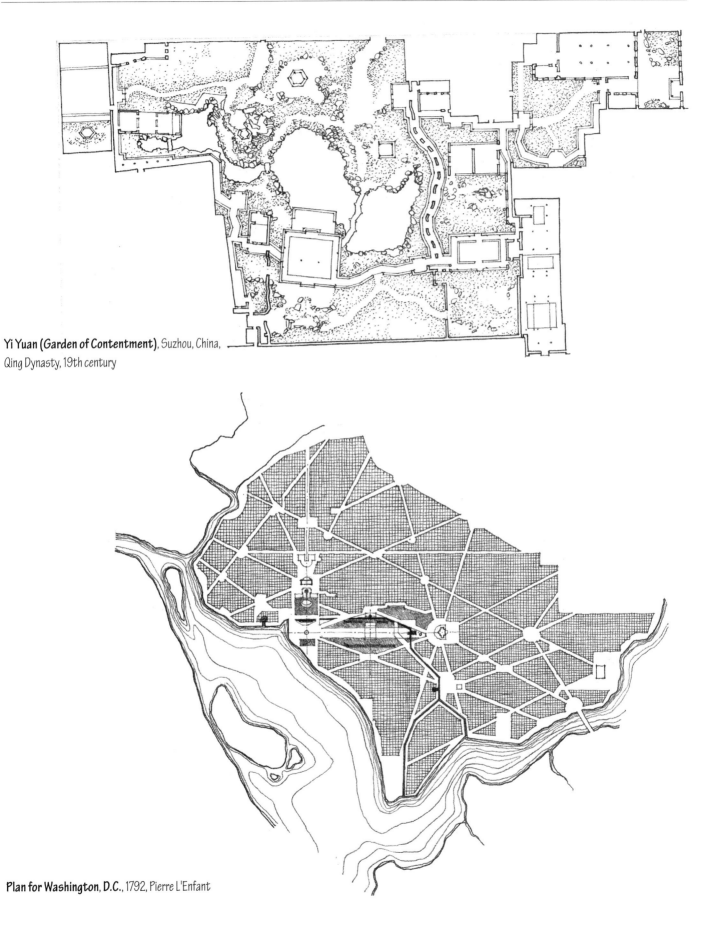

**Yi Yuan (Garden of Contentment)**, Suzhou, China,
Qing Dynasty, 19th century

**Plan for Washington, D.C.**, 1792, Pierre L'Enfant

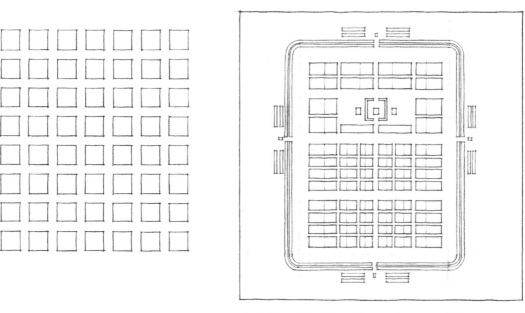

Typical Layout for a **Roman Camp**, c. 1st century A.D.

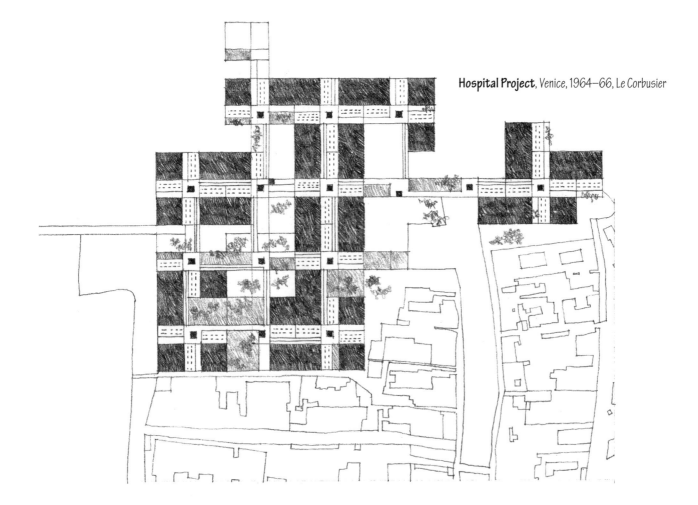

**Hospital Project**, Venice, 1964—66, Le Corbusier

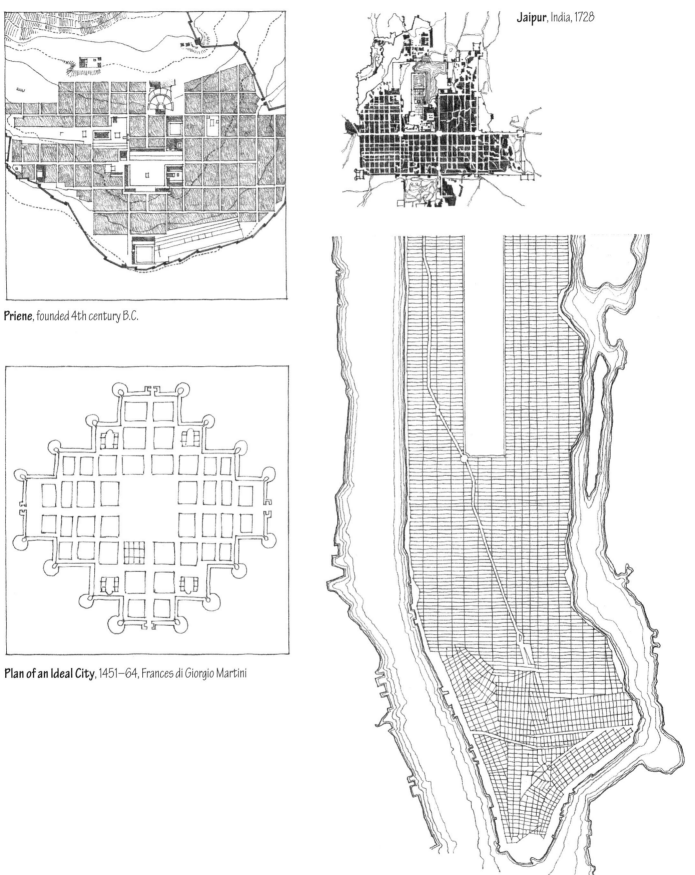

Jaipur, India, 1728

**Priene**, founded 4th century B.C.

**Plan of an Ideal City**, 1451–64, Frances di Giorgio Martini

**Manhattan**, New York City

Paths may be related to the spaces they link in the following ways. They may:

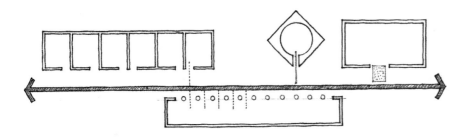

## Pass by Spaces

- The integrity of each space is maintained.
- The configuration of the path is flexible.
- Mediating spaces can be used to link the path with the spaces.

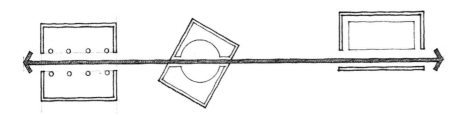

## Pass through Spaces

- The path may pass though a space axially, obliquely, or along its edge.
- In cutting through a space, the path creates patterns of rest and movement within it.

## Terminate in a Space

- The location of the space establishes the path.
- This path-space relationship is used to approach and enter functionally or symbolically important spaces.

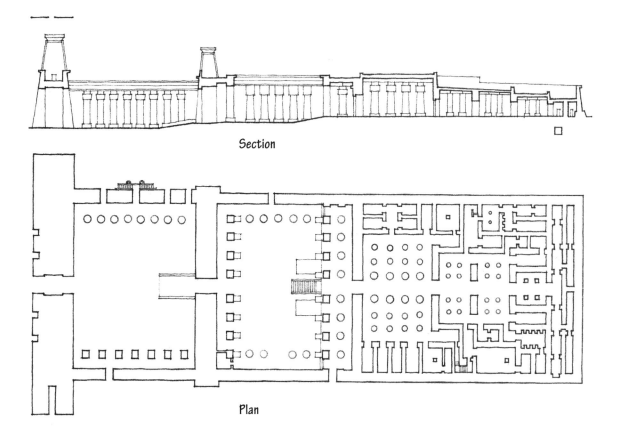

Section

Plan

**Mortuary Temple of Rameses III**, Medînet-Habu, 1198 B.C.

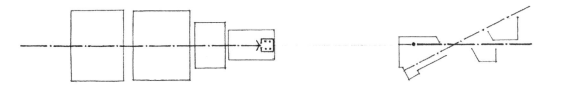

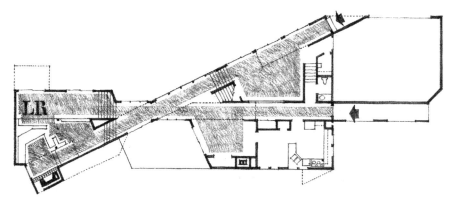

LR

**Stern House**, Woodbridge, Connecticut, 1970, Charles Moore Associates

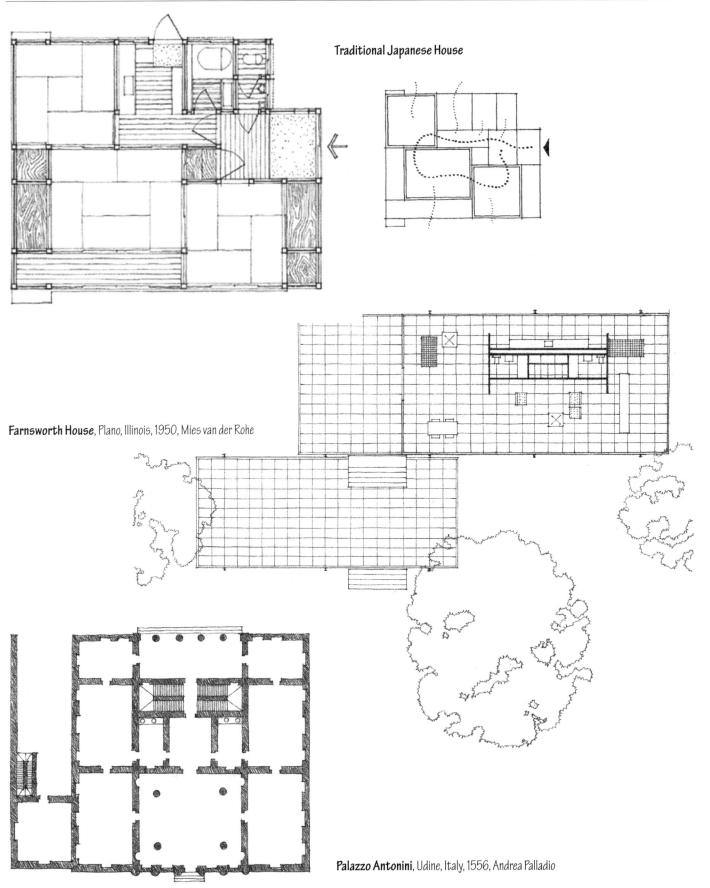

Traditional Japanese House

Farnsworth House, Plano, Illinois, 1950, Mies van der Rohe

Palazzo Antonini, Udine, Italy, 1556, Andrea Palladio

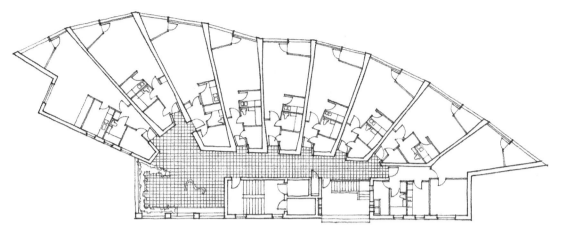

**Neur Vahr Apartment Building**, Bremen, Germany, 1958–62, Alvar Aalto

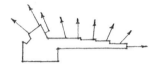

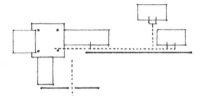

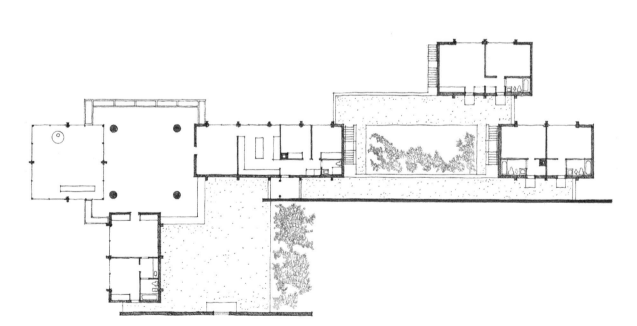

**Eric Boissonas House II**, Cap Benat, France, 1964, Philip Johnson

After a drawing by William R. Ware of
a vaulted staircase

Spaces for movement form an integral part of any building organization and occupy a significant amount of the volume of a building. If considered merely as functional linking devices, then circulation paths would be endless, corridor-like spaces. The form and scale of a circulation space, however, should accommodate the movement of people as they promenade, pause, rest, or take in a view along a path.

The form of a circulation space varies according to how:
- its boundaries are defined
- its form relates to the form of the spaces it links
- its qualities of scale, proportion, light, and view are articulated
- entrances open onto it
- it handles changes in level with stairs and ramps

A circulation space may be:

## Enclosed

forming a public galleria or private corridor that relates to the spaces it links though entrances in a wall plane;

## Open on One Side

forming a balcony or gallery that provides visual and spatial continuity with the spaces it links;

## Open on Both Sides

forming a colonnaded passageway that becomes a physical extension of the space it passes through.

The width and height of a circulation space should be proportionate with the type and amount of movement it must handle. A distinction in scale should be established between a public promenade, a more private hall, and a service corridor.

A narrow, enclosed path naturally encourages forward motion. To accommodate more traffic as well as to create spaces for pausing, resting, or viewing, sections of a path can be widened. The path can also be enlarged by merging with the spaces it passes through.

Within a large space, a path can be random, without form or definition, and be determined by the activities and arrangement of furnishings within the space.

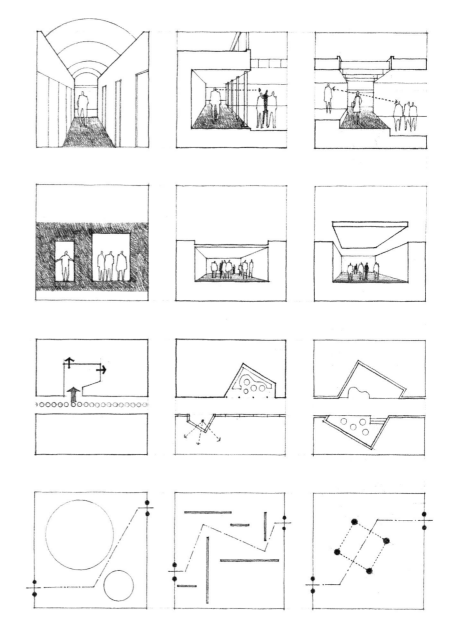

**Cloister of S. Maria della Pace**, Rome, 1500–04, Donato Bramante

**Hallway of Okusu Residence**, Todoroki, Tokyo, 1976–78, Tadao Ando

**Vestibule of Renaissance Palace**

Examples of various forms of spaces used for movement through a building.

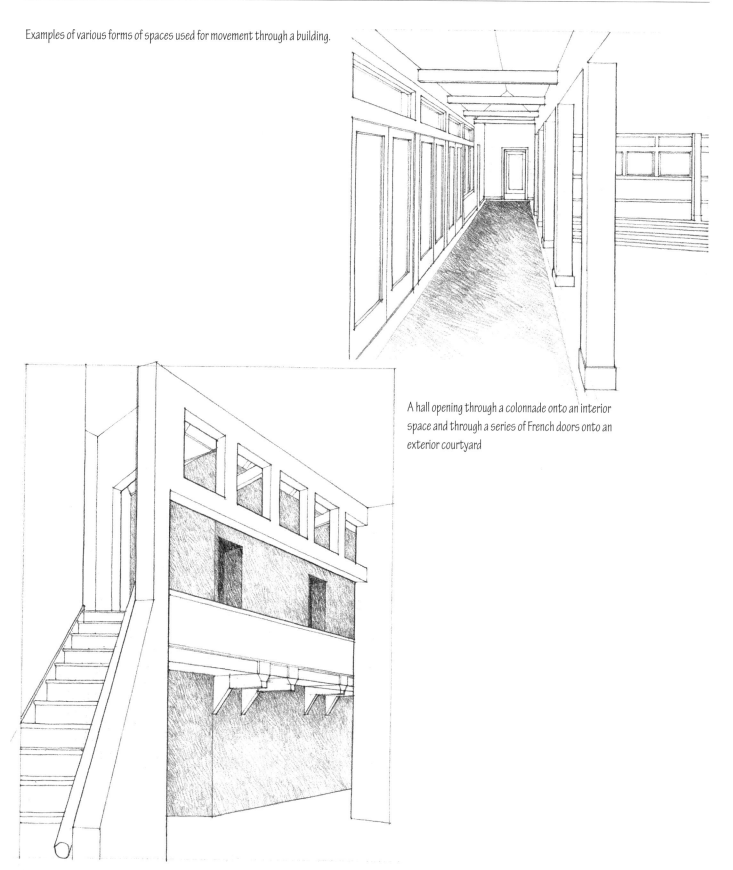

A hall opening through a colonnade onto an interior space and through a series of French doors onto an exterior courtyard

**Raised hall, Residence in Morris County**, New Jersey, 1971, Moore, Lyndon, Turnbull & Whitaker

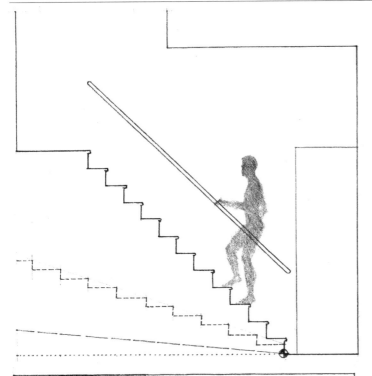

Stairs and stairways provide for our vertical movement between the levels of a building or outdoor space. The slope of a stairway, determined by the dimensions of its risers and treads, should be proportioned to fit our body movement and capability. If steep, a stair can make ascent physically tiring as well as psychologically forbidding, and can make descent precarious. If shallow, a stair must have treads deep enough to fit our stride.

A stairway should be wide enough to comfortably accommodate our passage as well as any furnishings and equipment that must be moved up or down the steps. The width of a stairway also provides a visual clue to the public or private nature of the stairway. Wide, shallow steps can serve as an invitation, while a narrow, steep stairway can lead to more private places.

While the act of traversing up a stairway may convey privacy, aloofness, or detachment, the process of going down can imply moving toward secure, protected, or stable ground.

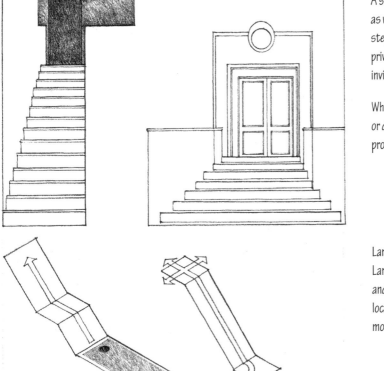

Landings interrupt the run of a stair and enable it to change direction. Landings also provide opportunities for rest and possibilities for access and outlook from the stairway. Together with the pitch of a stair, the locations of landings determine the rhythm and choreography of our movements as we ascend or descend its steps.

Stairs, in accommodating a change in level, can reinforce the path of movement, interrupt it, accommodate a change in its course, or terminate it prior to entering a major space.

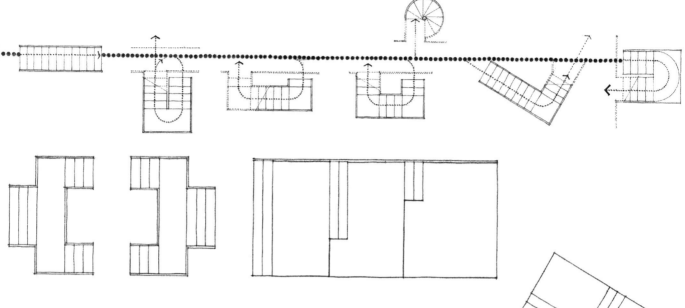

The configuration of a stairway determines the direction of our path as we ascend or descend its steps. There are several basic ways in which to configure the runs of a stairway.

- straight-run stair
- L-shaped stair
- U-shaped stair
- circular stair
- spiral stair

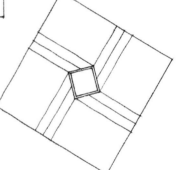

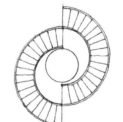

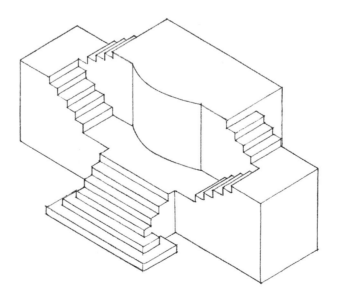

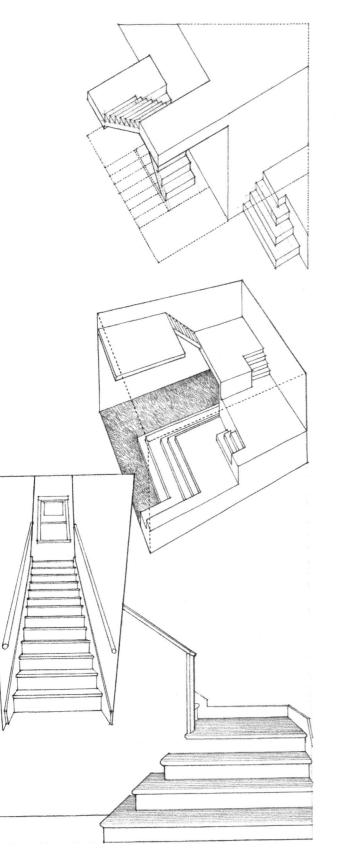

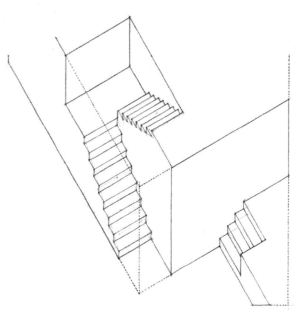

The space a stairway occupies can be great, but its form can be fitted into an interior in several ways. It can be treated as an additive form or as a volumetric solid from which space for movement as well as rest have been carved out.

The stairway can run along one of the edges of a room, wrap around the space, or fill its volume. It can be woven into the boundaries of a space or be extended into a series of platforms for seating or terraces for activity.

A stairway can be an organizing element and meander through and weave together a series of spaces at different levels of a building or outdoor space.

Landings which are visible on approach invite ascent, as do treads which spill out at the bottom of a stairway. On the other hand, to offer access to a private place or signify unapproachability, the path of a stair can rise steeply between walls through a narrow shaft of space.

Stairs are three-dimensional forms just as moving up or down a stairway is a three-dimensional experience. This three-dimensional quality can be exploited when we treat it as sculpture, freestanding within a space or attached to a wall plane. Further, a space can itself become an oversized elaborated stairway.

**Grand Staircase, Paris Opera House,** 1861–74, Charles Garnier

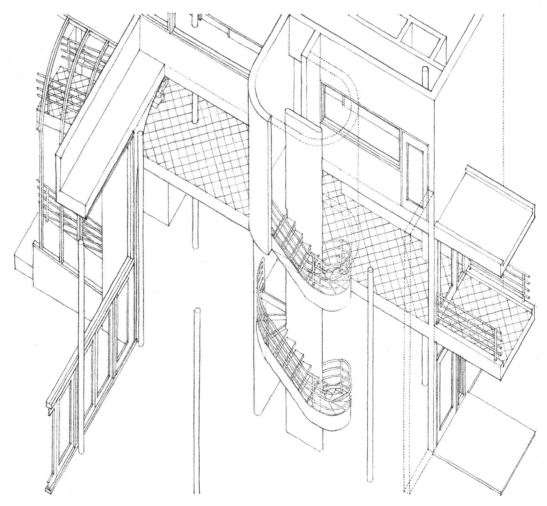

Axonometric of Living Room Stair, **House in Old Westbury,** New York, 1969–71, Richard Meier

# 6
# Proportion & Scale

". . . Within the Villa Foscari you are aware of the thickness of the walls that separate the rooms, each of which has been given definitive and precise form. At either end of the cross-arm of the central hall is a square room measuring 16 x 16 feet. It lies between a larger and a smaller rectangular room, the one 12 x 16, the other 16 x 24 feet, or twice as large. The smaller has its longer wall, the larger its shorter, in common with the square room. Palladio placed great emphasis on these simple ratios: 3:4, 4:4, and 4:6, which are those found in musical harmony. The width of the central hall is also based on 16. Its length is less exact because the thickness of the walls must be added to the simple dimensions of the rooms. The special effect of the hall in this firmly interlocked composition is produced by its great height, the barrel-vaulted ceiling towering high above the side rooms into the mezzanine. But, you may ask, does the visitor actually experience these proportions? The answer is yes—not the exact measurements but the fundamental idea behind them. You receive an impression of a noble, firmly integrated composition in which each room presents an ideal form within a greater whole. You also feel the the rooms are related in size. Nothing is trivial— all is great and whole."

Steen Eiler Rasmussen
*Experiencing Architecture*
1962

This chapter discusses the interrelated issues of proportion and scale. While scale alludes to the size of something compared to a reference standard or to the size of something else, proportion refers to the proper or harmonious relation of one part to another or to the whole. This relationship may not only be one of magnitude, but also of quantity or degree. While the designer usually has a range of choices when determining the proportions of things, some are given to us by the nature of materials, by how building elements respond to forces, and by how things are made.

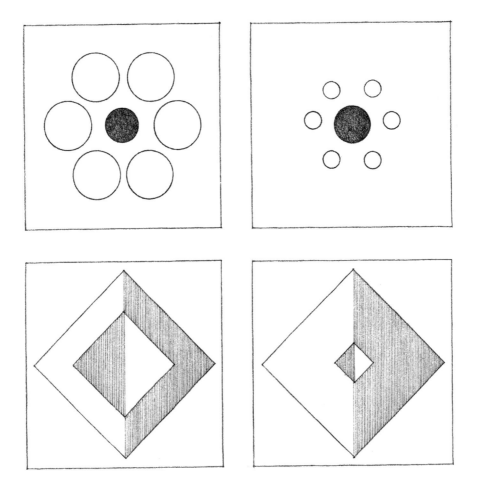

All building materials in architecture have distinct properties of elasticity, hardness, and durability. And they all have an ultimate strength beyond which they cannot extend themselves without fracturing, breaking, or collapsing. Since the stresses in a material resulting from the force of gravity increase with size, all materials also have rational dimensions beyond which they cannot go. For example, a stone slab that is four-inches thick and eight-feet long can be reasonably expected to support itself as a bridge between two supports. But if its size were to increase fourfold, to sixteen-inches thick and thirty-two-feet long, it would probably collapse under its own weight. Even a strong material like steel has lengths beyond which it cannot span without exceeding its ultimate strength.

All materials also have rational proportions which are dictated by their inherent strengths and weaknesses. Masonry units like brick, for example, are strong in compression and depend on their mass for strength. Such materials are therefore volumetric in form. Materials like steel are strong in both compression and tension and can therefore be formed into linear columns and beams as well as planar sheet materials.
Wood, being a flexible and fairly elastic material, can be used as linear posts and beams, planar boards, and as a volumetric element in log cabin construction.

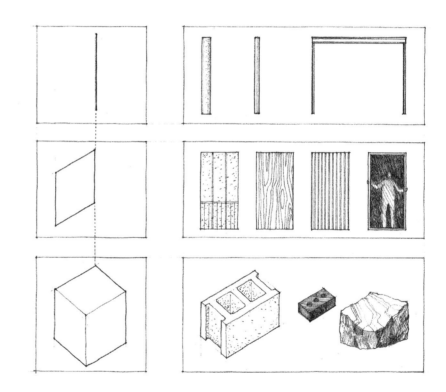

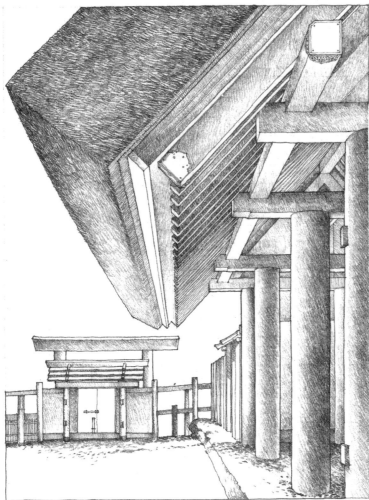

South gateway of the third fence of **Naigu**, **the inner shrine**, **Ise Shrine**, Mie Prefecture, Japan, A.D. 690

In the construction of architecture, structural elements are called upon to span spaces and transmit their loads through vertical supports to the foundation system of a building. The size and proportion of these elements are directly related to the structural tasks they perform and can therefore be visual indicators of the size and scale of the spaces they help enclose.

Beams, for example, transmit their loads horizontally across space to their vertical supports. If the span or load of a beam were doubled, its bending stresses would likewise double, possibly causing it to collapse. But if its depth were doubled, its strength would increase fourfold. Depth, therefore, is the critical dimension of a beam and its depth-to-span ratio can be a useful indicator of its structural role.

In a similar manner, columns become thicker as their loads and unsupported height increase. Together, beams and columns form a skeletal structural framework that defines modules of space. By their size and proportion, columns and beams articulate space and give it scale and a hierarchical structure. This can be seen in the way joists are supported by beams, which in turn are supported by girders. Each element increases in depth as its load and span increase in size.

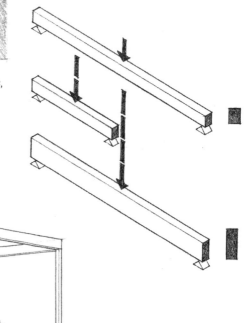

The proportions of other structural elements, as bearing walls, floor and roof slabs, vaults, and domes, also give us visual clues to their role in a structural system as well as the nature of their material. A masonry wall, being strong in compression but relatively weak in bending, will be thicker than a reinforced concrete wall doing the same work. A steel column will be thinner than a wood post supporting the same load. A four-inch-thick reinforced concrete slab will span farther than four-inch wood decking.

As a structure depends less on the weight and stiffness of a material and more on its geometry for stability, as in the case of a membrane structure or a space frame, its elements will get thinner and thinner until they lose their ability to give a space scale and dimension.

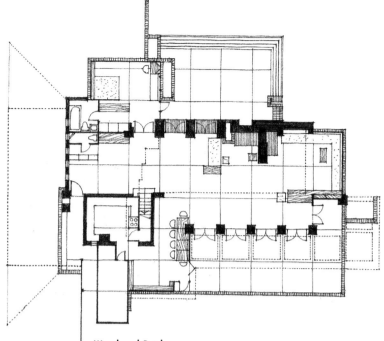

### Wood and Brick
**Schwartz House**, Two Rivers, Wisconsin, 1939, Frank Lloyd Wright

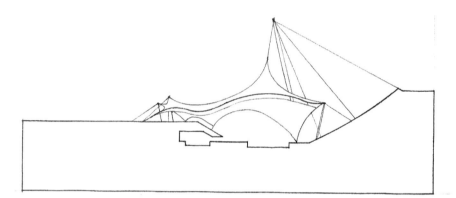

### Membrane
Roof of **Olympic Swimming Arena**, Munich, Germany, 1972, Fred Otto

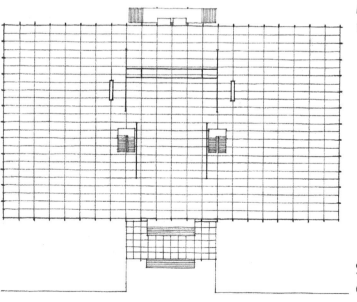

### Steel
**Crown Hall**, Illinois Institute of Technology, Chicago, 1956, Mies van der Rohe

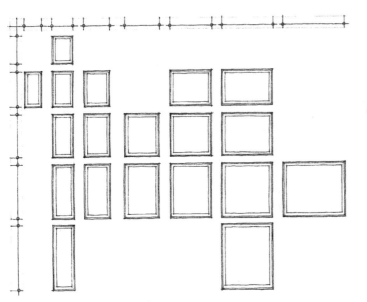

**Standard Casement Window Units**

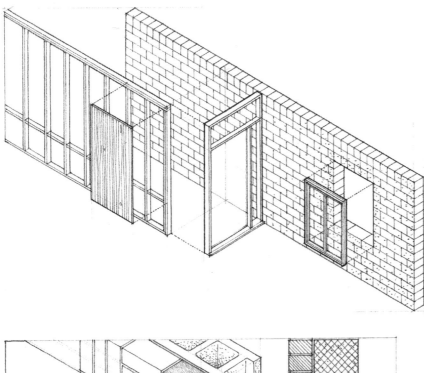

Many architectural elements are sized and proportioned not only according to their structural properties and function, but also by the process through which they are manufactured. Because these elements are mass-produced in factories, they have standard sizes and proportions imposed on them by the individual manufacturers or by industry standards.

Concrete block and common brick, for example, are produced as modular building units. Although they differ from each other in size, both are proportioned on a similar basis. Plywood and other sheathing materials also are manufactured as modular units with fixed proportions. Steel sections have fixed proportions generally agreed upon by the steel manufacturers and the American Institute of Steel Construction. Windows and doors have proportions that are set by the individual manufacturers of the units.

Since these and other materials must ultimately come together and achieve a high degree of fit in the construction of a building, the standard sizes and proportions of factory-produced elements affect the size, proportion, and spacing of other materials as well. Standard door and window units are sized and proportioned to fit into modular masonry openings. Wood or metal studs and joists are spaced to accept modular sheathing materials.

Even considering the proportional constraints imposed on a form by the nature of its material, its structural function, or by the manufacturing process, the designer still has the ability to control the proportion of the forms and spaces within and around a building. The decision to make a room square or oblong in plan, intimate or lofty in scale, or to endow a building with an imposing, higher-than-normal facade, legitimately falls to the designer. But on what basis are these decisions made?

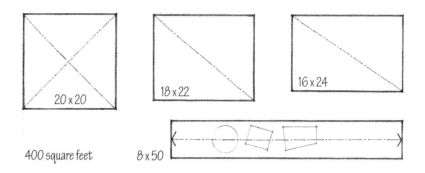

400 square feet          8 x 50

If a space 400 square feet in area were required, what dimensions—what ratios of width-to-length and length-to-height—should it have? Of course, the functioning of the space and the nature of the activities to be accommodated will influence its form and proportion.

A square space, having four equal faces, is static in nature. If its length expands and dominates its width, it becomes more dynamic. While square and oblong spaces define places for activity, linear spaces encourage movement and are susceptible to subdivision into a number of zones.

A technical factor, such as its structure, might limit one or more of its dimensions. Its context—the exterior environment or an adjacent interior space—might pressure its form. The decision might be to recall a space from another time and place and to simulate its proportions. Or the decision might be based finally on an aesthetic, visual judgment of the "desirable" relationships among the dimensions of the parts and the whole of a building.

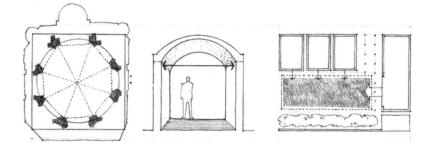

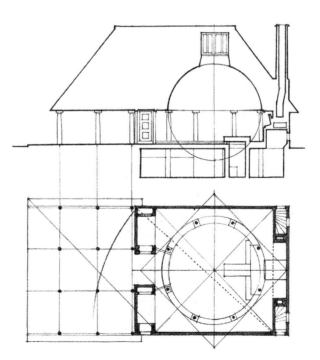

**Woodland Chapel**,
Stockholm, Sweden, 1918–1920, Erik Gunnar Asplund

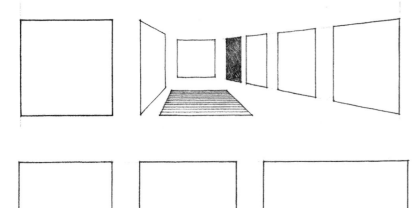

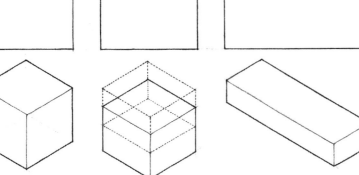

Ratio: $\dfrac{a}{b}$

Proportion: $\dfrac{a}{b} = \dfrac{c}{d}$ or $\dfrac{a}{b} = \dfrac{b}{c} = \dfrac{c}{d} = \dfrac{d}{e}$

Proportion is the equality between two ratios in which the first of the four terms divided by the second equals the third divided by the fourth.

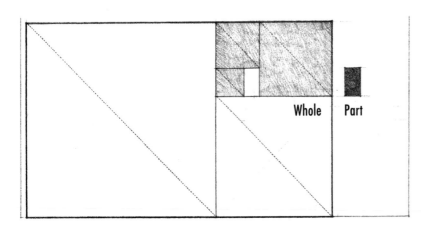

Whole    Part

In truth, our perception of the physical dimensions of architecture, of proportion and scale, is imprecise. It is distorted by the foreshortening of perspective and distance, and by cultural biases, and is thus difficult to control and predict in an objective and precise manner.

Small or slight differences in the dimensions of a form are especially difficult to discern. While a square, by definition, has four equal sides and four right angles, a rectangle can appear to be exactly square, almost a square, or very much unlike a square. It can appear to be long, short, stubby, or squat, depending on our point of view. We use these terms to give a form or figure a visual quality that is largely a result of how we perceive its proportions. It is not, however, an exact science.

If the precise dimensions and relationships of a design that is regulated by a proportioning system cannot be objectively perceived in a similar manner by everyone, why are proportioning system useful and of particular significance in architectural design?

The intent of all theories of proportions is to create a sense of order and harmony among the elements in a visual construction. According to Euclid, a ratio refers to the quantitative comparison of two similar things, while proportion refers to the equality of ratios. Underlying any proportioning system, therefore, is a characteristic ratio, a permanent quality that is transmitted from one ratio to another. Thus, a proportioning system establishes a consistent set of visual relationships between the parts of a building, as well as between the parts and the whole. Although these relationships may not be immediately perceived by the casual observer, the visual order they create can be sensed, accepted, or even recognized through a series of repetitive experiences. Over a period of time, we might begin to see the whole in the part, and the part in the whole.

Proportioning systems go beyond the functional and technical determinants of architectural form and space to provide an aesthetic rationale for their dimensions. They can visually unify the multiplicity of elements in an architectural design by having all of its parts belong to the same family of proportions. They can provide a sense of order in, and heighten the continuity of, a sequence of spaces. They can establish relationships between the exterior and interior elements of a building.

A number of theories of "desirable" proportions have been developed in the course of history. The notion of devising a system for design and communicating its means is common to all periods. Although the actual system varies from time to time, the principles involved and their value to the designer remain the same.

**Theories of Proportion:**

• Golden Section

• Classical Orders

• Renaissance Theories

• Modulor

• Ken

• Anthropometry

• Scale    A fixed proportion used in determining measurements and dimensions

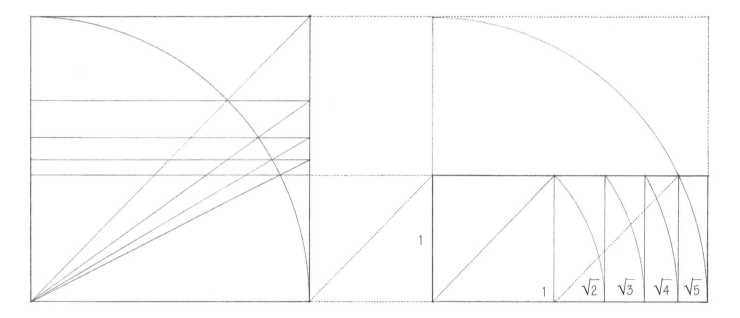

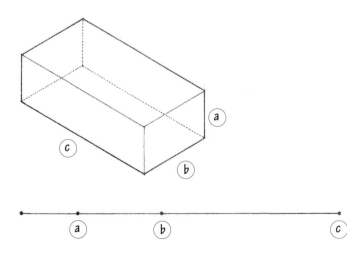

**Types of Proportion:**

Arithmetic    $\dfrac{c-b}{b-a} = \dfrac{c}{c}$    (e.g., 1, 2, 3)

Geometric    $\dfrac{c-b}{b-a} = \dfrac{c}{b}$    (e.g., 1, 2, 4)

Harmonic    $\dfrac{c-b}{b-a} = \dfrac{c}{a}$    (e.g., 2, 3, 6)

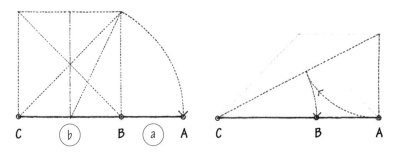

The geometric construction of the Golden Section, first by extension, and then by division.

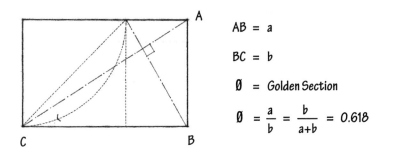

AB = a

BC = b

Ø = Golden Section

$$\text{Ø} = \frac{a}{b} = \frac{b}{a+b} = 0.618$$

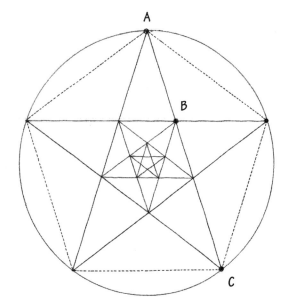

Mathematical systems of proportion originate from the Pythagorean concept of 'all is number' and the belief that certain numerical relationships manifest the harmonic structure of the universe. One of these relationships that has been in use ever since the days of antiquity is the proportion known as the Golden Section. The Greeks recognized the dominating role the Golden Section played in the proportions of the human body. Believing that both humanity and the shrines housing their deities should belong to a higher universal order, they utilized these same proportions in their temple structures. Renaissance architects also explored the Golden Section in their work. In more recent times, Le Corbusier based his Modulor system on the Golden Section. Its use in architecture endures even today.

The Golden Section can be defined as the ratio between two sections of a line, or the two dimensions of a plane figure, in which the lesser of the two is to the greater as the greater is to the sum of both. It can be expressed algebraically by the equation of two ratios:

$$\frac{a}{b} = \frac{b}{a+b}$$

The Golden Section has some remarkable algebraic and geometric properties that account for its existence in architecture as well as in the structures of many living organisms. Any progression based on the Golden Section is at once additive and geometrical.

Another progression that closely approximates the Golden Section in whole numbers is the Fibonacci Series: 1, 1, 2, 3, 5, 8, 13 …. Each term again is the sum of the two preceding ones, and the ratio between two consecutive terms tends to approximate the Golden Section as the series progresses to infinity.

In the numerical progression: $1, \text{Ø}^1, \text{Ø}^2, \text{Ø}^3 \ldots \text{Ø}^n$, each term is the sum of the two preceding ones.

A rectangle whose sides are proportioned according to the Golden Section is known as a Golden Rectangle. If a square is constructed on its smaller side, the remaining portion of the original rectangle would be a smaller but similar Golden Rectangle. This operation can be repeated indefinitely to create a gradation of squares and Golden Rectangles. During this transformation, each part remains similar to all of the other parts, as well as to the whole. The diagrams on this page illustrate this additive and geometrical growth pattern of progressions based on the Golden Section.

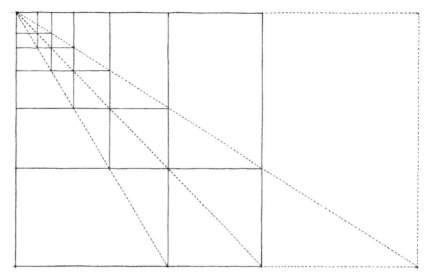

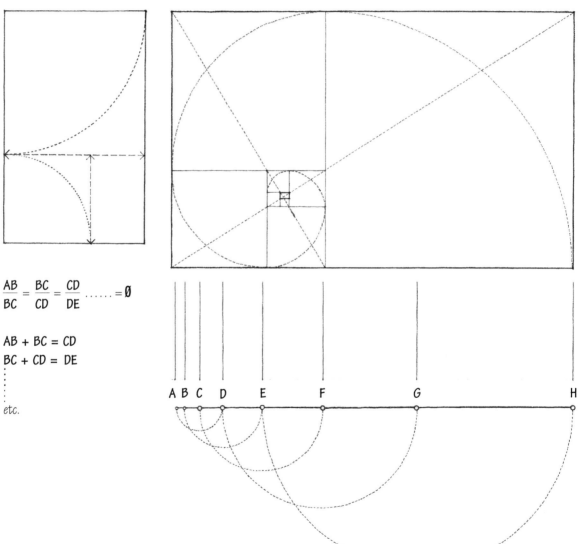

$$\frac{AB}{BC} = \frac{BC}{CD} = \frac{CD}{DE} \dots\dots = \emptyset$$

$$AB + BC = CD$$
$$BC + CD = DE$$
$$\vdots$$
etc.

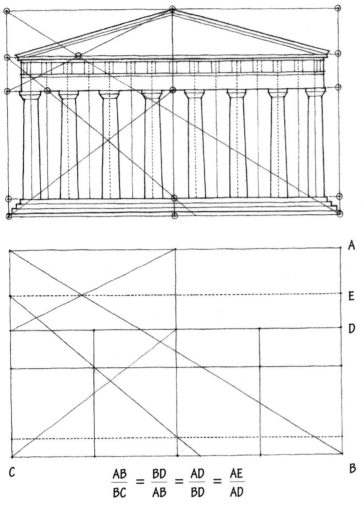

The Parthenon, Athens, 447–432 B.C., Ictinus and Callicrates

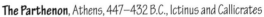

$$\frac{AB}{BC} = \frac{BD}{AB} = \frac{AD}{BD} = \frac{AE}{AD}$$

These two graphic analyses illustrate the use of the Golden Section in the proportioning of the facade of the Parthenon. It is interesting to note that while both analyses begin by fitting the facade into a Golden Rectangle, each analysis then varies from the other in its approach to proving the existence of the Golden Section and its effect on the dimensions and distribution of elements across the facade.

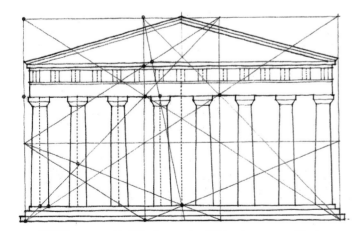

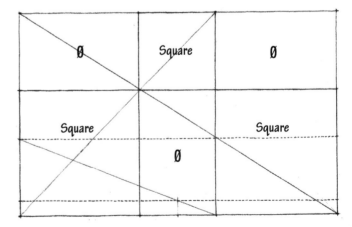

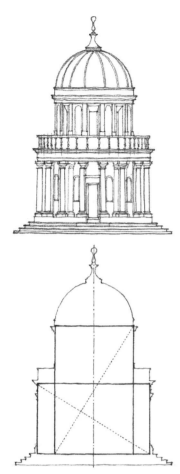

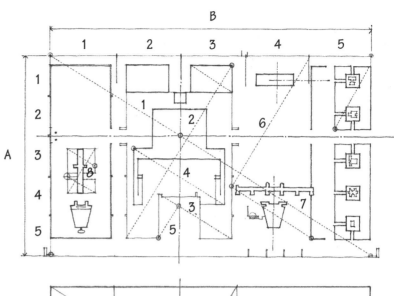

**Tempietto of S. Pietro** in Montorio, Rome, 1502–10, Donato Bramante

**World Museum** (Project), Geneva, 1929, Le Corbusier

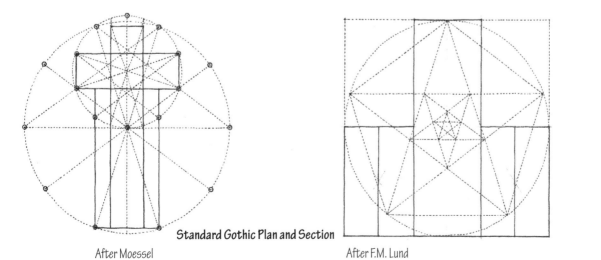

**Standard Gothic Plan and Section**

After Moessel

After F.M. Lund

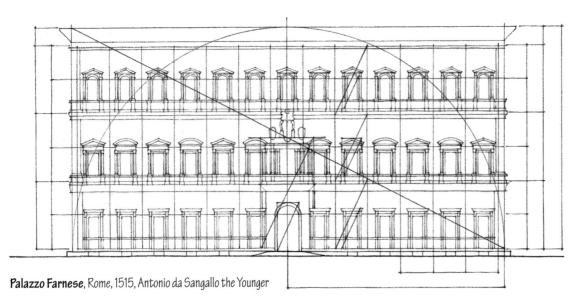

**Palazzo Farnese**, Rome, 1515, Antonio da Sangallo the Younger

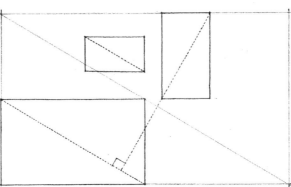

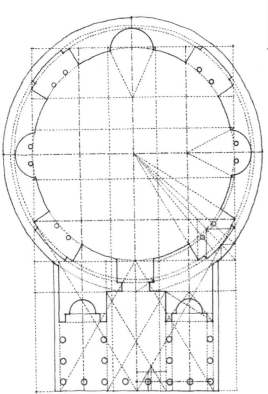

**The Pantheon**, Rome, A.D. 120–124

If the diagonals of two rectangles are either parallel or perpendicular to each other, they indicate that the two rectangles have similar proportions. These diagonals, as well as lines that indicate the common alignment of elements, are called regulating lines. They were seen previously in the discussion of the Golden Section, but they can also be used to control the proportion and placement of elements in other proportioning systems as well. Le Corbusier, in *Towards a New Architecture*, stated the following:

"A regulating line is an assurance against capriciousness; it is a means of verification which can ratify all work created in fervour . . . It confers on the work the quality of rhythm. The regulating line brings in this tangible form of mathematics which gives the reassuring perception of order. The choice of a regulating line fixes the fundamental geometry of the work . . . It is a means to an end; it is not a recipe."

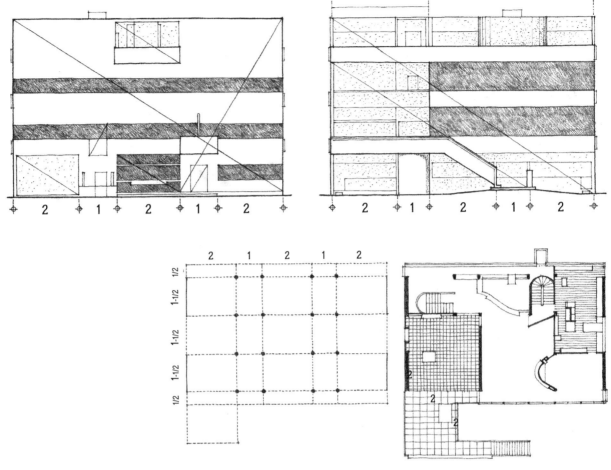

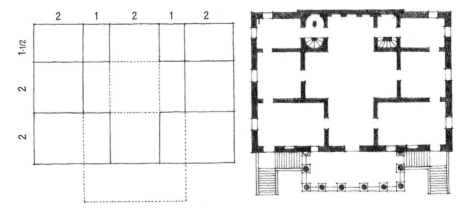

**Villa Garches**, Vaucresson, France, 1926–27, Le Corbusier

In his essay, *The Mathematics of the Ideal Villa*, 1947, Colin Rowe pointed out the similarity between the spatial subdivision of a Palladian villa and the structural grid of a villa by Le Corbusier. While both villas shared a similar proportioning system and a relationship to a higher mathematical order, Palladio's villa consisted of spaces with fixed shapes and harmonic interrelationships. Le Corbusier's villa was composed of horizontal layers of free space defined by the floor and roof slabs. The rooms varied in shape and were asymmetrically arranged at each level.

**Villa Foscari**, Malcontenta, Italy, 1558, Andrea Palladio

**Ionic Order**, from the **Temple on the Ilissus**, Athens, 449 B.C., Callicrates. After a drawing by William R. Ware.

To the Greeks and Romans of classical antiquity, the Orders represented in their proportioning of elements the perfect expression of beauty and harmony. The basic unit of dimension was the diameter of the column. From this module were derived the dimensions of the shaft, the capital, as well as the pedestal below and the entablature above, down to the smallest detail. Intercolumniation — the system of spacing between columns—was also based on the diameter of the column.

Because the sizes of columns varied according to the extent of a building, the Orders were not based on a fixed unit of measurement. Rather, the intention was to ensure that all of the parts of any one building were proportionate and in harmony with one another.

Vitruvius, in the time of Augustus, studied actual examples of the Orders and presented his 'ideal' proportions for each in his treatise, *The Ten Books on Architecture*. Vignola recodified these rules for the Italian Renaissance and his forms for the Orders are probably the best known today.

Tuscan    Doric    Ionic    Corinthian    Composite

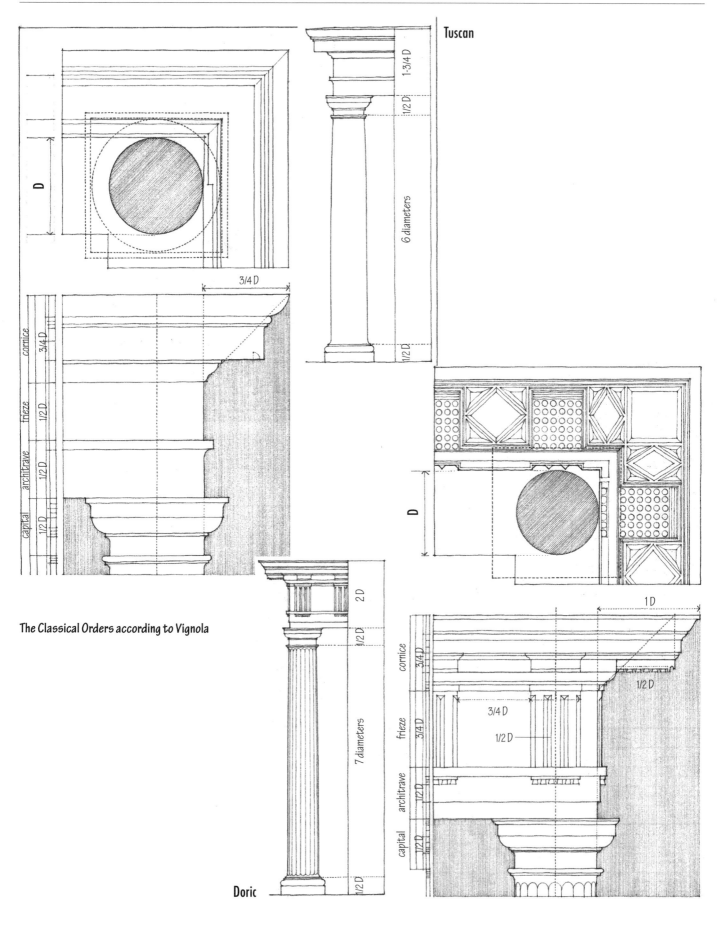

Tuscan

D

3/4 D

1-3/4 D

1/2 D

6 diameters

1/2 D

cornice 3/4 D

frieze 1/2 D

architrave 1/2 D

capital 1/2 D

D

The Classical Orders according to Vignola

2 D

1/2 D

7 diameters

1/2 D

Doric

1 D

cornice 3/4 D

1/2 D

frieze 3/4 D

3/4 D

1/2 D

architrave 1/2 D

capital 1/2 D

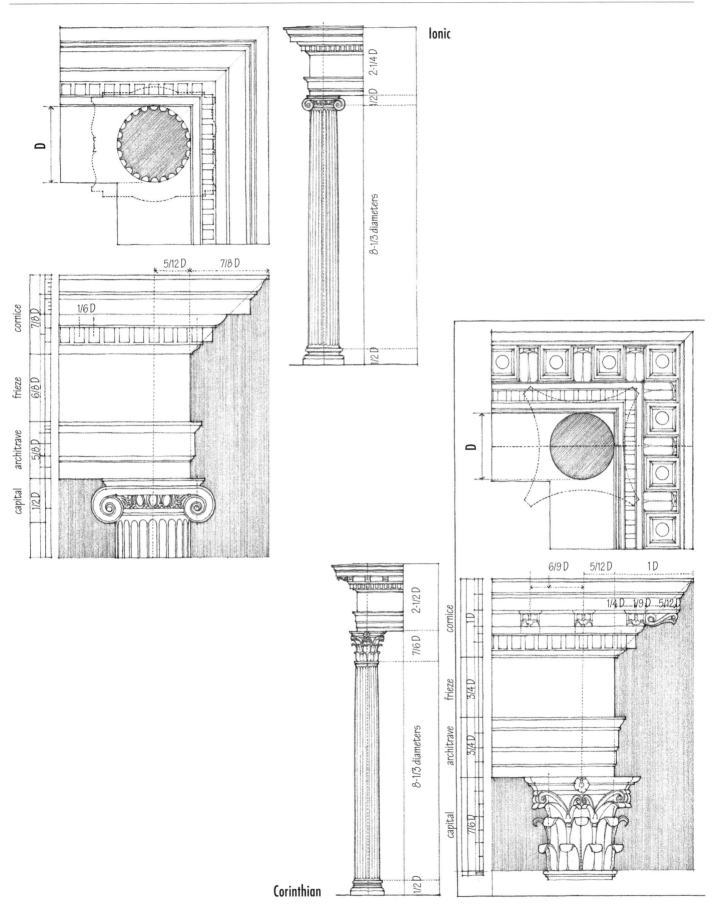

Ionic

2-1/4 D

1/2 D

8-1/3 diameters

1/2 D

5/12 D     7/8 D

1/6 D

cornice  7/8 D

frieze  6/8 D

architrave  5/8 D

capital  1/2 D

6/9 D     5/12 D     1 D

1/4 D   1/9 D   5/12 D

cornice  1 D

frieze  3/4 D

architrave  3/4 D

capital  7/6 D

2-1/2 D

7/6 D

8-1/3 diameters

1/2 D

Corinthian

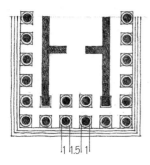

Pycnostyle

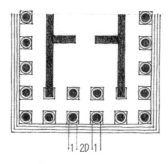

Systyle

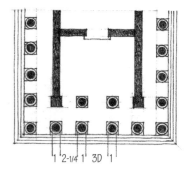

Eustyle

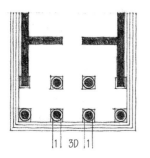

Diastyle

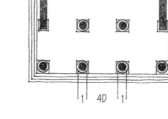

Araeostyle

Classification of Temples according to their **Intercolumniation**

**Vitruvius'** Rules for the Diameter, Height, and Spacing of Columns

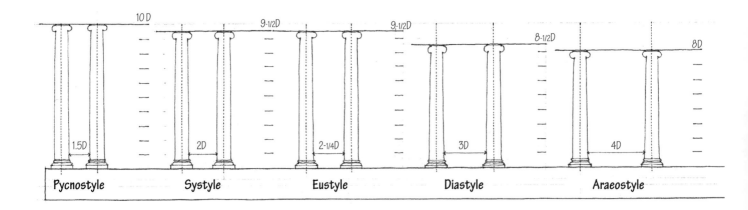

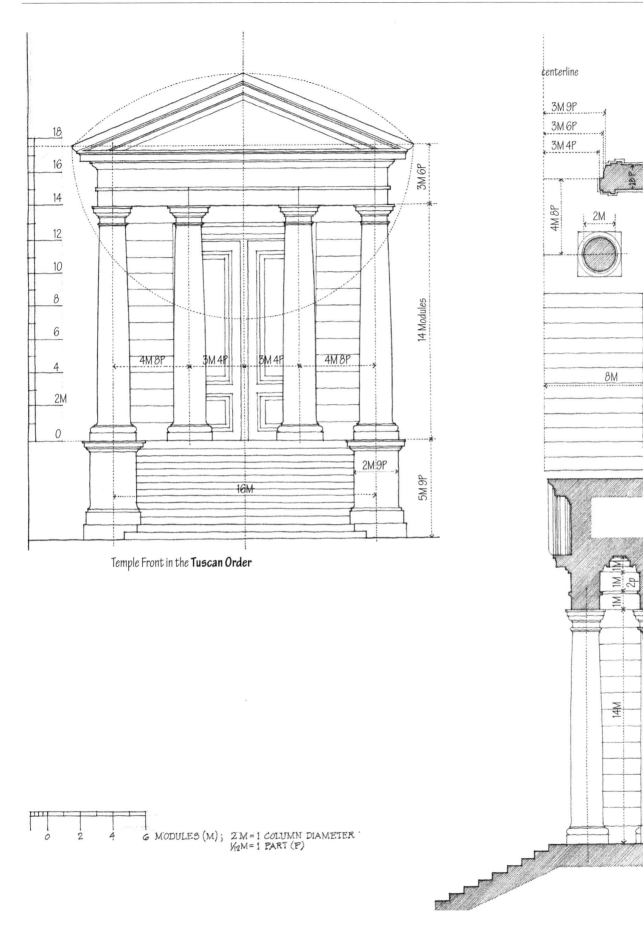

18
16
14
12
10
8
6
4
2M
0

3M 6P

14 Modules

4M 8P    3M 4P    3M 4P    4M 8P

2M 9P

5M 9P

16M

Temple Front in the **Tuscan Order**

0   2   4   6 MODULES (M); 2 M = 1 COLUMN DIAMETER
 1/12 M = 1 PART (P)

centerline

3M 9P
3M 6P
3M 4P

18P

18P

4M 8P

2M

8M

3M 6P

1M 1M
2p
1M 1M

14M

17M 2P

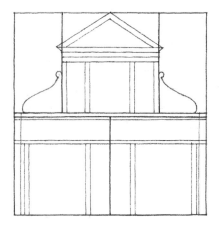
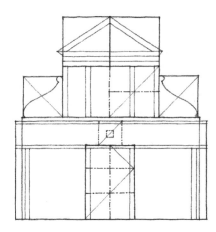

S. Maria Novella, Florence, Italy.
Alberti designed the Renaissance facade (1456–70)
to complete a Gothic church (1278–1350).

Pythagoras discovered that the consonances of the Greek musical system could be expressed by the simple numerical progression—1, 2, 3, 4—and their ratios, 1:2, 1:3, 2:3, 3:4. This relationship led the Greeks to believe they had found the key to the mysterious harmony that pervaded the universe. The Pythagorean creed was "Everything is arranged according to numbers." Plato later developed Pythagoras' aesthetics of numbers into an aesthetics of proportion. He squared and cubed the simple numerical progression to produce the double and triple progressions, 1, 2, 4, 8, and 1, 3, 9, 27. For Plato, these numbers and their ratios not only contained the consonances of the Greek musical scale but also expressed the harmonic structure of his universe.

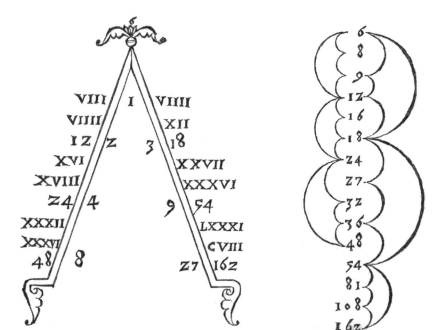

Diagram by Francesco Giorgi, 1525, illustrating the series of interlocking ratios that results from applying Pythagoras' theory of means to the intervals of the Greek musical scale.

The architects of the Renaissance, believing that their buildings had to belong to a higher order, returned to the Greek mathematical system of proportions. Just as the Greeks conceived music to be geometry translated into sound, Renaissance architects believed that architecture was mathematics translated into spatial units. Applying Pythagoras' theory of means to the ratios of the intervals of the Greek musical scale, they developed an unbroken progression of ratios that formed the basis for the proportions of their architecture. These series of ratios manifested themselves not only in the dimensions of a room or a facade, but also in the interlocking proportions of a sequence of spaces or an entire plan.

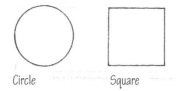

Circle          Square

**7 Ideal Plan Shapes for Rooms.**

Andrea Palladio (1508–80) was probably the most influential architect of the Italian Renaissance. In *The Four Books on Architecture*, first published in Venice in 1570, he followed in the footsteps of his predecessors, Alberti and Serlio, and proposed these seven "most beautiful and proportionable manners of rooms."

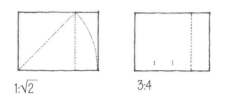

$1:\sqrt{2}$          3:4

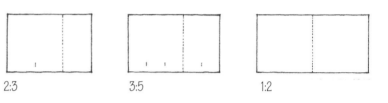

2:3          3:5          1:2

**Determining the Heights of Rooms.**

Palladio also proposed several methods for determining the height of a room so that it would be in proper proportion to the room's width and length. The height of rooms with flat ceilings would be equal to their width. The height of square rooms with vaulted ceilings would be one-third greater than their width. For other rooms, Palladio used Pythagoras' theory of means to determine their heights. Accordingly, there were three types of means: arithmetic, geometric, and harmonic.

Arithmetic:
$$\frac{c-b}{b-a} = \frac{c}{c} \quad (e.g., 1, 2, 3 \ldots \text{ or } 6, 9, 12)$$

Geometric:
$$\frac{c-b}{b-a} = \frac{c}{b} \quad (e.g., 1, 2, 4 \ldots \text{ or } 4, 6, 9)$$

Harmonic:
$$\frac{c-b}{b-a} = \frac{c}{a} \quad (e.g., 2, 3, 6 \ldots \text{ or } 6, 8, 12)$$

In each case, the height of a room is equal to the mean (b) between the two extremes of the width (a) and length (c) of the room.

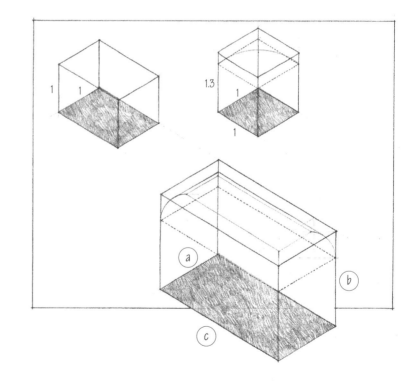

"Beauty will result from the form and correspondence of the whole, with respect to the several parts, of the parts with regard to each other, and of these again to the whole; that the structure may appear an entire and complete body, wherein each member agrees with the other, and all necessary to compose what you intend to form."

Andrea Palladio, *The Four Books on Architecture*, Book I, Chapter 1.

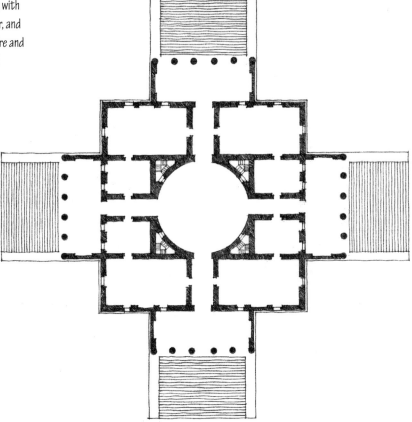

**Villa Capra (The Rotunda)**, Vicenza, Italy, 1552–67, Andrea Palladio
12 x 30, 6 x 15, 30 x 30

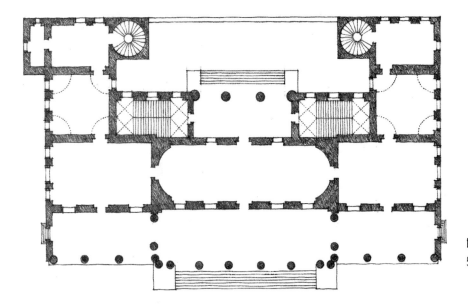

**Palazzo Chiericati**, Vicenza, Italy, 1550, Andrea Palladio
54 x 16 (18), 18 x 30, 18 x 18, 18 x 12

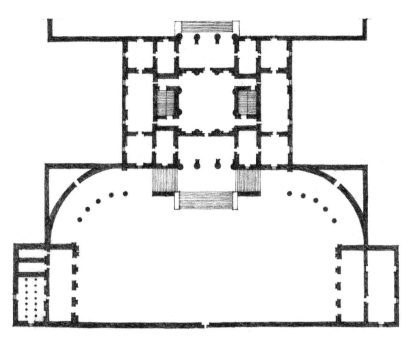

**Villa Thiene**, Cicogna, Italy, 1549, Andrea Palladio
18 x 36, 36 x 36, 36 x 18, 18 x 18, 18 x 12

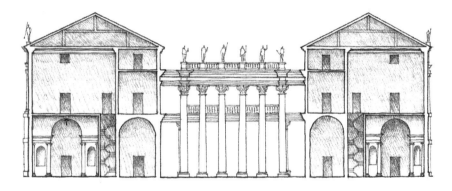

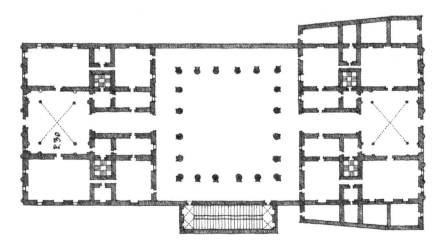

**Palazzo Iseppo Porto**, Vicenza, Italy, 1552, Andrea Palladio
30 x 30, 20 x 30, 10 x 30, 45 x 45

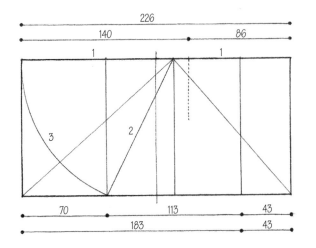

Le Corbusier developed his proportioning system, the Modulor, to order "the dimensions of that which contains and that which is contained." He saw the measuring tools of the Greeks, Egyptians, and other high civilizations as being "infinitely rich and subtle because they formed part of the mathematics of the human body, gracious, elegant, and firm, the source of that harmony which moves us, beauty." He therefore based his measuring tool, the Modulor, on both mathematics (the aesthetic dimensions of the Golden Section and the Fibonacci Series), and the proportions of the human body (functional dimensions).

Le Corbusier began his study in 1942, and published *The Modulor: A Harmonious Measure to the Human Scale Universally Applicable to Architecture and Mechanics* in 1948. A second volume, *Modulor II*, was published in 1954.

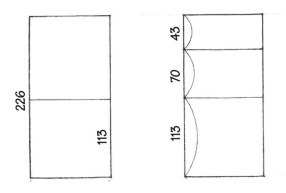

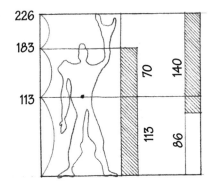

The basic grid consist of three measures, 113, 70, and 43 centimeters, proportioned according to the Golden Section.

$$43 + 70 = 113$$
$$113 + 70 = 183$$
$$113 + 70 + 43 = 226 \ (2 \times 113)$$

113, 183, and 226 define the space occupied by the human figure. From 113 and 226, Le Corbusier developed the Red and Blue series, diminishing scales of dimensions that were related to the stature of the human figure.

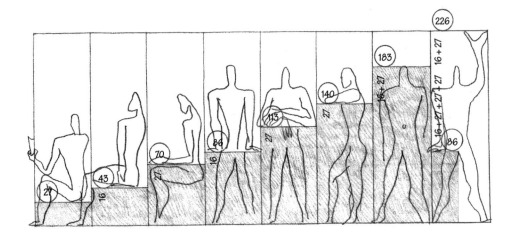

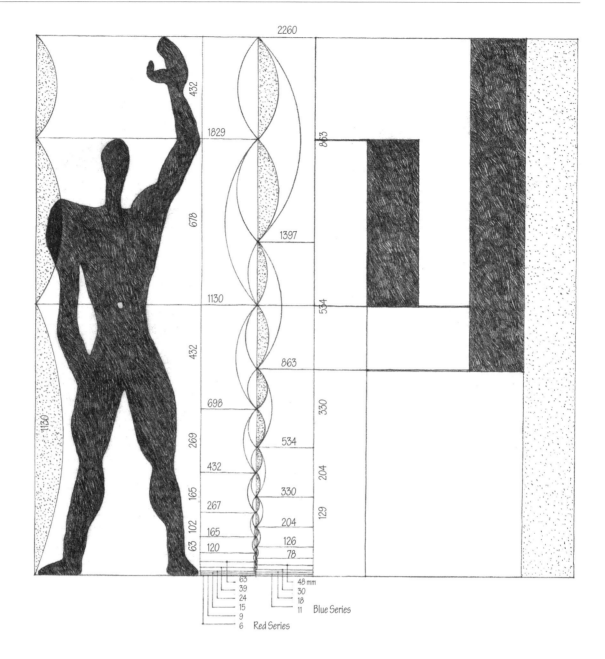

Le Corbusier saw the Modulor not merely as a series of numbers with an inherent harmony, but as a system of measurements that could govern lengths, surfaces, and volumes, and "maintain the human scale everywhere." It could "lend itself to an infinity of combinations; it ensures unity with diversity . . . the miracle of numbers."

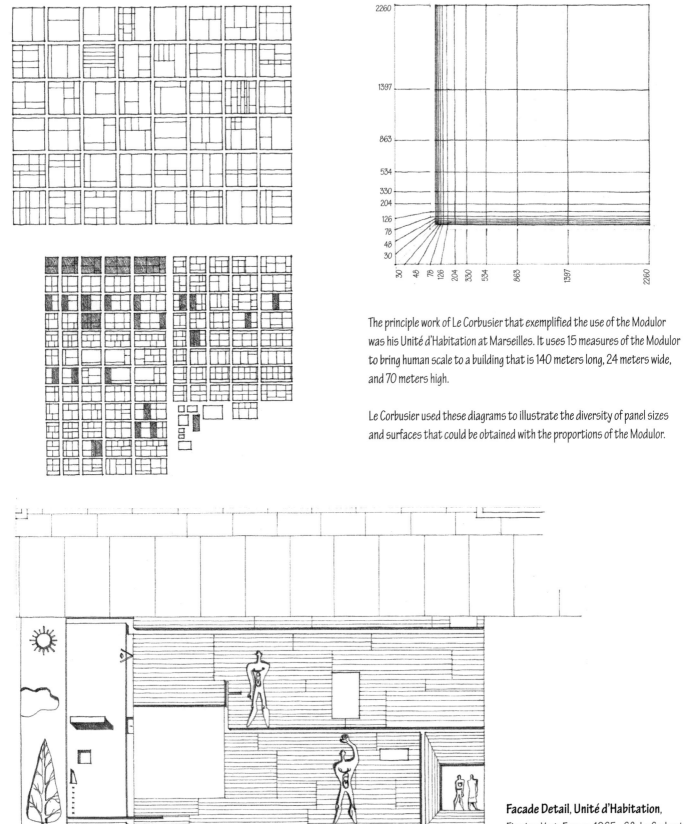

The principle work of Le Corbusier that exemplified the use of the Modulor was his Unité d'Habitation at Marseilles. It uses 15 measures of the Modulor to bring human scale to a building that is 140 meters long, 24 meters wide, and 70 meters high.

Le Corbusier used these diagrams to illustrate the diversity of panel sizes and surfaces that could be obtained with the proportions of the Modulor.

**Facade Detail**, **Unité d'Habitation**, Firminy-Vert, France, 1965–68, Le Corbusier

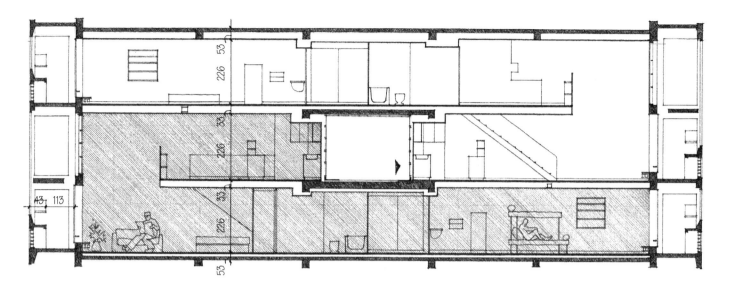

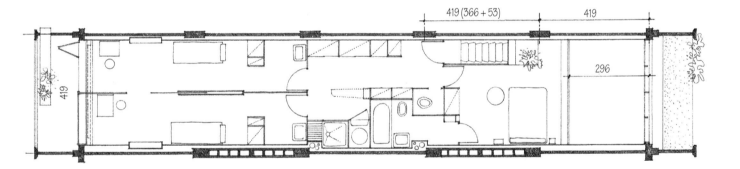

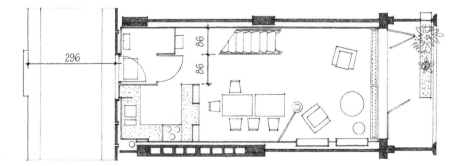

Plans and Section of Typical Apartment Unit,
Unité d'Habitation, Marseilles, 1946–52, Le Corbusier

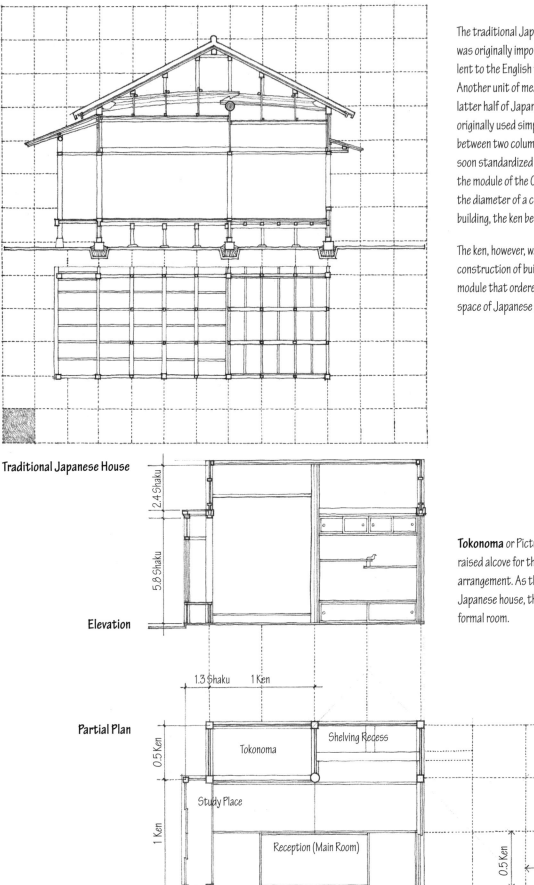

The traditional Japanese unit of measure, the shaku, was originally imported from China. It is almost equivalent to the English foot and divisible into decimal units. Another unit of measure, the ken, was introduced in the latter half of Japan's Middle Ages. Although it was originally used simply to designate the interval between two columns and varied in size, the ken was soon standardized for residential architecture. Unlike the module of the Classical Orders, which was based on the diameter of a column and varied with the size of a building, the ken became an absolute measurement.

The ken, however, was not only a measurement for the construction of buildings. It evolved into an aesthetic module that ordered the structure, materials, and space of Japanese architecture.

Traditional Japanese House

2.4 Shaku

5.8 Shaku

Elevation

**Tokonoma** or Picture Recess, a shallow, slightly raised alcove for the display of a kakemono or flower arrangement. As the spiritual center of a traditional Japanese house, the tokonoma is located in its most formal room.

1.3 Shaku        1 Ken

Partial Plan

0.5 Ken

1 Ken

Tokonoma

Shelving Recess

Study Place

Reception (Main Room)

0.5 Ken

0.5 Ken

Two methods of designing with the ken modular grid developed that affected its dimension. In the Inaka-ma method, the ken grid of 6 shaku determined the center-to-center spacing of columns. Therefore, the standard tatami floor mat (3 x 6 shaku or $\frac{1}{2}$ x 1 ken) varied slightly to allow for the thickness of the columns.

In the Kyo-ma method, the floor mat remained constant (3.15 x 6.30 shaku) and the column spacing (ken module) varied according to the size of the room and ranged from 6.4 to 6.7 shaku.

The size of a room is designated by the number of its floor mats. The traditional floor mat was originally proportioned to accommodate two persons sitting or one person sleeping. As the ordering system of the ken grid developed, however, the floor mat lost its dependence on human dimensions and was subjected to the demands of the structural system and its column spacing.

Because of their 1:2 modularity, the floor mats can be arranged in a number of ways for any given room size. And for each room size, a different ceiling height is established according to the following:
height of the ceiling (shaku), measured from the top of the frieze board = number of mats x 0.3.

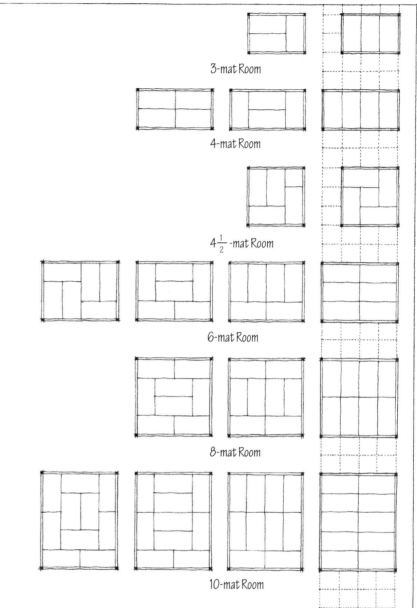

3-mat Room

4-mat Room

$4\frac{1}{2}$ -mat Room

6-mat Room

8-mat Room

10-mat Room

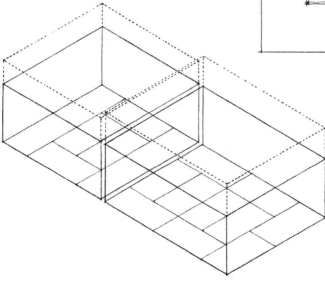

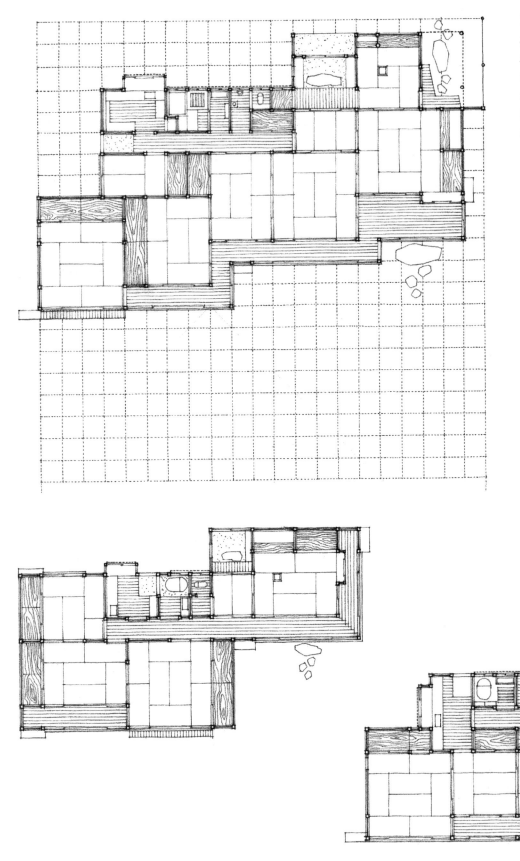

In a typical Japanese residence, the ken grid orders the structure as well as the additive, space-to-space sequence of rooms. The relatively small size of the module allows the rectangular spaces to be freely arranged in linear, staggered, or clustered patterns.

Elevations of a Traditional Japanese Residence

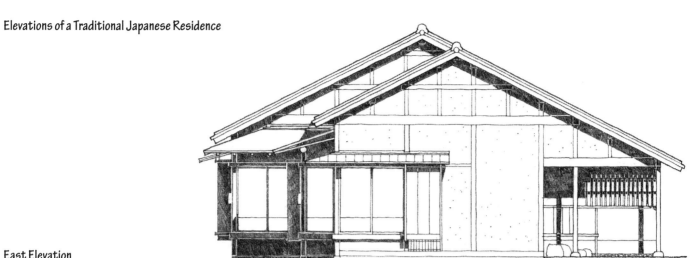

East Elevation

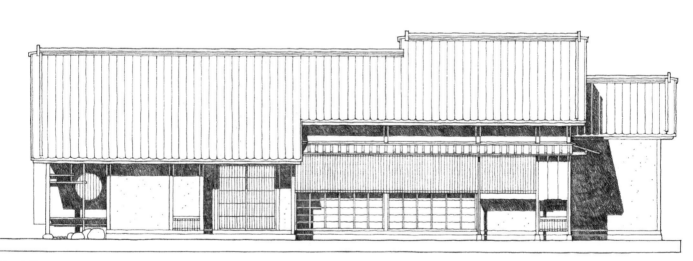

North Elevation

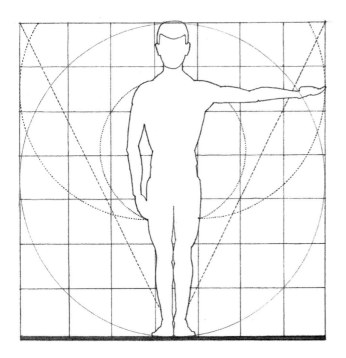

Anthropometry refers to the measurement of the size and proportions of the human body. While the architects of the Renaissance saw the proportions of the human figure as a reaffirmation that certain mathematical ratios reflected the harmony of their universe, anthropometric proportioning methods seek not abstract or symbolic ratios, but functional ones. They are predicated on the theory that forms and spaces in architecture are either containers or extensions of the human body and should therefore be determined by its dimensions.

The difficulty with anthropometric proportioning is the nature of the data required for its use. For example, the dimensions given here in millimeters are average measurements and are merely guidelines which should be modified to satisfy specific user needs. Average dimensions must always be treated with caution since variations from the norm will always exist due to the difference between men and women, among various age and racial groups, even from one individual to the next.

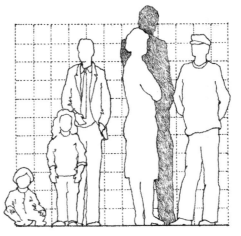

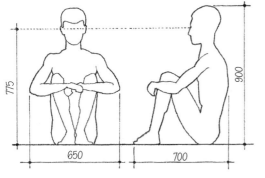

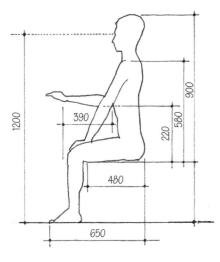

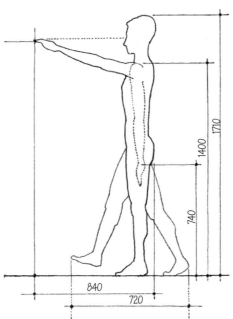

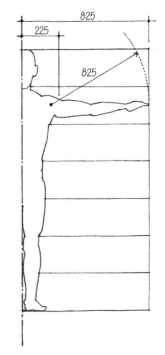

The dimensions and proportions of the human body affect the proportion of things we handle, the height and distance of things we try to reach, and the dimensions of the furnishings we use for sitting, working, eating, and sleeping. There is a difference between our structural dimensions and those dimensional requirements which result from how we reach for some-thing on a shelf, sit down at a table, walk down a set of stairs, or interact with other people. These are functional dimensions and will vary according to the nature of the activity engaged in and the social situation.

A special field that has developed from a concern with human factors is ergonomics—the applied science that coordinates the design of devices, systems, and environments with our physiological and psychological capacities and requirements.

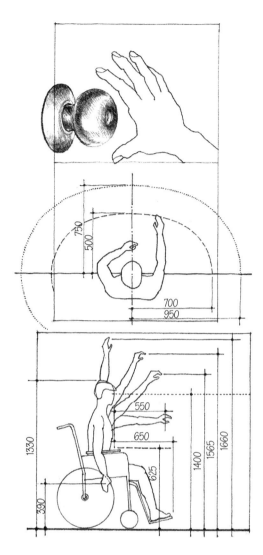

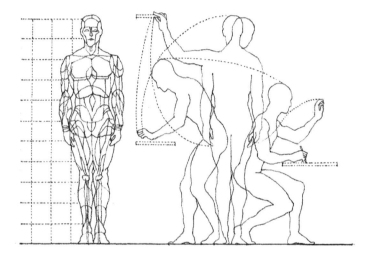

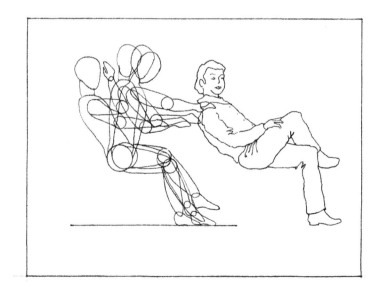

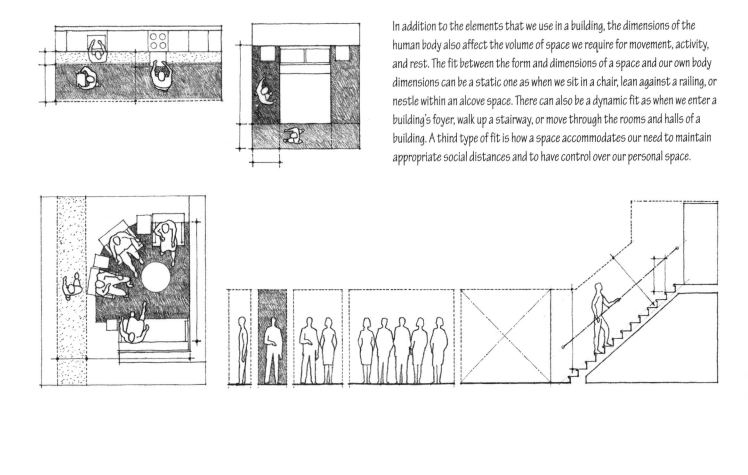

In addition to the elements that we use in a building, the dimensions of the human body also affect the volume of space we require for movement, activity, and rest. The fit between the form and dimensions of a space and our own body dimensions can be a static one as when we sit in a chair, lean against a railing, or nestle within an alcove space. There can also be a dynamic fit as when we enter a building's foyer, walk up a stairway, or move through the rooms and halls of a building. A third type of fit is how a space accommodates our need to maintain appropriate social distances and to have control over our personal space.

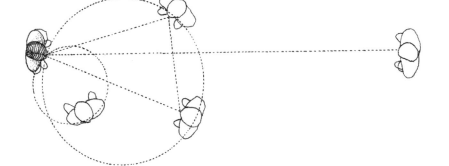

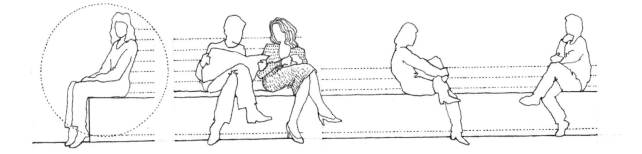

While proportion pertains to an ordered set of mathematical relationships among the dimensions of a form or space, scale refers to how we perceive or judge the size of something in relation to something else. In dealing with the issue of scale, therefore, we are always comparing one thing to another.

The entity an object or space is being compared to may be an accepted unit or standard of measurement. For example, we can say that a table is, according to the U.S. Customary System, 3 feet wide, 6 feet long, and 29 inches high. Using the International Metric System, the same table would measure 914 mm wide, 1829 mm long, and 737 mm high. The physical dimensions of the table have not changed, just the system used to calculate its size.

In drawing, we use a scale to specify the ratio that determines the relationship between an illustration to that which it represents. For example, the scale of an architectural drawing notes the size of a depicted building in comparison to the real thing.

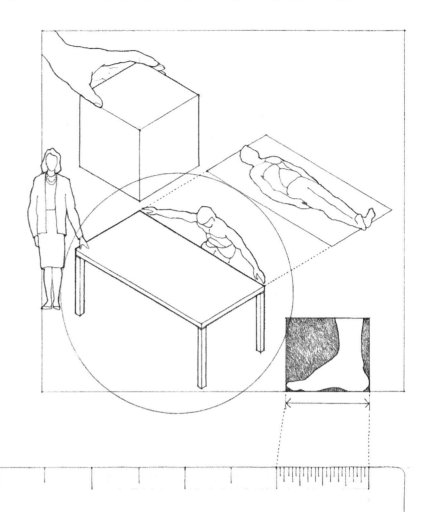

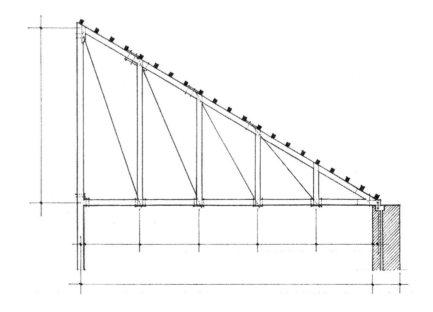

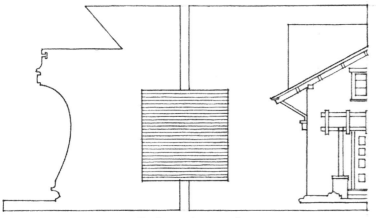

How large is this square?

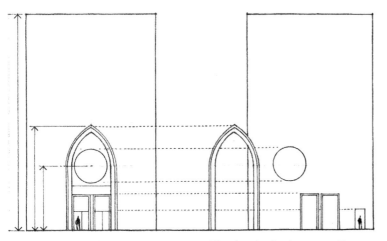

**Mechanical scale:** the size or proportion of something relative to an accepted standard of measurement.

**Visual scale:** the size or proportion an element appears to have relative to other elements of known or assumed size.

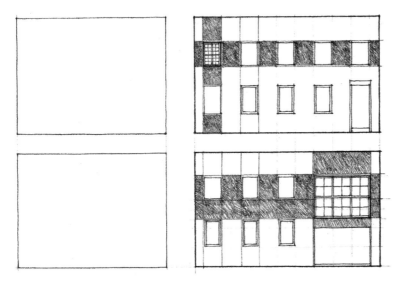

Of particular interest to designers is the notion of visual scale, which refers not to the actual dimensions of things, but rather to how small or large something appears to be in relation to its normal size or to the size of other things in its context.

When we say something is small-scale or miniature, we usually mean that thing appears to be smaller than its usual size. Likewise, something that is large-scale is perceived as being larger than what is normal or expected.

We speak of urban scale when we refer to the size of a project in the context of a city, or neighborhood scale when we judge a building appropriate to its locale within a city, or street scale when we note the relative sizes of elements fronting a roadway.

At the scale of a building, all elements, no matter how plain or unimportant they may be, have a certain size. Its dimensions may be predetermined by the manufacturer, or they may be selected by the designer from a range of choices. Nevertheless, we perceive the size of each element in relation to other parts or to the whole of a composition.

For example, the size and proportion of windows in a building facade are visually related to one another as well as to the spaces between them and the overall dimensions of the facade. If the windows are all of the same size and shape, they establish a scale relative to the size of the facade.

If, however, one of the windows is larger than the others, it would create another scale within the composition of the facade. The jump in scale could indicate the size or significance of the space behind the window, or it could alter our perception of the size of the other windows or the overall dimensions of the facade.

Many building elements have sizes and characteristics that are familiar to us and which we use to gauge the sizes of other elements around them. Such elements as residential window units and doorways help give us an idea of how large a building is and how many stories it has. Stairs and certain modular materials, such as brick and concrete block, help us measure the scale of a space. Because of their familiarity, these elements, if oversized, can also be used to deliberately alter our perception of the size of a building form or space.

Some buildings and spaces have two or more scales operating simultaneously. The entrance portico of the library at the University of Virginia, modeled after the Pantheon in Rome, is scaled to the overall building form while the doorway and windows behind it are scaled to the size of the spaces within the building.

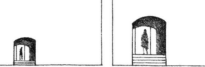

**University of Virginia,** Charlottesville, 1817–26, Thomas Jefferson

The recessed entry portals of Reims Cathedral are scaled to the dimensions of the facade and can be seen and recognized at a distance as the entrances to the interior space of the church. As we get closer, however, we see that the actual entrances are really simple doors within the larger portals and are scaled to our dimensions, to a human scale.

**Reims Cathedral,** 1211–1290

Human scale in architecture is based on the dimensions and proportions of the human body. It has already been mentioned in the section on anthropometric proportioning that our dimensions vary from individual to individual and should not be used as an absolute measuring device. We can, however, gauge a space whose width is such that we can reach out and touch its walls. Similarly, we can judge its height if we can reach up and touch the ceiling plane overhead. Once we can no longer do these things, we must rely on visual rather than tactile clues to give us a sense of the scale of a space.

For these clues, we can use elements that have human meaning and whose dimensions are related to the dimensions of our posture, pace, reach, or grasp. Such elements as a table or chair, the risers and treads of a stairway, the sill of a window, and the lintel over a doorway, not only help us judge the size of a space but also give it a human scale.

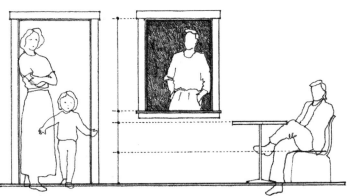

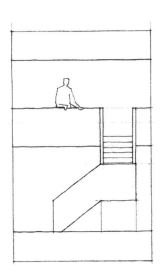

While something that is monumental in scale makes us feel small in comparison, a space that is intimate in scale describes an environment in which we feel comfortable, in control, or important. Intimate settings of tables and lounge chairs in a large hotel lobby tell us something about the expansiveness of the space as well as define comfortable, human-scale areas within it. A stairway leading up to a second-story balcony or loft can give us an idea of the vertical dimension of a room as well as suggest a human presence. A window in a blank wall conveys something about the space behind it and also leaves the impression that it is inhabited.

Of a room's three dimensions, its height has a greater effect on its scale than either its width or length. While the walls of the room provide enclosure, the height of the ceiling plane overhead determines its qualities of shelter and intimacy.

Raising the ceiling height of a 12 X 16-foot room from 8 to 9 feet will be be more noticeable and affect its scale more than if its width were increased to 13 feet or its length to 17 feet. While the 12 X 16-foot room with a 9-foot ceiling might feel comfortable to most people, a 50 X 50 foot space with the same ceiling height would begin to feel oppressive.

In addition to the vertical dimension of a space, other factors that affect its scale are:
• the shape, color, and pattern of its bounding surfaces
• the shape and disposition of its openings
• the nature and scale of the elements placed within it

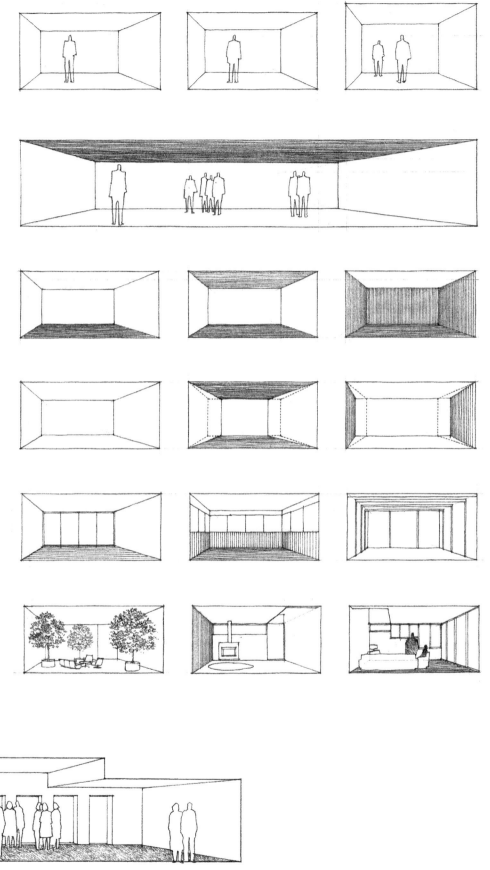

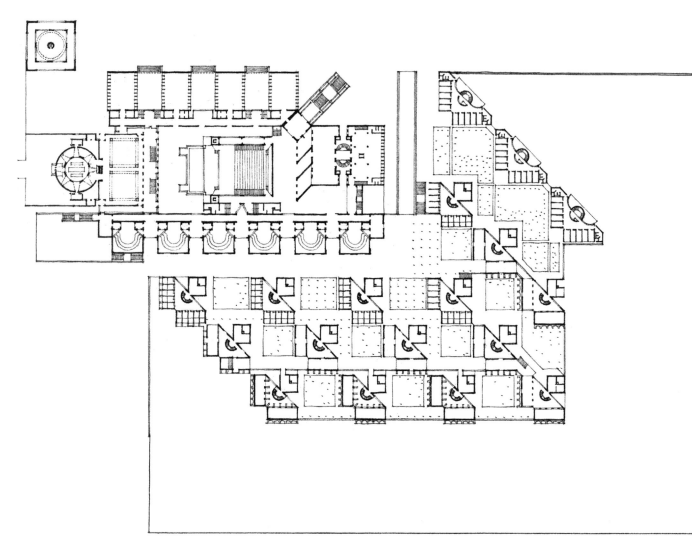

**Indian Institute of Management**, Ahmedabad, India, 1965, Louis Kahn

# 7
# Principles

"...Nothing but confusion can result when order is considered a quality that can equally well be accepted or abandoned, something that can be forgone and replaced by something else. Order must be understood as indispensable to the functioning of any organized system, whether its function be physical or mental. Just as neither an engine nor an orchestra nor a sports team can perform without the integrated cooperation of all its parts, so a work of art or architecture cannot fulfill its function and transmit its message unless it presents an ordered pattern. Order is possible at any level of complexity: in statues as simple as those on Easter Island or as intricate as those by Bernini, in a farmhouse and in a Borromini church. But if there is not order, there is no way of telling what the work is trying to say."

Rudolf Arnheim
*The Dynamics of Architectural Form*
1977

While Chapter 4 employed a geometric basis for organizing the forms and spaces of a building, this chapter discusses additional principles that can be utilized to create order in an architectural composition. Order refers not simply to geometric regularity, but rather to a condition in which each part of a whole is properly disposed with reference to other parts and to its purpose so as to produce a harmonious arrangement.

There exists a natural diversity and complexity in the program requirements for buildings. The forms and spaces of any building should acknowledge the hierarchy inherent in the functions they accommodate, the users they serve, the purposes or meaning they convey, and the scope or context they address. It is in recognition of this natural diversity, complexity, and hierarchy in the programming, designing, and making of buildings that ordering principles are discussed.

Order without diversity can result in monotony or boredom; diversity without order can produce chaos. A sense of unity with variety is the ideal. The following ordering principles are seen as visual devices that allow the varied and diverse forms and spaces of a building to coexist perceptually and conceptually within an ordered, unified, and harmonious whole.

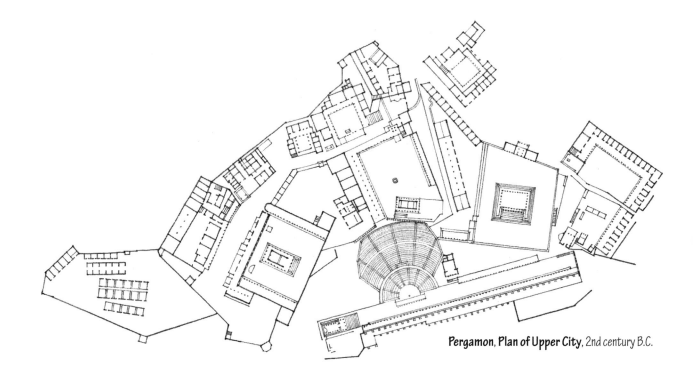

**Pergamon**, **Plan of Upper City**, 2nd century B.C.

**Axis**

A line established by two points in space, about which forms and spaces can be arranged in a symmetrical or balanced manner.

**Symmetry**

The balanced distribution and arrangement of equivalent forms and spaces on opposite sides of a dividing line or plane, or about a center or axis.

**Hierarchy**

The articulation of the importance or significance of a form or space by its size, shape, or placement relative to the other forms and spaces of the organization.

**Rhythm**

A unifying movement characterized by a patterned repetition or alternation of formal elements or motifs in the same or a modified form.

**Datum**

A line, plane, or volume that, by its continuity and regularity, serves to gather, measure, and organize a pattern of forms and spaces.

**Transformation**

The principle that an architectural concept, structure, or organization can be altered through a series of discrete manipulations and permutations in response to a specific context or set of conditions without a loss of identity or concept.

This Florentine street flanked by the **Uffizi Palace** links the River Arno to the Piazza della Signoria.

The axis is perhaps the most elementary means of organizing forms and spaces in architecture. It is a line established by two points in space, about which forms and spaces can be arranged in a regular or irregular manner. Although imaginary and not visible except to the mind's eye, an axis can be a powerful, dominating, regulating device. Although it implies symmetry, it demands balance. The specific disposition of elements about an axis will determine whether the visual force of an axial organization is subtle or overpowering, loosely structured or formal, picturesque or monotonous.

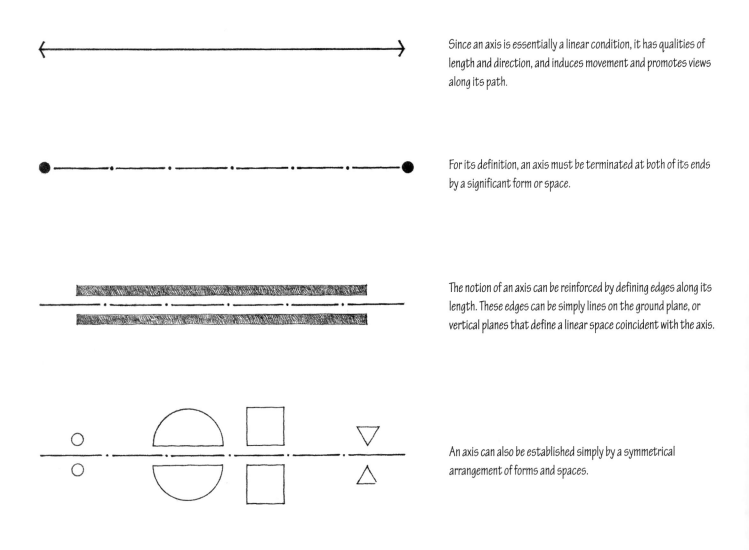

Since an axis is essentially a linear condition, it has qualities of length and direction, and induces movement and promotes views along its path.

For its definition, an axis must be terminated at both of its ends by a significant form or space.

The notion of an axis can be reinforced by defining edges along its length. These edges can be simply lines on the ground plane, or vertical planes that define a linear space coincident with the axis.

An axis can also be established simply by a symmetrical arrangement of forms and spaces.

The terminating elements of an axis serve to both send and receive its visual thrust. These culminating elements can be any of the following:

- points in space established by vertical, linear elements or centralized building forms

- vertical planes, such as symmetrical building facades or fronts, preceded by a forecourt or similar open space

- well-defined spaces, generally centralized or regular in form

- gateways that open outward toward a view or vista beyond

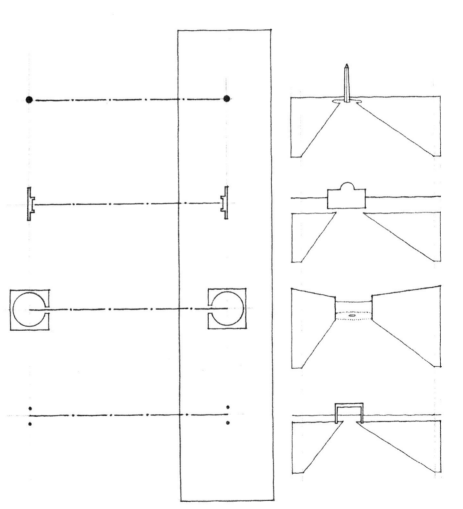

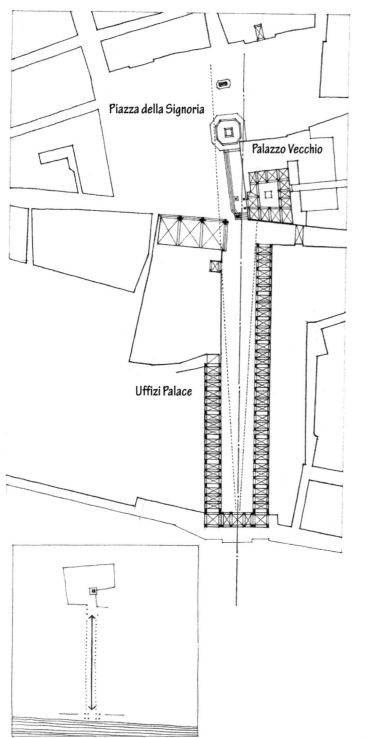

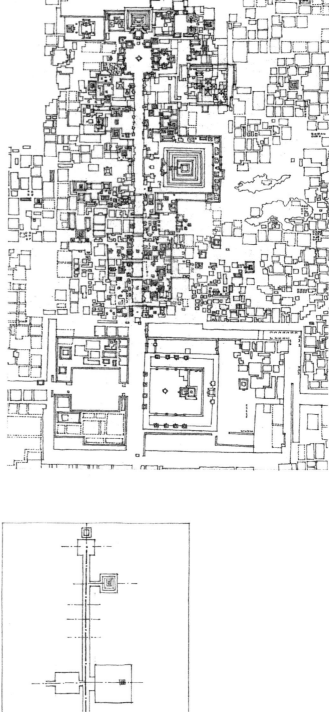

The wings of the **Uffizi Palace** in Florence, Italy, (1560, Giorgio Vasari) frame an axial space which leads from the River Arno, through the Uffizi arch, to the Piazza della Signoria and the **Palazzo Vecchio** (1298–1314, Arnolfo di Cambio).

**Teotihuacan, City of the Gods.** Located near Mexico city, Teotihuacan was the largest and most influential ritual center of Mesoamerica, founded c. 100 B.C. and flourishing until about A.D. 750. The site was dominated by two massive temple-pyramids, the Pyramid of the Sun and the smaller Pyramid of the Moon, from which the Avenue of the Dead runs south to the citadel and market compound in the center of the city.

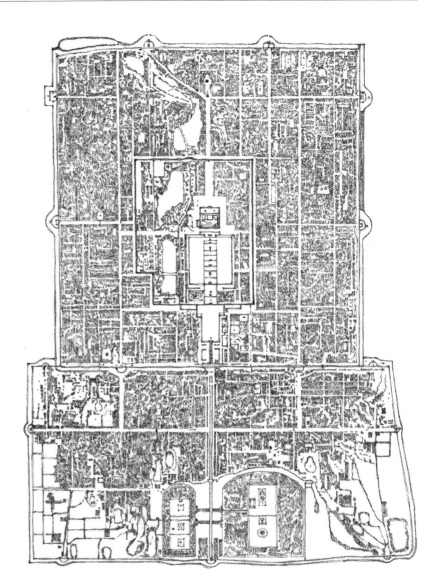

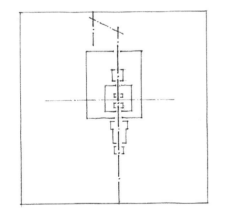

**Plan of Peking (Beijing), China.** Located on its north-south axis is the Forbidden City, a walled section within the inner city, built in the 15th century and containing the Imperial Palace and other buildings of the imperial government of China. It was so named because it was formerly closed to the public.

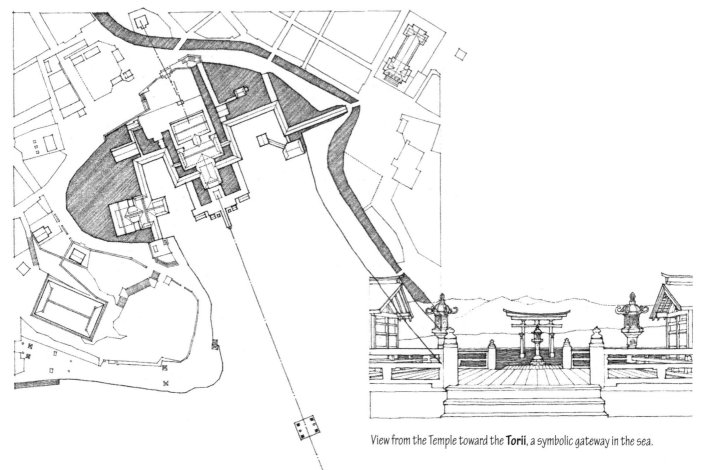

View from the Temple toward the **Torii**, a symbolic gateway in the sea.

**Itsukushima Temple**, Hiroshima Prefecture, Japan, 13th century

**Torii** is a monumental, freestanding gateway on the approach to a Shinto shrine, consisting of two pillars connected at the top by a horizontal crosspiece and a lintel above it, usually curving upward.

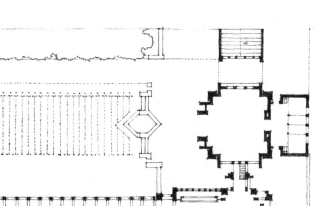

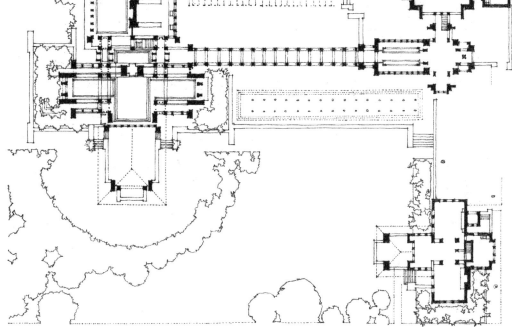

**Darwin D. Martin House and Estate**, Buffalo, New York, 1904, Frank Lloyd Wright

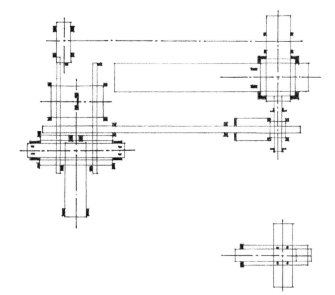

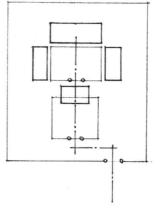

**Chinese Courtyard House**, Peking (Beijing), China

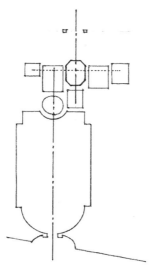

**Hôtel de Matignon**, Paris, 1721, J. Courtonne

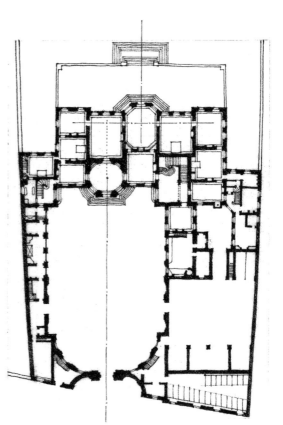

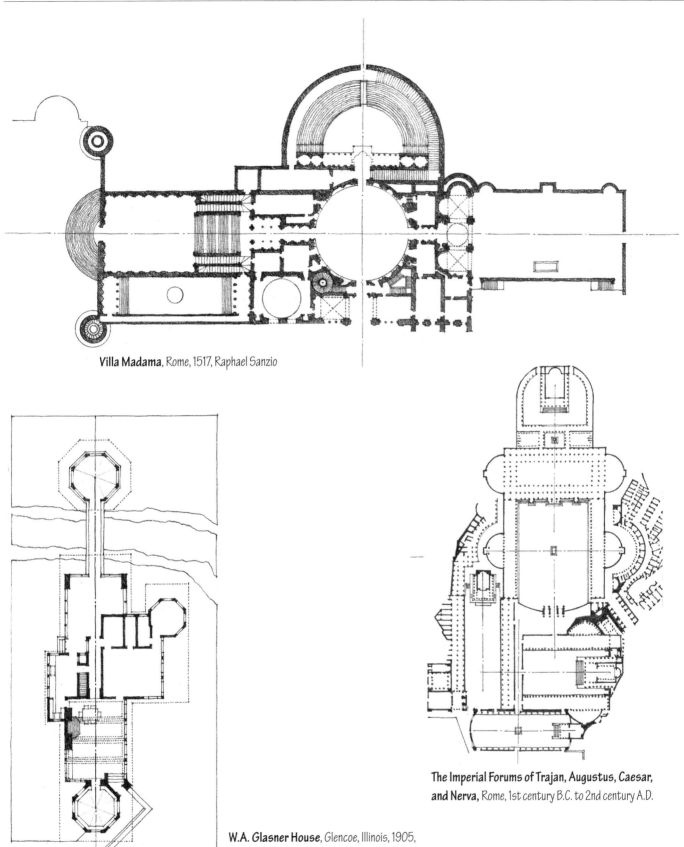

**Villa Madama**, Rome, 1517, Raphael Sanzio

**W.A. Glasner House**, Glencoe, Illinois, 1905,
Frank Lloyd Wright

**The Imperial Forums of Trajan, Augustus, Caesar,
and Nerva,** Rome, 1st century B.C. to 2nd century A.D.

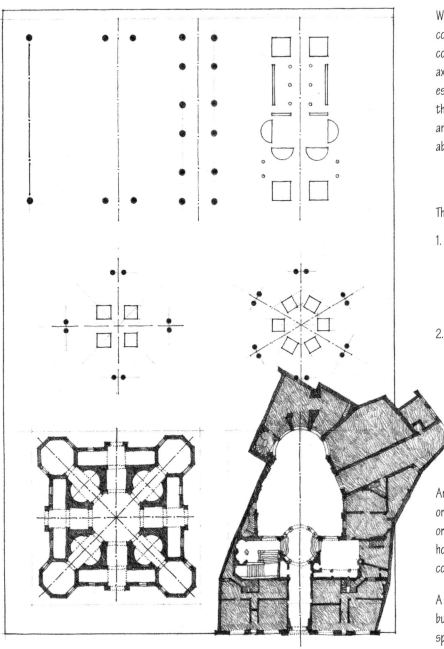

While an axial condition can exist without a symmetrical condition being simultaneously present, a symmetrical condition cannot exist without implying the existence of an axis or center about which it is structured. An axis is established by two points; a symmetrical condition requires the balanced arrangement of equivalent patterns of form and space on opposite sides of a dividing line or plane, or about a center or axis.

There are two fundamental types of symmetry:

1. Bilateral symmetry refers to the balanced arrangement of similar or equivalent elements on opposite sides of a median axis so that only one plane can divide the whole into essentially identical halves.

2. Radial symmetry refers to the balanced arrangement of similar, radiating elements such that the composition can be divided into similar halves by passing a plane at any angle around a centerpoint or along a central axis.

**Plan of an Ideal Church**, 1460, Antonio Filarete

**Hôtel de Beauvais**, Paris, 1656, Antoine Le Pautre

An architectural composition can utilize symmetry to organize its forms and spaces in two ways. An entire building organization can be made symmetrical. At some point, however, any totally symmetrical arrangement must confront and resolve the asymmetry of its site or context.

A symmetrical condition can occur in only a portion of the building and organize an irregular pattern of forms and spaces about itself. The latter case of local symmetry allows a building to respond to exceptional conditions of its site or program. The symmetrical condition itself can be reserved for significant or important spaces within the organization.

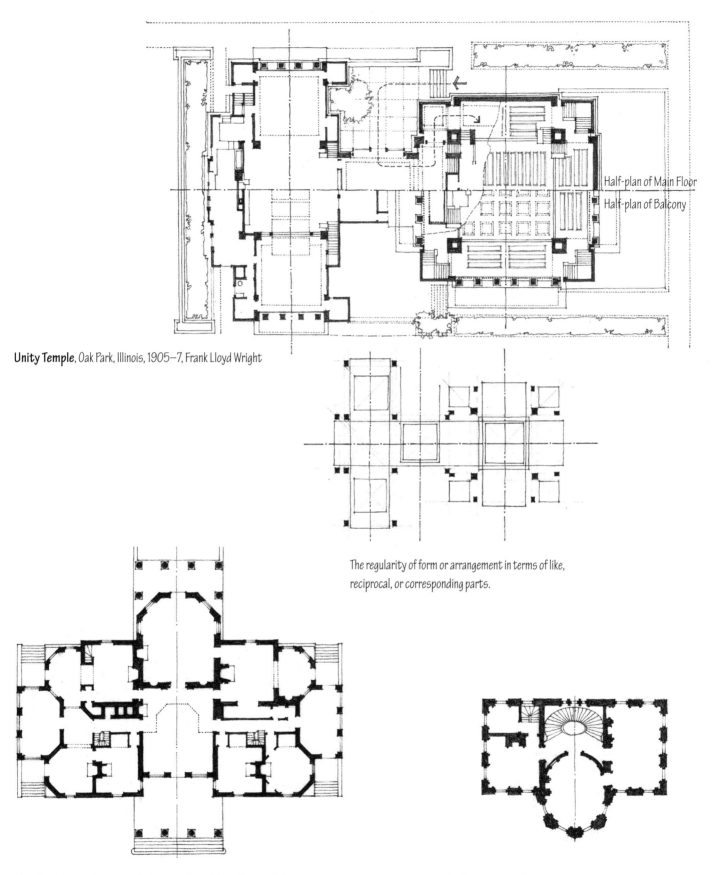

**Unity Temple**, Oak Park, Illinois, 1905–7, Frank Lloyd Wright

Half-plan of Main Floor

Half-plan of Balcony

The regularity of form or arrangement in terms of like, reciprocal, or corresponding parts.

**Monticello**, near Charlottesville, Virginia, 1770-1808, Thomas Jefferson

**Nathaniel Russell House**, Charleston, South Carolina, 1809

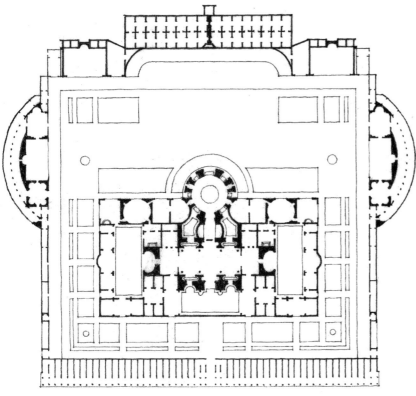

Baths (Thermae) of Caracalla, Rome, A.D. 211-17

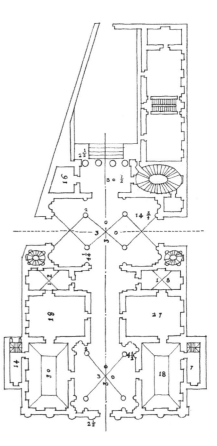

Palazzo No. 52, Andrea Palladio

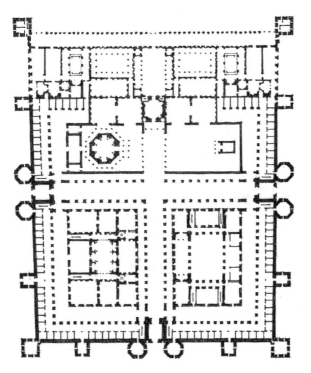

Palace of Diocletian, Spalato, Yugoslavia, c. A.D. 300

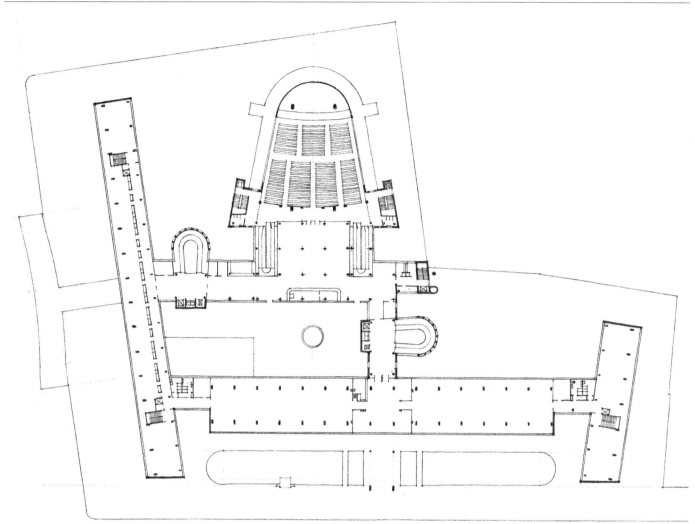

**Third Floor Plan**, **Centrosoyus Building**, Kirova Ulitsa, Moscow, 1929–33, Le Corbusier

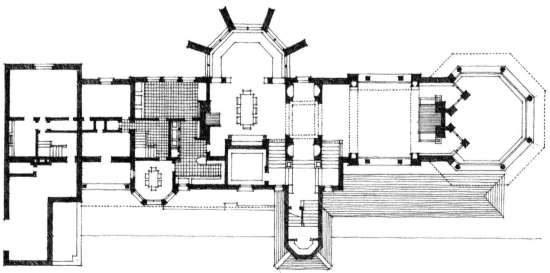

**Husser House**, Chicago, Illinois, 1899, Frank Lloyd Wright

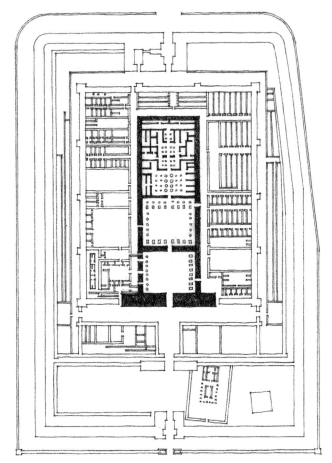

**Mortuary Temple of Rameses III**, Medinet-Habu, 1198 B.C.

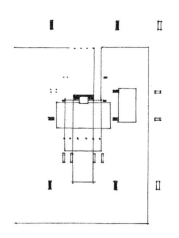

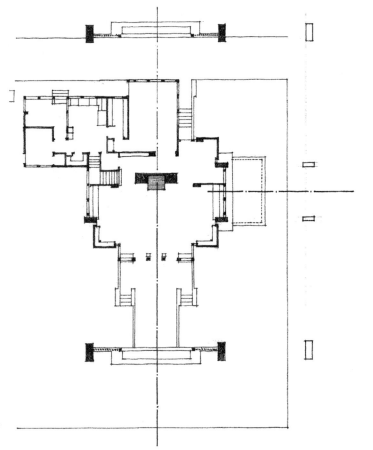

**Robert W. Evans House**, Chicago, Illinois, 1908, Frank Lloyd Wright

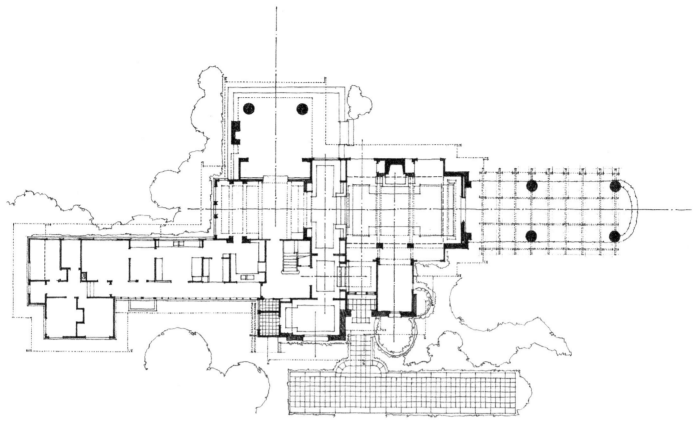

**A.E. Bingham House**, Near Santa Barbara, California, 1916, Bernard Maybeck

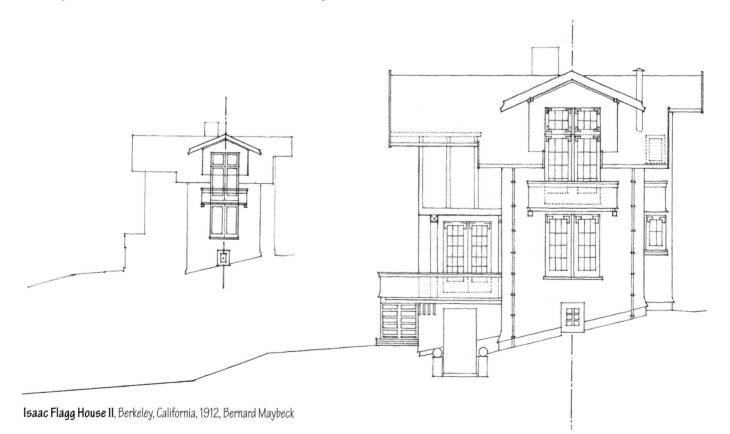

**Isaac Flagg House II**, Berkeley, California, 1912, Bernard Maybeck

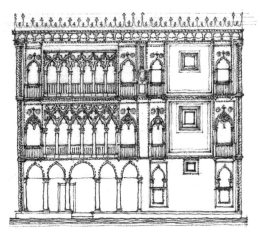

**Frank Lloyd Wright Studio,** Oak Park, Illinois, 1889

**Ca d'Oro**, Venice, 1424–36, Giovanni and Bartolomeo Buon

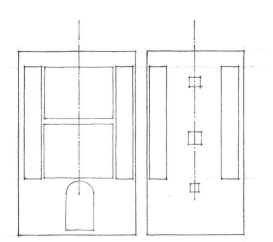

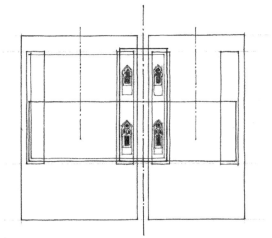

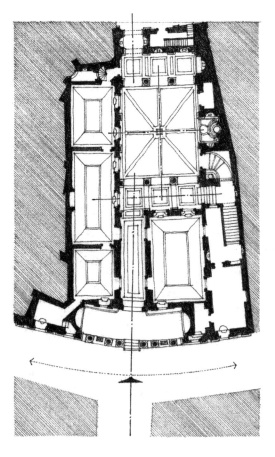

**Palazzo Pietro Massimi**, Rome, 1532–36, Baldassare Peruzzi.
A symmetrical facade leading into an asymmetrical interior.

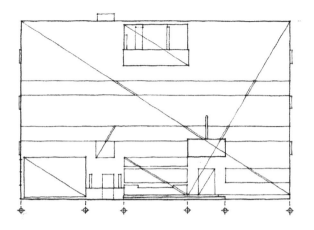

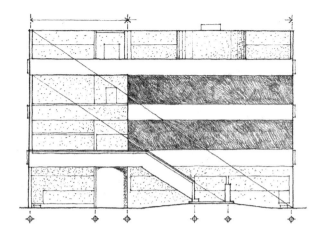

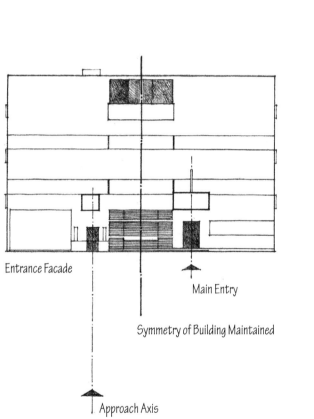

Entrance Facade

Main Entry

Symmetry of Building Maintained

Approach Axis

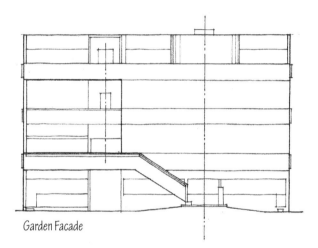

Garden Facade

**Villa Garches**, Vaucresson, France, 1926–27, Le Corbusier

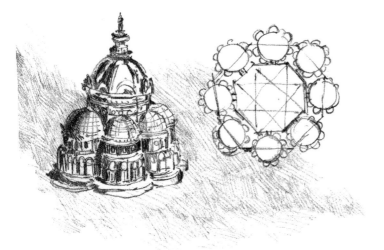

After a sketch of an ideal church by Leonardo da Vinci

The principle of hierarchy implies that in most if not all architectural compositions, real differences exist among their forms and spaces. These differences reflect the degree of importance of these forms and spaces, as well as the functional, formal, and symbolic roles they play in the organization. The value system by which relative importance is measured will of course depend on the specific situation, the needs and desires of the users, and the decisions of the designer. The values expressed may be individual or collective, personal or cultural. In any case, the manner in which the functional or symbolic differences among a building's elements are revealed is critical to the establishment of a visible, hierarchical order among its forms and spaces.

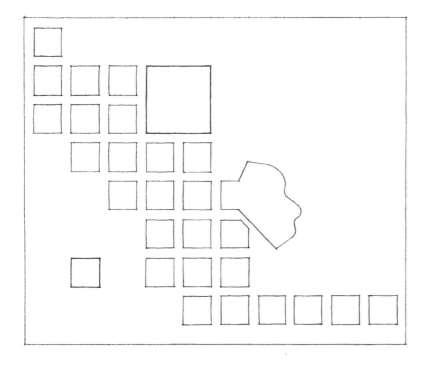

For a form or space to be articulated as being important or significant to an organization, it must be made uniquely visible. This visual emphasis can be achieved by endowing a form or shape with:

· exceptional size
· a unique shape
· a strategic location

In each case, the hierarchically important form or space is given meaning and significance by being an exception to the norm, an anomaly within an otherwise regular pattern.

In an architectural composition, there can be more than a single dominant element. Secondary points of emphasis which have less attention value than the primary focal point create visual accents. These distinctive but subordinate elements can both accommodate variety and create visual interest, rhythm, and tension in a composition. If carried too far, however, this interest may be replaced by confusion. When everything is emphasized, nothing is emphasized.

## Hierarchy by Size

A form or space may dominate an architectural composition by being significantly different in size from all the other elements in the composition. Normally, this dominance is made visible by the sheer size of an element. In some cases, an element can dominate by being significantly smaller than the other elements in the organization, but placed in a well-defined setting.

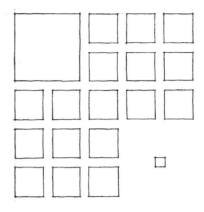

## Hierarchy by Shape

A form or space can be made visually dominant and thus important by clearly differentiating its shape from that of the other elements in the composition. A discernible contrast in shape is critical, whether the differentiation is based on a change in geometry or regularity. Of course, it is also important that the shape selected for the hierarchically significant element be compatible with its functional use.

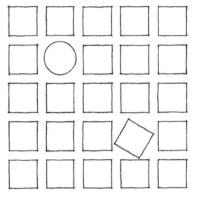

## Hierarchy by Placement

A form or space may be strategically placed to call attention to itself as being the most important element in a composition. Hierarchically important locations for a form or space include:

- the termination of a linear sequence or axial organization
- the centerpiece of a symmetrical organization
- the focus of a centralized or radial organization
- being offset above, below, or in the foreground of a composition

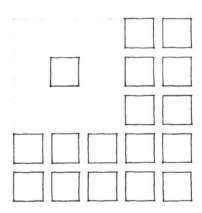

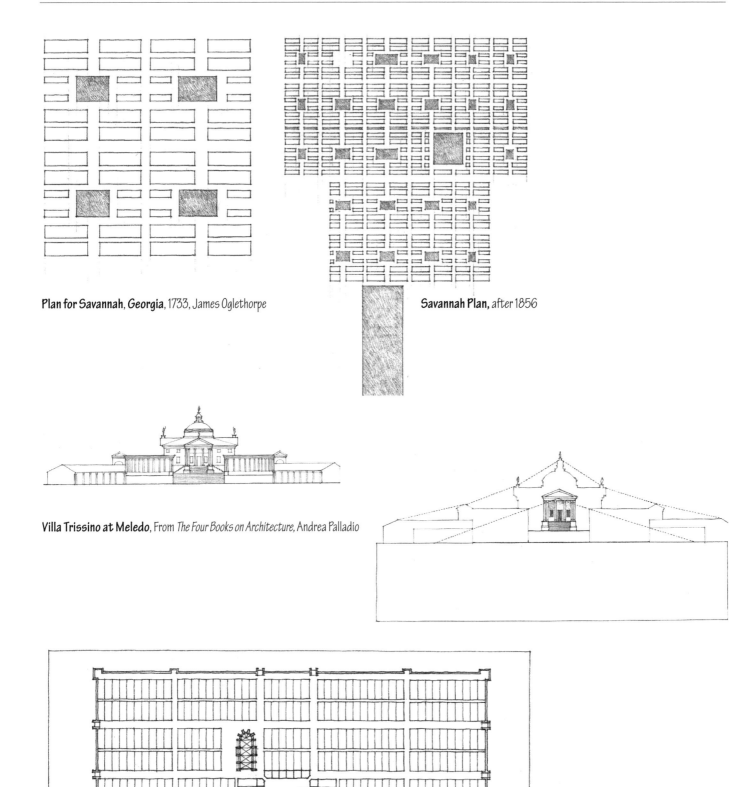

**Plan for Savannah, Georgia**, 1733, James Oglethorpe

**Savannah Plan,** after 1856

**Villa Trissino at Meledo**, From *The Four Books on Architecture*, Andrea Palladio

**Plan of Montfazier**, France, a Medieval town founded in 1284

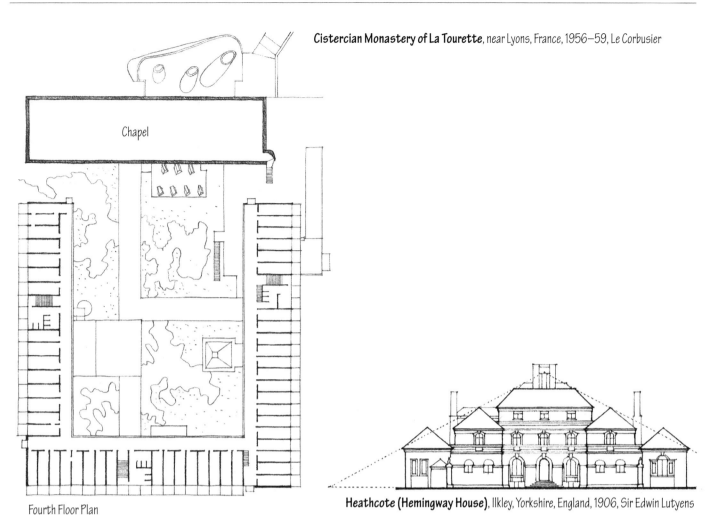

**Cistercian Monastery of La Tourette**, near Lyons, France, 1956–59, Le Corbusier

Chapel

Fourth Floor Plan

**Heathcote (Hemingway House)**, Ilkley, Yorkshire, England, 1906, Sir Edwin Lutyens

**View of Florence** illustrating the dominance of the cathedral over the urban landscape

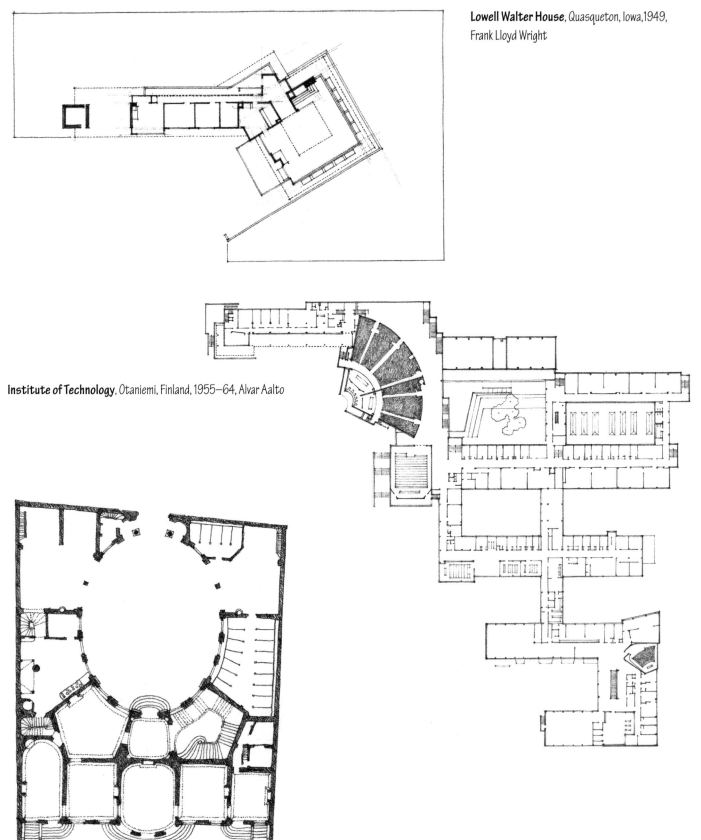

**Lowell Walter House**, Quasqueton, Iowa, 1949, Frank Lloyd Wright

**Institute of Technology**, Otaniemi, Finland, 1955–64, Alvar Aalto

**Hôtel Amelot**, Paris, 1710–13, Germain Boffrand

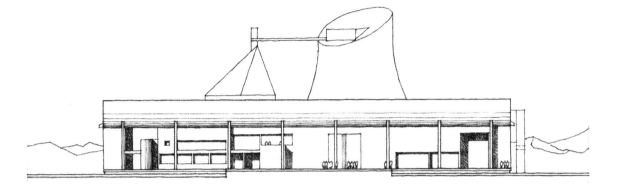

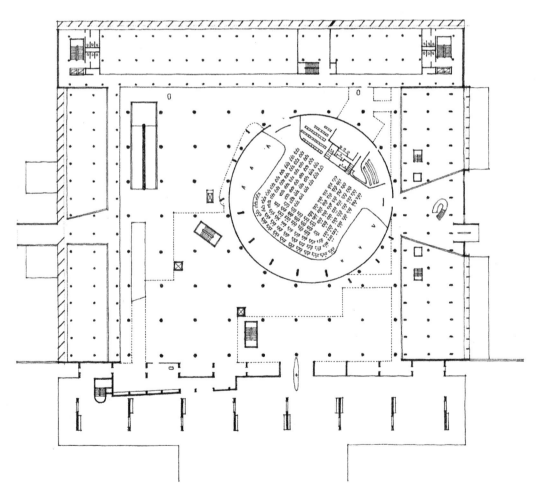

**Legislative Assembly Building**, Chandigarh, Capitol Complex of Punjab, India, 1956–59, Le Corbusier

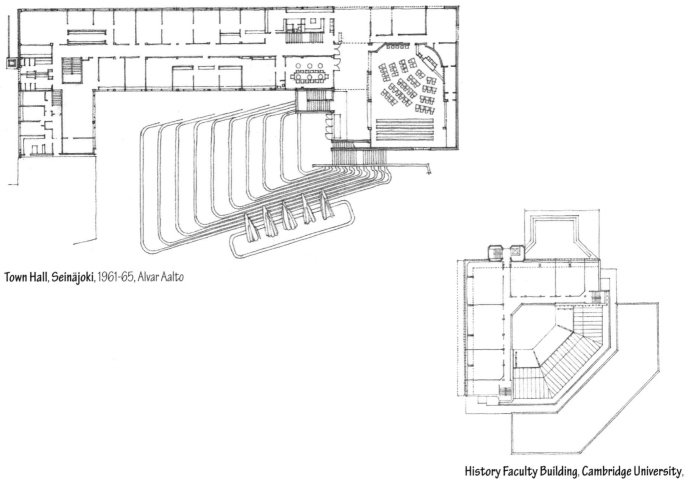

**Town Hall**, **Seinäjoki**, 1961-65, Alvar Aalto

**History Faculty Building**, **Cambridge University**,
England, 1964–67, James Stirling

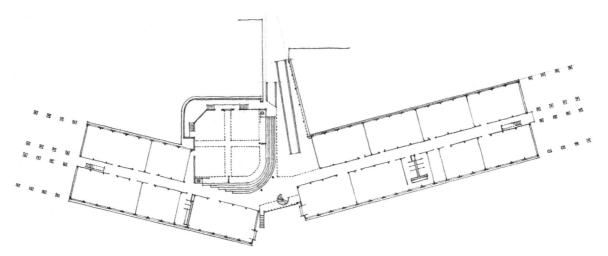

**Olivetti Training School**, Haslemere, England, 1969–72, James Stirling

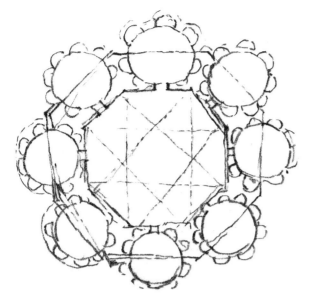

**Plan of an Ideal Church**, c. 1490, Leonardo da Vinci

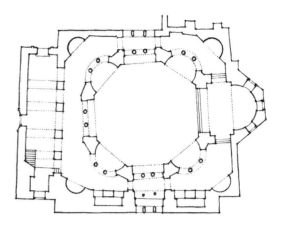

**S.S. Sergius and Bacchus**, Constantinople (Istanbul), A.D. 525–30

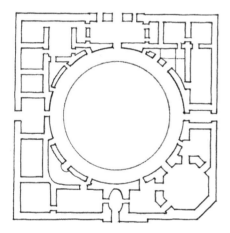

**Palace of Charles V**, Granada, 1527–68, Pedro Machuca

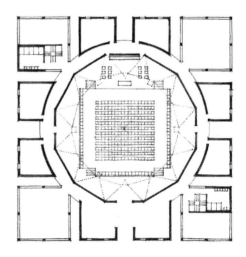

**First Unitarian Church**, First Design, Rochester, New York, 1959, Louis Kahn

Excerpt from **Gavotte I, Sixth Cello Suite,** by Johann Sebastian Bach (1685–1750). Transcribed for classical guitar by Jerry Snyder.

A datum refers to a line, plane, or volume of reference to which other elements in a composition can relate. It organizes a random pattern of elements through its regularity, continuity, and constant presence. For example, the lines of a musical staff serve as a datum in providing the visual basis for reading notes and the relative pitches of their tones. The regularity of their spacing and their continuity organizes, clarifies, and accentuates the differences between the series of notes in a musical composition.

A preceding section illustrated the ability of an axis to organize a series of elements along its length. In effect, the axis was serving as a datum. A datum, however, need not be a straight line. It can also be planar or volumetric in form.

To be an effective ordering device, a linear datum must have sufficient visual continuity to cut through or bypass all of the elements being organized. If planar or volumetric in form, a datum must have sufficient size, closure, and regularity to be seen as a figure that can embrace or gather together the elements being organized within its field.

Given a random organization of dissimilar elements, a datum can organize the elements in the following ways:

Line

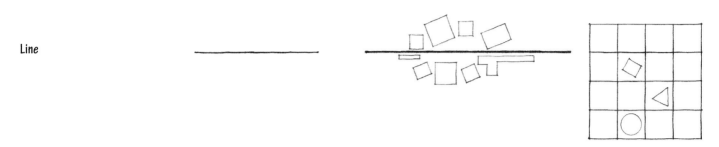

A line can cut through or form a common edge for the pattern, while a grid of lines can form a neutral, unifying field for the pattern.

Plane

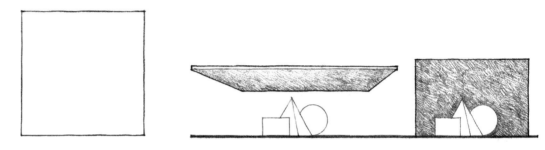

A plane can gather the pattern of elements beneath it or serve as an encompassing background for the elements and frame them in its field.

Volume

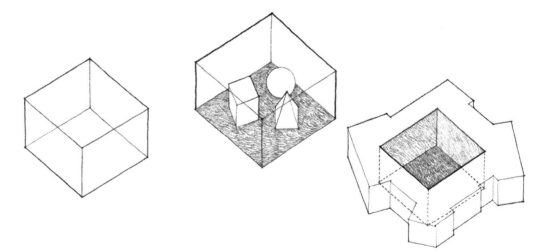

A volume can collect the pattern of elements within its boundaries or organize them along its perimeter.

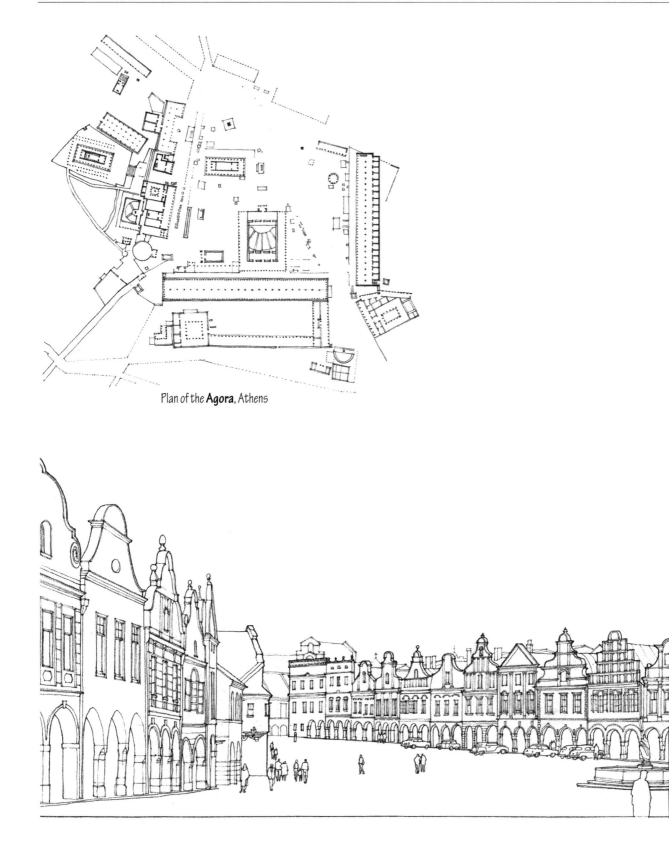

Plan of the **Agora**, Athens

**Arcades** unify the facades of houses that front the town square of Telo, Czechoslovakia.

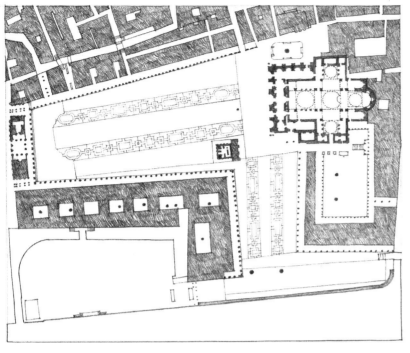

Piazza San Marco, Venice

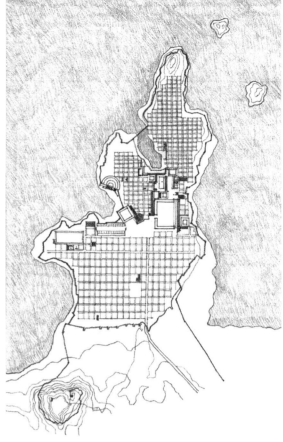

Plan of Miletus, 5th century B.C.

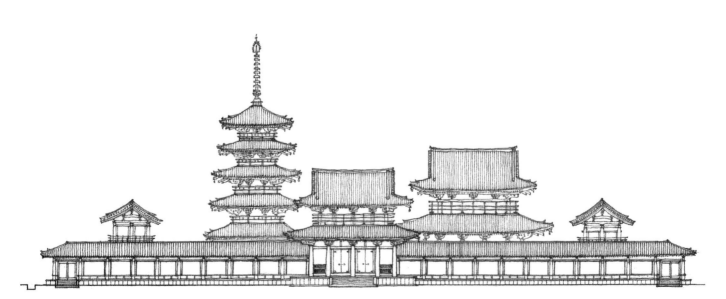

Horyu-Ji Temple Group, Nara Prefecture, Japan, A.D. 607–746

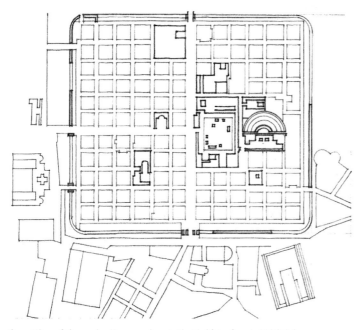

**Town Plan of Timgad**, a Roman colony in North Africa founded 100 B.C.

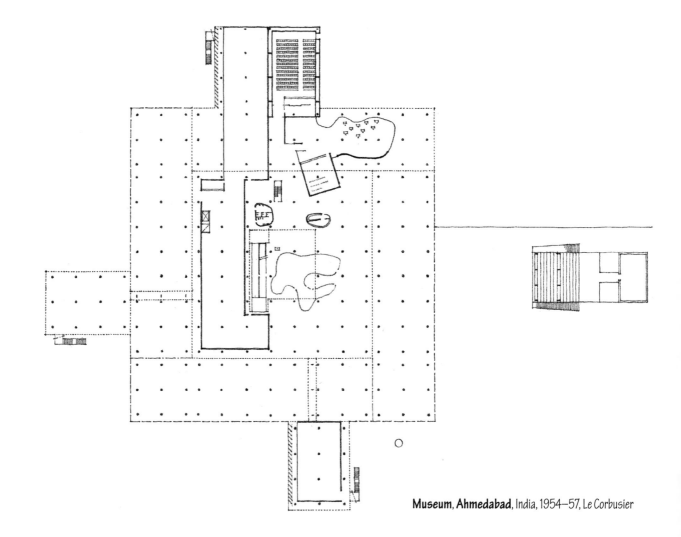

**Museum, Ahmedabad**, India, 1954–57, Le Corbusier

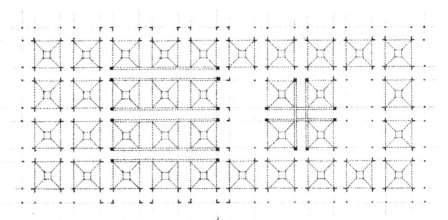

Structural Grid of Main Building, **Jewish Community Center,** Trenton, New Jersey, 1954–59, Louis Kahn

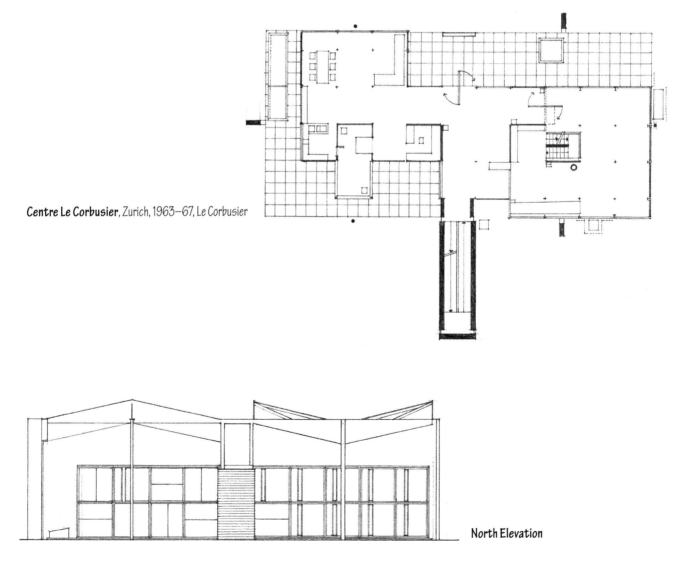

**Centre Le Corbusier**, Zurich, 1963–67, Le Corbusier

**North Elevation**

**Section**

**German Pavilion, Montreal World Exposition,**
1966–67, Rolf Gutbrod and Frei Otto

**Ground Floor Plan**

**DeVore House** (Project), Montgomery County, Pennsylvania, 1954, Louis Kahn

Cultural Center (Competition Entry), Leverkusen, Germany, 1962, Alvar Aalto

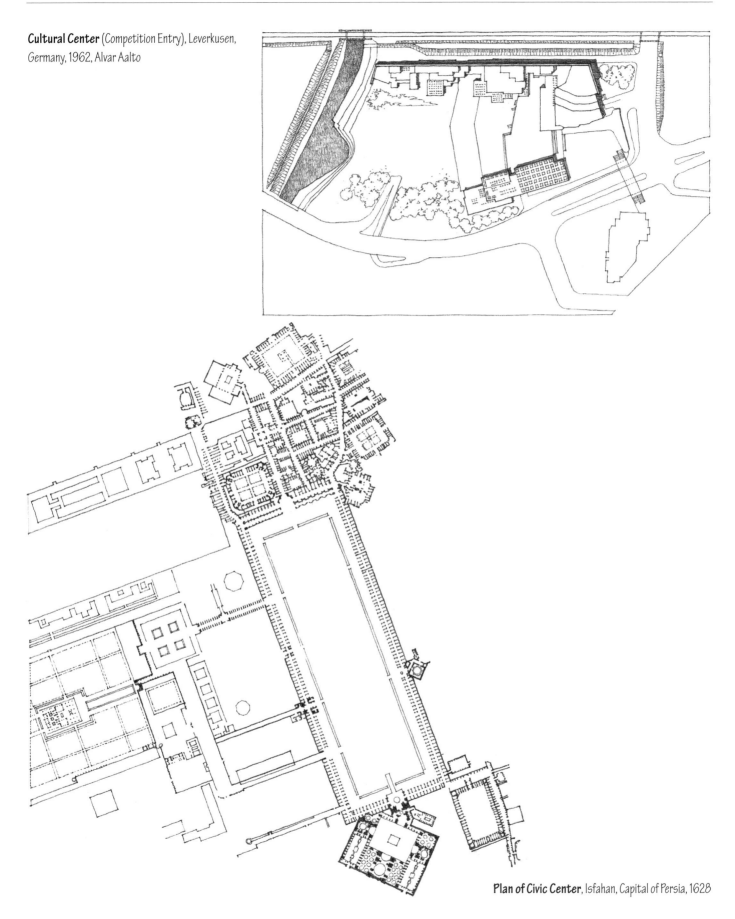

Plan of Civic Center, Isfahan, Capital of Persia, 1628

**Salvation Army Hostel**, Paris, 1928–33, Le Corbusier

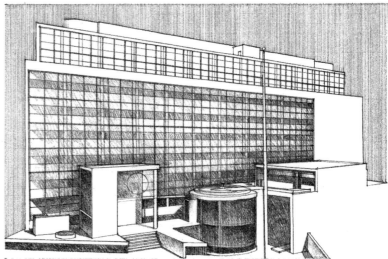

**Plan of Huánoco**, an Inca Town in central Peru

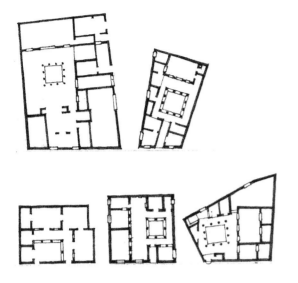

**Plan of Peristyle Courtyard Houses on Delos**, a Greek island in the Aegean

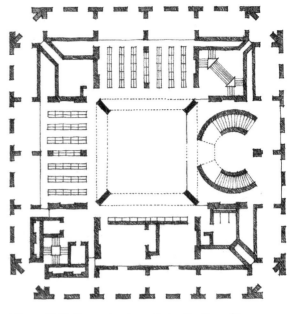

**Library, Philip Exeter Academy**, Exeter, New Hampshire, 1967–72, Louis Kahn

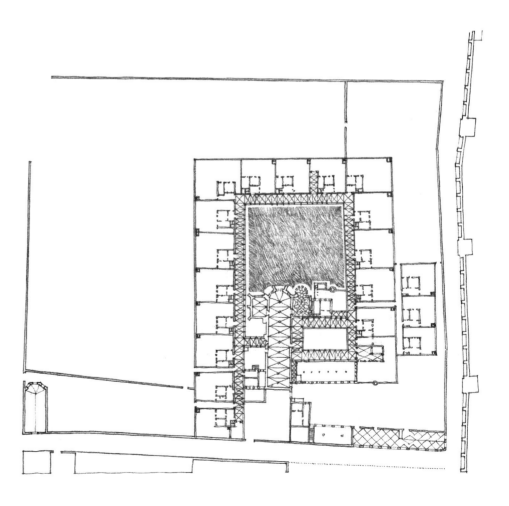

**Nuremberg Charterhouse**, 1383

Column Details, **Notre Dame la Grande**, Poitiers, France, 1130—45

Rhythm refers to any movement characterized by a patterned recurrence of elements or motifs at regular or irregular intervals. The movement may be of our eyes as we follow recurring elements in a composition, or of our bodies as we advance through a sequence of spaces. In either case, rhythm incorporates the fundamental notion of repetition as a device to organize forms and spaces in architecture.

Almost all building types incorporate elements that are by their nature repetitive. Beams and columns repeat themselves to form repetitive structural bays and modules of space. Windows and doors repeatedly puncture the surfaces of a building to allow light, air, views, and people to enter the interior. Spaces often recur to accommodate similar or repetitive functional requirements in the building program. This section discusses the patterns of repetition that can be utilized to organize a series of recurring elements, and the resultant visual rhythms these patterns create.

We tend to group elements in a random composition according to:

- their closeness or proximity to one another
- the visual characteristics they share in common

The principle of repetition utilizes both of these concepts of visual perception to order recurring elements in a composition.

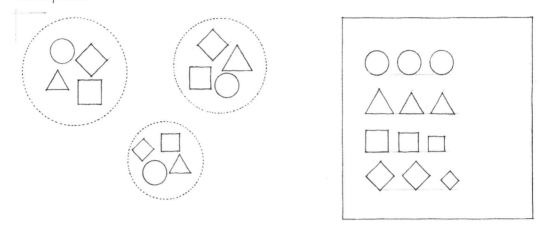

The simplest form of repetition is a linear pattern of redundant elements. Elements need not be perfectly identical, however, to be grouped in a repetitive fashion. They may merely share a common trait or a common denominator, allowing each element to be individually unique, yet belong to the same family.

- Size

- Shape

- Detail Characteristics

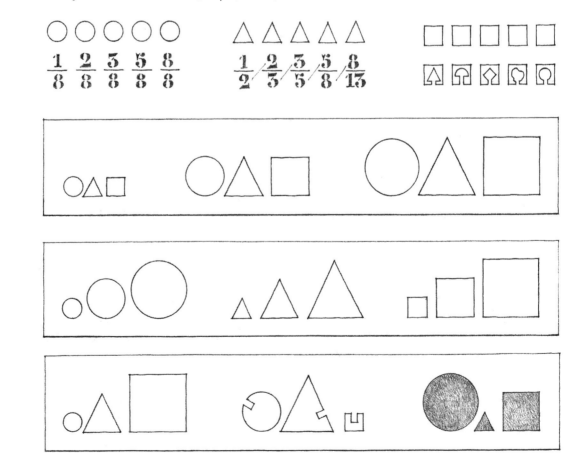

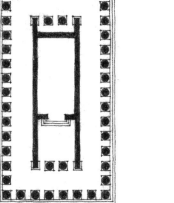

Distyle in Antis

Prostyle

Amphiprostyle

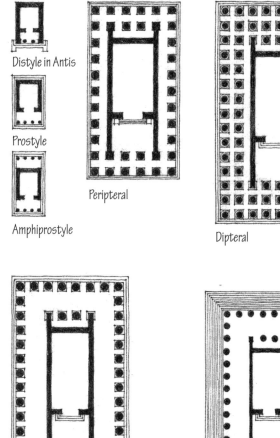

Peripteral

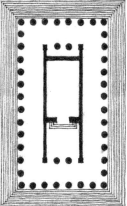

Dipteral

Pseudodipteral

The Smitheum

**Classification of Temples** according to the arrangements of the colonnades. From Book III, Chapter II of Vitruvius' *Ten Books on Architecture.*

Structural patterns often incorporate the repetition of vertical supports at regular or harmonious intervals which define modular bays or divisions of space. Within such repetitive patterns, the importance of a space can be emphasized by its size and placement.

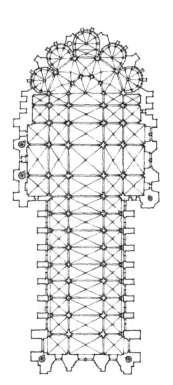

**Cathedral at Reims**, 1211–1290

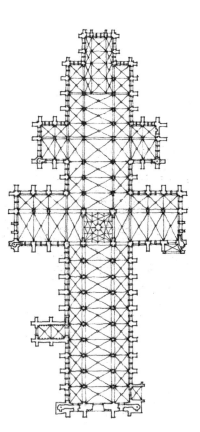

**Cathedral at Salisbury**, 1220–60

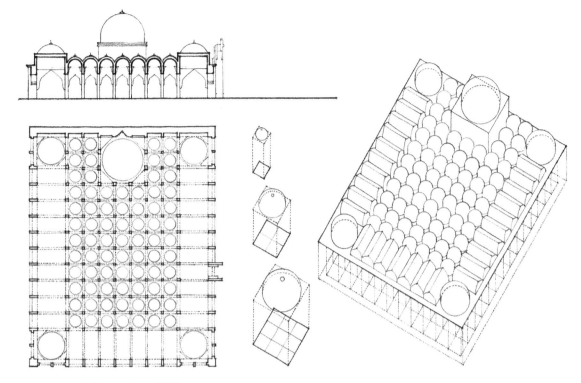

**Jami Masjid**, Gulbarga, India, 1367

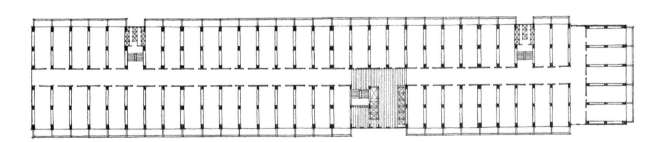

Typical Floor Plan, **Unité d'Habitation**, Marseilles, 1946–52, Le Corbusier

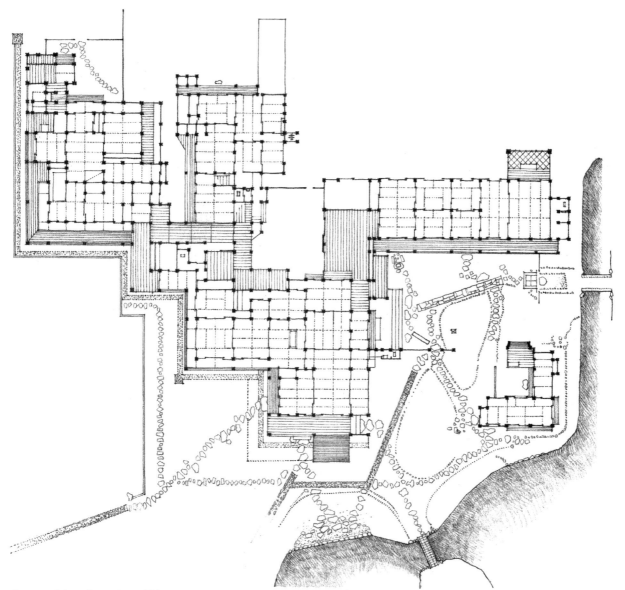

**Katsura Palace**, Kyoto, Japan, 17th century

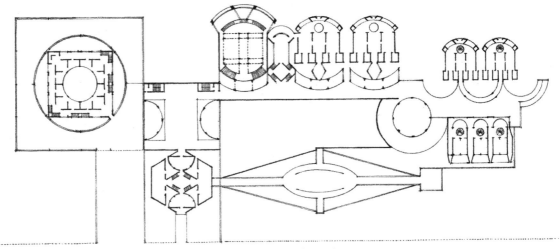

**Capitol Complex** (Project), **Islamabad**, Pakistan, 1965, Louis Kahn

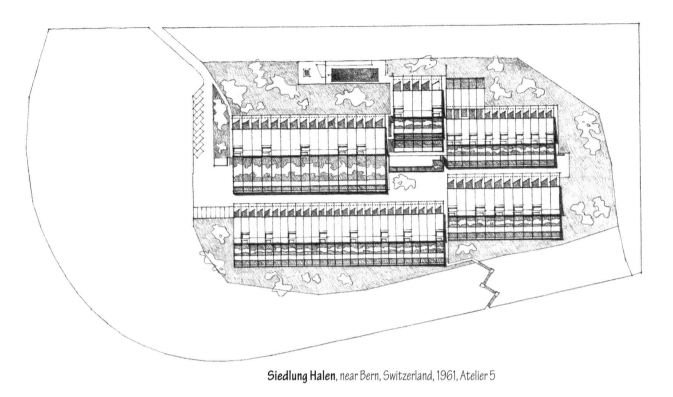

**Siedlung Halen**, near Bern, Switzerland, 1961, Atelier 5

As in music, a rhythmic pattern may be legato, continuous, and flowing, or staccato and abrupt in its pace or cadence.

View of Spanish Hill Town of **Mojácar**

Rhythm created by connecting points in space

Contrasting rhythms

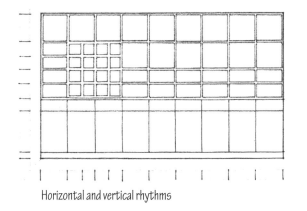

Horizontal and vertical rhythms

View of **Villa Hermosa**, Spain

**Külliye of Beyazid II**, Bursa, Turkey, 1398–1403

Rhythmic patterns provide continuity and lead us to anticipate what comes next. Any break in the pattern announces and emphasizes the importance of the interrupting element or interval.

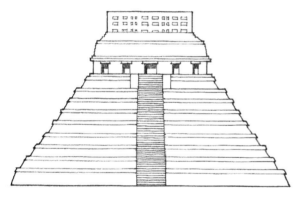

**Temple of the Inscriptions**, Palenque, Mexico, c. A.D. 550

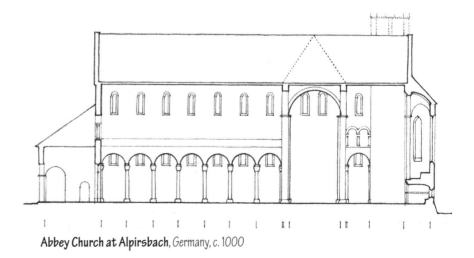

**Abbey Church at Alpirsbach**, Germany, c. 1000

**Victorian Facades** Fronting a San Francisco street

Multiple rhythms can be laid over one another in the facade of a building.

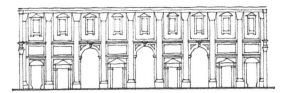

a · b · a · b · a · b · a · b · a . . . . . . . .
a · a · b · a · b · a · b · a · a . . . . . . . .
A · B · C · B · C · B · C · B · A . . . . . .

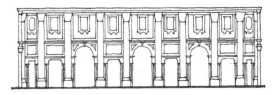

a · b · b · b · b · b · b · a . . . . . .
c · a · b · a · b · a · b · a · c . . . . . .
A · B · C · B · C · B · C · B · A . . . . . .

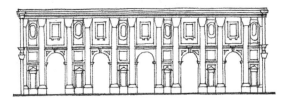

a · b · a · b · a · b · a · b · a · b · a . . . . .
a · b · a · b · a · b · a · b · a · b · a . . . . .
A · B · A · B · A · C · A · B · A · B · A . . . . .

Studies of **Internal Facade of a Basilica** by Francesco Borromini

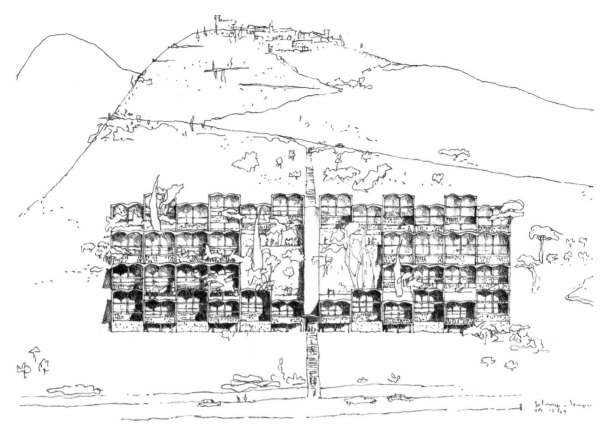

**Roq Housing Project**, Cap-Martin, on the French Riviera near Nice, 1949, Le Corbusier

More complex rhythmic patterns can be created by introducing points of emphasis or exceptional intervals into a sequence. These accents or beats help differentiate between the major and minor themes in a composition.

**Bedford Park**, London, 1875, Maurice Adams, E.W. Goodwin, E.J. May, Norman Shaw

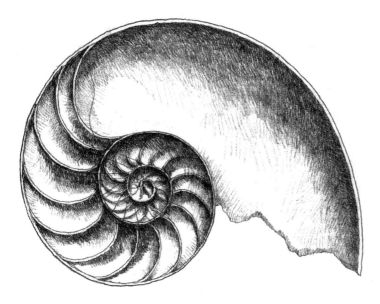

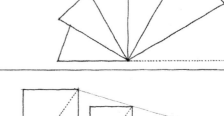

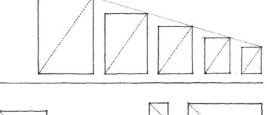

The radial segments of a nautilus shell spiral outward in a reverberating manner from its center and maintain the shell's organic unity through this pattern of additive growth. Using the mathematical ratio of the Golden Section, a series of rectangles can be generated to form a unified organization wherein each rectangle is proportionate to the others as well as to the overall structure. In each of these examples, the principle of reverberation creates a sense of order among a group of elements which are similar in shape but hierarchically graded in size.

Progressive, reverberating patterns of forms and spaces can be organized in the following ways:

* in a radial or concentric manner about a point
* sequentially according to size in a linear fashion
* randomly but related by proximity as well as similarity of form

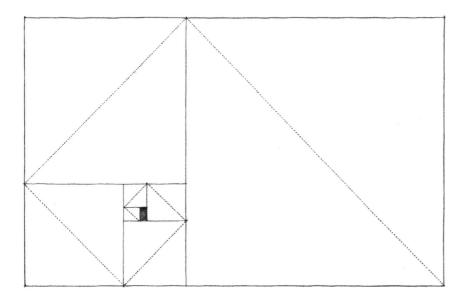

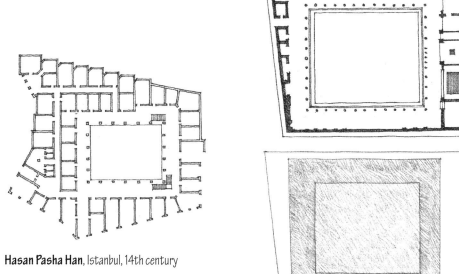

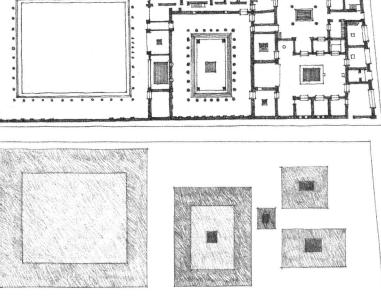

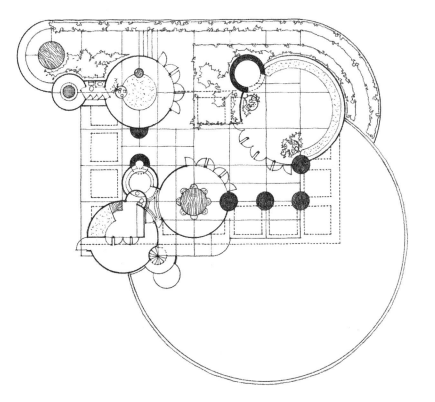

**Hasan Pasha Han**, Istanbul, 14th century

**House of the Faun**, Pompeii, c. 2nd century B.C.

**Jester House** (Project), Palos Verdes, California, 1938, Frank Lloyd Wright

**Sydney Opera House**, Sydney, Australia, designed 1957, completed 1973, Jorn Utzon

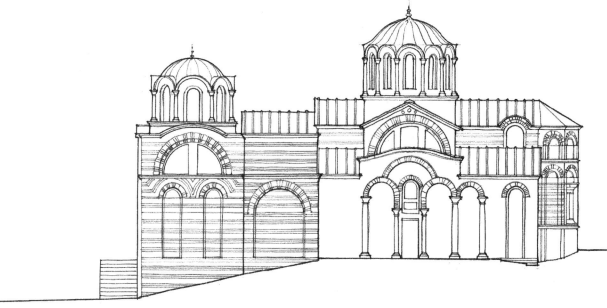

**S. Theodore** (now **Kilisse Mosque**), Constantinople (Istanbul), c. 1100

**Cultural Center, Wolfsburg**, Germany, 1948–62, Alvar Aalto

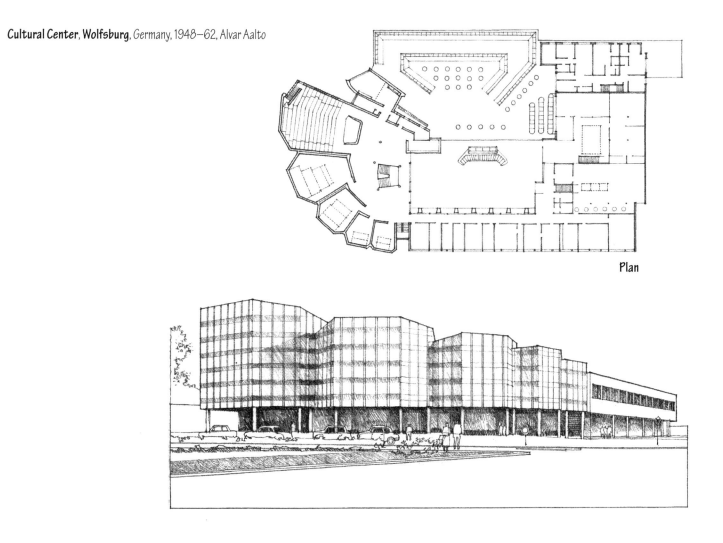

Plan

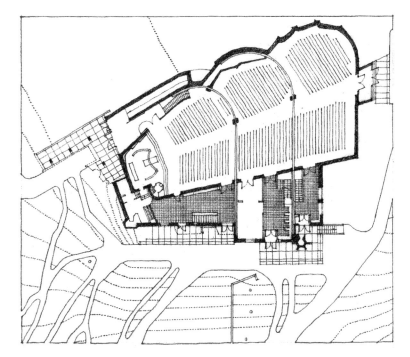

**Church at Vuoksenniska**, Finland, 1956, Alvar Aalto

The study of architecture, as with other disciplines, should legitimately involve the study of its past, of prior experiences, endeavors, and accomplishments from which much can be learned and emulated. The principle of transformation accepts this notion; this book, and all of the examples it contains, is predicated on it.

The principle of transformation allows a designer to select a prototypical architectural model whose formal structure and ordering of elements might be appropriate and reasonable, and to transform it through a series of discrete manipulations in order to respond to the specific conditions and context of the design task at hand.

Design is a generative process of analysis and synthesis, of trial and error, of trying out possibilities and seizing opportunities. In the process of exploring an idea and probing its potential, it is essential that a designer understand the fundamental nature and structure of the concept. If the ordering system of a prototypical model is perceived and understood, then the original design concept can, through a series of finite permutations, be clarified, strengthened, and built upon, rather than destroyed.

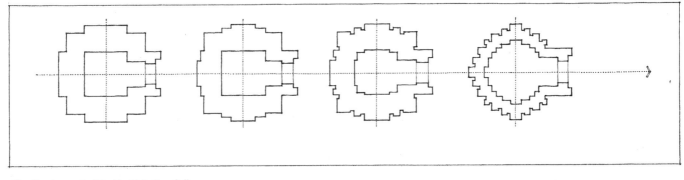

Plan Development of the **North Indian Cella**

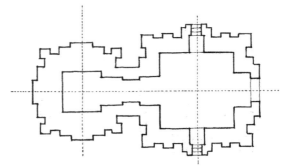

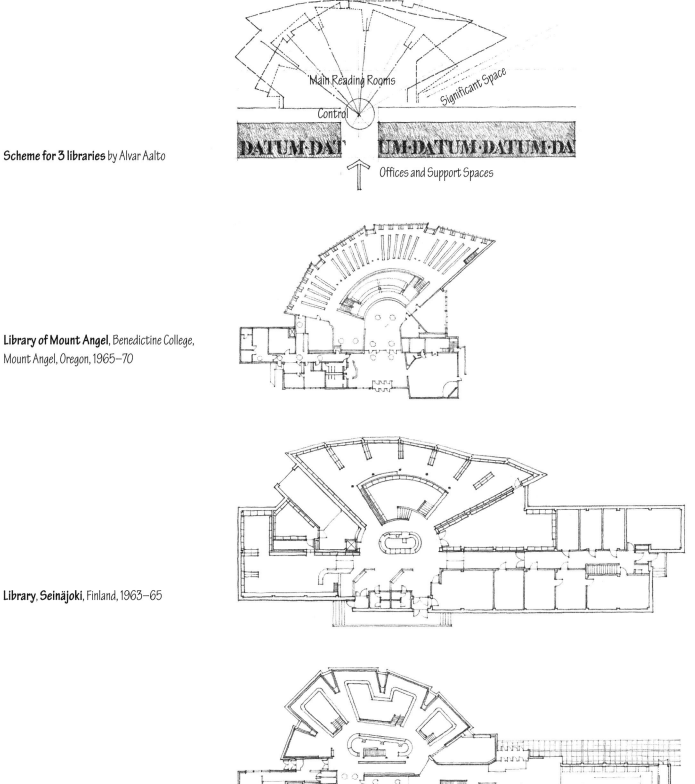

**Scheme for 3 libraries** by Alvar Aalto

Main Reading Rooms

Significant Space

Control

DATUM·DAT    UM·DATUM·DATUM·DA

Offices and Support Spaces

**Library of Mount Angel**, Benedictine College,
Mount Angel, Oregon, 1965–70

**Library**, **Seinäjoki**, Finland, 1963–65

**Library**, **Rovaniemi**, Finland, 1963–68

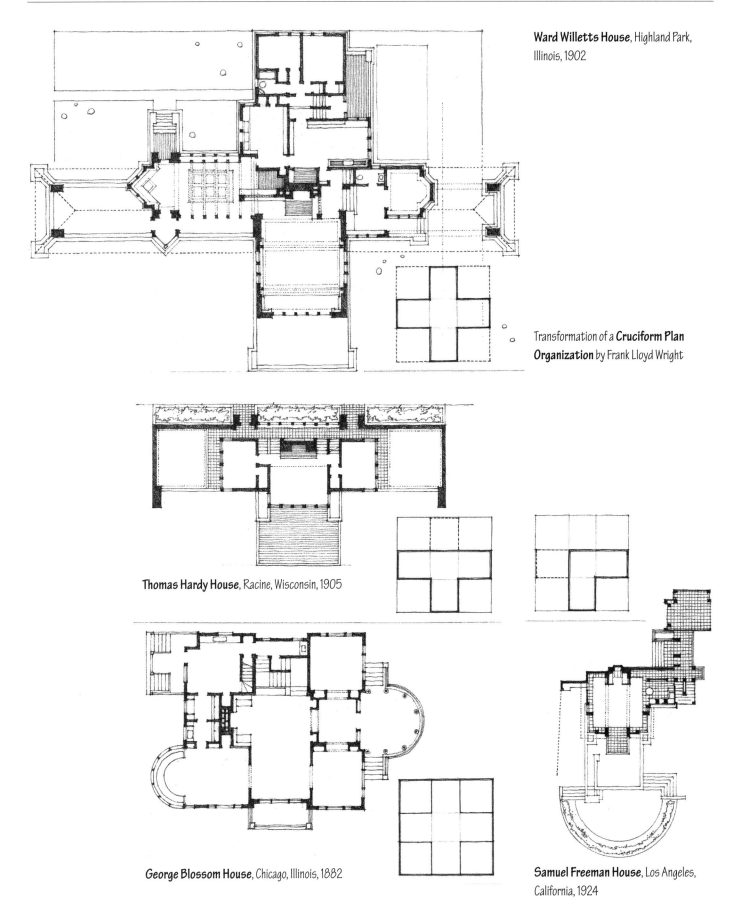

**Ward Willetts House**, Highland Park, Illinois, 1902

Transformation of a **Cruciform Plan Organization** by Frank Lloyd Wright

**Thomas Hardy House**, Racine, Wisconsin, 1905

**George Blossom House**, Chicago, Illinois, 1882

**Samuel Freeman House**, Los Angeles, California, 1924

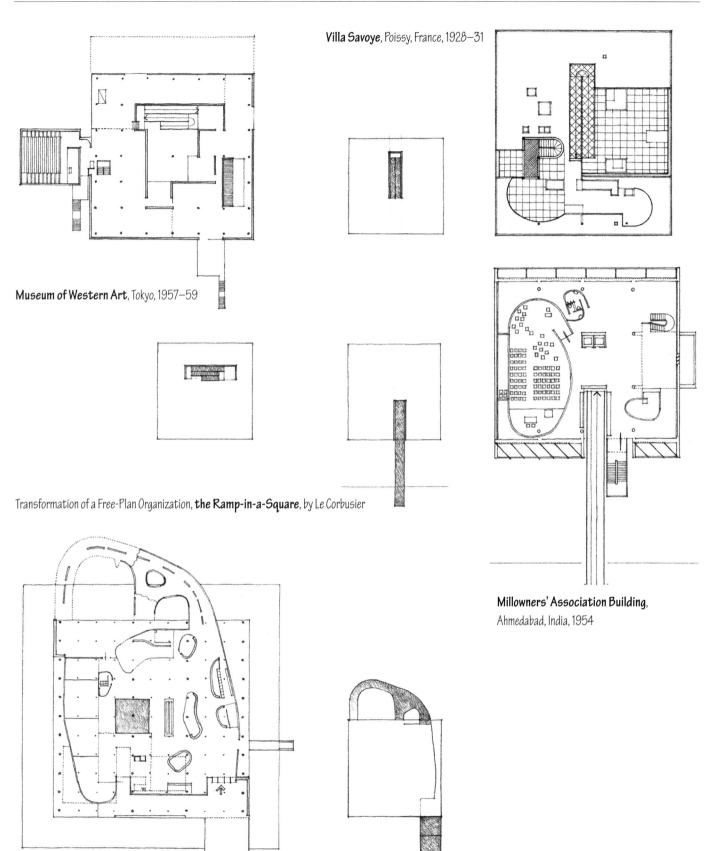

Villa Savoye, Poissy, France, 1928–31

Museum of Western Art, Tokyo, 1957–59

Transformation of a Free-Plan Organization, **the Ramp-in-a-Square**, by Le Corbusier

Millowners' Association Building,
Ahmedabad, India, 1954

**Congress Hall** (Project), Strasbourg, 1964

### Meaning in Architecture

This book, throughout its presentation of the elements of form and space, has been concerned primarily with the visual aspects of their physical reality in architecture. Points, moving through space and defining lines, lines defining planes, planes defining volumes of form and space. Beyond these visual functions, these elements, by their relationships to one another and the nature of their organization, also communicate notions of domain and place, entry and path of movement, hierarchy and order. These are presented as the literal, denotative meanings of form and space in architecture.

As in language, however, architectural forms and spaces also have connotative meanings: associative values and symbolic content that are subject to personal and cultural interpretation, which can change with time. The spires of a Gothic cathedral can stand for the realm, values, or goals of Christianity. The Greek column can convey the notion of democracy, or, as in America in the early 19th century, the presence of civilization in a new world.

Although the study of connotative meanings, of semiotics and symbology in architecture, is beyond the scope of this book, it should be noted here that architecture, in combining form and space into a single essence, not only facilitates purpose but communicates meaning. The art of architecture makes our existence not only visible but meaningful.

"You employ stone, wood, and concrete, and with these materials you build house and palaces. That is construction. Ingenuity is at work.

But suddenly, you touch my heart, you do me good. I am happy and I say: 'This is beautiful.' That is architecture. Art enters in.

My house is practical. I thank you, as I might thank Railway engineers, or the Telephone service. You have not touched my heart.

But suppose that walls rise toward heaven in such a way that I am moved. I perceive your intentions. Your mood has been gentle, brutal, charming, or noble. The stones you have erected tell me so. You fix me to the place and my eyes regard it. They behold something which expresses a thought. A thought which reveals itself without wood or sound, but solely by means of shapes which stand in a certain relationship to one another. These shapes are such that they are clearly revealed in light. The relationships between them have not necessarily any reference to what is practical or descriptive. They are a mathematical creation of our mind. They are the language of Architecture. By the use of raw materials and starting from conditions more or less utilitarian, you have established certain relationships which have aroused my emotions. This is Architecture."

Le Corbusier
*Towards a New Architecture*
1927

Aalto, Alvar. *Complete Works.* 2 volumes. Zurich: Les Editions d'Architecture Artemis, 1963.

Arnheim, Rudolf. *Art and Visual Perception.* Berkeley: University of California Press, 1965.

Ashihara, Yoshinobu. *Exterior Design in Architecture.* New York: Van Nostrand Reinhold Co., 1970.

Bacon, Edmund. *Design of Cities.* New York: The Viking Press, 1974.

Collins, George R., gen. ed. *Planning and Cities Series.* New York: George Braziller, 1968.

Clark, Roger H. and Pause, Michael. *Precedents in Architecture.* New York: Van Nostrand Reinhold Co., 1985.

Engel, Heinrich. *The Japanese House: A Tradition for Contemporary Architecture.* Tokyo: Charles E. Tuttle, Co., 1964.

Fletcher, Sir Banister. *A History of Architecture.* 18th ed. Revised by J.C. Palmes. New York: Charles Schriber's Sons, 1975.

Giedion, Siegfried. *Space, Time and Architecture.* 4th ed. Cambridge: Harvard University Press, 1963.

Giurgola, Romaldo and Mehta, Jarmini. *Louis I. Kahn.* Boulder: Westview Press, 1975.

Hall, Edward T. *The Hidden Dimension.* Garden City, N.Y.: Doubleday & Company, Inc., 1966.

Halprin, Lawrence. *Cities.* Cambridge: The MIT Press, 1972.

Hitchcock, Henry Russell. *In the Nature of Materials.* New York: Da Capo Press, 1975.

Jencks, Charles. *Modern Movements in Architecture.* Garden City, N.Y.: Anchor Press, 1973.

Laseau, Paul and Tice, James. *Frank Lloyd Wright: Between Principle and Form.* New York: Van Nostrand Reinhold Co., 1992.

Le Corbusier. *Oeuvre Complete.* 8 Volumes. Zurich: Les Editions d'Architecture, 1964-70.

—. *Towards a New Architecture.* London: The Architectural Press, 1946.

Lyndon, Donlyn and Moore, Charles. *Chambers for a Memory Palace.* Cambridge: The MIT Press, 1994.

Martienssen, Heather. *The Shapes of Structure.* London: Oxford University Press, 1976.

Moore, Charles; Allen, Gerald; Lyndon, Donlyn. *The Place of Houses.* New York: Holt, Rinehardt and Winston, 1974.

Mumford, Lewis. *The City in History.* New York: Harcourt, Brace & World, Inc., 1961.

Norberg-Schulz, Christian. *Meaning in Western Architecture.* New York: Praeger Publishers, 1975.

Palladio, Andrea. *The Four Books of Architecture.* New York: Dover Publications, 1965.

Pevsner, Nikolaus. *A History of Building Types.* Princeton: Princeton University Press, 1976.

Pye, David. *The Nature and Aesthetics of Design.* New York: Van Nostrand Reinhold Co., 1978.

Rapoport, Amos. *House Form and Culture.* Englewood Cliffs, N.J.: Prentice-Hall, Inc., 1969.

Rasmussen, Steen Eiler. *Experiencing Architecture.* Cambridge: The MIT Press, 1964.

—. *Towns and Buildings.* Cambridge: The MIT Press, 1969.

Rowe, Colin. *The Mathematics of the Ideal Villa and Other Essays.* Cambridge: The MIT Press, 1976.

Rudofsky, Bernard. *Architecture Without Architects.* Garden City, N.Y.: Doubleday & Co., 1964.

Simonds, John Ormsbee. *Landscape Architecture.* New York: McGraw Hill Book Co., Inc., 1961.

Stierlin, Henry, gen. ed. *Living Architecture Series.* New York: Grosset & Dunlap, 1966.

Venturi, Robert. *Complexity and Contradiction in Architecture.* New York: The Museum of Modern Art, 1966.

Vitruvius. *The Ten Books of Architecture.* New York: Dover Publications, 1960.

von Meiss, Pierre. *Elements of Architecture.* New York: Van Nostrand Reinhold Co., 1990.

Wilson, Forrest. *Structure: the Essence of Architecture.* New York: Van Nostrand Reinhold Co., 1971.

Wittkower, Rudolf. *Architectural Principles in the Age of Humanism.* New York: W.W. Norton & Co., Inc., 1971.

Wong, Wucius. *Principles of Two-Dimensional Design.* New York: Van Nostrand Reinhold Co., 1972.

Wright, Frank Lloyd. *Writings and Buildings.* New York: Meridian Books, 1960.

Zevi, Bruno. *Architecture as Space.* New York: Horizon Press, 1957.

**acropolis** The fortified high area or citadel of an ancient Greek city, esp. the citadel of Athens and site of the Parthenon.

**aedicule** A canopied opening or niche flanked by two columns, piers, or pilasters supporting a gable, lintel, or entablature.

**agora** A marketplace or public square in an ancient Greek city, usually surrounded with public buildings and porticoes and commonly used as a place for popular or political assembly.

**allée** French term for a narrow passage between houses, or a broad walk planted with trees.

**anomaly** A deviation from the normal or expected form, order, or arrangement.

**anthropology** The science of human beings: specif. the study of the origins, physical and cultural development, and environmental and social relations of humankind.

**anthropometry** The measurement and study of the size and proportions of the human body.

**anthropomorphism** A conception or representation resembling the human form or having human attributes.

**apse** A semicircular or polygonal projection of a building, usually vaulted and used esp. at the sanctuary or east end of a church.

**arbor** A shady shelter of shrubs and branches or of latticework intertwined with climbing vines and flowers.

**arcade** A series of arches supported on piers or columns. Also, an arched, roofed gallery or passageway with shops on one or both sides.

**arch** A curved structure for spanning an opening, designed to support a vertical load primarily by axial compression.

**architrave** The lowermost division of a classical entablature, resting directly on the column capitals and supporting the frieze.

**atrium** Originally, the main or central inner hall of an ancient Roman house, open to the sky at the center and usually having a pool for the collection of rainwater. Later, the forecourt of an early Christian church, flanked or surrounded by porticoes. Now, an open, skylit court around which a house or building is built.

**axis** A central line that bisects a two-dimensional body or figure or about which a three-dimensional body or figure is symmetrical. Also, a straight line to which elements in a composition are referred for measurement or symmetry.

**background** The part of an image represented as being at the maximum distance from the frontal plane.

**balance** A state of equilibrium between contrasting, opposing, or interacting elements. Also, the pleasing or harmonious arrangement or proportion of parts or elements in a design or composition.

**balcony** An elevated platform projecting from the wall of a building and enclosed by a railing or parapet.

**baldachin** An ornamental canopy of stone or marble permanently placed over the high altar in a church.

**base** The lowermost portion of a wall, column, pier, or other structure, usually distinctively treated and considered as an architectural unit.

**basilica** A large oblong building used as a hall of justice and public meeting place in ancient Rome, typically having a high central space lit by a clerestory and covered by timber trusses, and a raised dais in a semi-circular apse for the tribunal. The Roman basilica served as a model for early Christian basilicas, which were characterized by a long, rectangular plan, a high colonnaded nave lit by a clerestory and covered by a timbered gable roof, two or four lower side aisles, a semicircular apse at the end, a narthex, and often other features, as an atrium, a bema, and small semicircular apses terminating the aisles.

**bay** A major spatial division, usually one of a series, marked or partitioned off by the principal vertical supports of a structure. Also, any of a number of principal compartments or divisions of a wall, roof, or other part of a building marked off by vertical or transverse supports.

**beam** A rigid structural member designed to carry and transfer transverse loads across space to supporting elements.

**bearing wall** A wall capable of supporting an imposed load, as from a floor or roof of a building.

**belvedere** A building, or architectural feature of a building, designed and situated to look out upon a pleasing scene.

**bema** A transverse open space separating the nave and the apse of an early Christian church, developing into the transept of later cruciform churches.

**berm** A bank of earth placed against one or more exterior walls of a building as protection against extremes in temperature.

**bosket** A grove or thicket of trees in a garden or park.

**brise-soleil** A screen, usually of louvers, placed on the outside of a building to shield the windows from direct sunlight.

**campanile** A bell tower, usually one near but not attached to the body of a church.

**cantilever** A beam or other rigid structural member extending beyond a fulcrum and supported by a balancing member or a downward force behind the fulcrum.

**capital** The distinctively treated upper end of a column, pillar, or pier, crowning the shaft and taking the weight of the entablature or architrave.

**caravansary** An inn in the Near East for the overnight accommodation of caravans, usually having a large courtyard enclosed by a solid wall and entered through an imposing gateway.

**caryatid** A sculptured female figure used as a column.

**cathedral** The principal church of a diocese, containing the bishop's throne called the cathedra.

**ceiling** The overhead interior surface or lining of a room, often concealing the underside of the floor or roof above.

**cenotaph** A monument erected in memory of a deceased person whose remains are buried elsewhere.

**chaitya** A Buddhist shrine in India, usually carved out of solid rock on a hillside, having the form of an aisled basilica with a stupa at one end.

**chancel** The space about the altar of a church for the clergy and choir, often elevated above the nave and separated from it by a railing or screen.

**chapel** A subordinate or private place of worship or prayer.

**church** A building for public Christian worship.

**charterhouse** A Carthusian monastery.

**clerestory** A portion of an interior rising above adjacent rooftops and having windows admitting daylight to the interior.

**cloister** A covered walk having an arcade or colonnade on one side opening onto a courtyard.

**colonnade** A series of regularly spaced columns supporting an entablature and usually one side of a roof structure.

**column** A rigid, relatively slender structural member designed primarily to support compressive loads applied at the member ends. In classical architecture, a cylindrical support consisting of a capital, shaft, and usually a base, either monolithic or built up of drums the full diameter of the shaft.

**contrast** Opposition or juxtaposition of dissimilar elements in a work of art to intensify each element's properties and produce a more dynamic expressiveness.

**corbel** To set bricks or stones in an overlapping arrangement so that each course steps upward and outward from the vertical face of a wall.

**cornice** The uppermost member of a classical entablature, consisting typically of a cymatium, corona, and bed molding.

**corona** The projecting, slablike member of a classical cornice, supported by the bed molding and crowned by the cymatium.

**corridor** A narrow passageway or gallery connecting parts of a building, esp. one into which several rooms or apartments open.

**cortile** A large or principal courtyard of an Italian palazzo.

**court** An area open to the sky and mostly or entirely surrounded by walls or buildings.

**courtyard** A court adjacent to or within a building, esp. one enclosed on all four sides.

**cyma recta** A projecting molding having the profile of a double curve with the concave part projecting beyond the convex part.

**cymatium** The crowning member of a classical cornice, usually a cyma recta.

**dado** The major part of a pedestal between the base and the cornice or cap. Also, the lower portion of an interior wall when faced or treated differently from the upper section, as with paneling or wallpaper.

**datum** Any level surface, line, or point used as a reference for the positioning or arrangement of elements in a composition.

**emphasis** Stress or prominence given to an element of a composition by means of contrast, anomaly, or counterpoint.

**entablature** The horizontal section of a classical order that rests on the columns, usually composed of a cornice, frieze, and architrave.

**ergonomics** An applied science concerned with the characteristics of people that need to be considered in the design of devices and systems in order that people and things will interact effectively and safely.

**facade** The front of a building or any of its sides facing a public way or space, esp. one distinguished by its architectural treatment.

**field** A region or expanse of space characterized by a particular property, feature, or activity.

**figure** A shape or form, as determined by outlines or exterior surfaces. Also, a combination of geometric elements disposed in a particular form or shape.

**figure–ground** A property of perception in which there is a tendency to see parts of a visual field as solid, well-defined objects standing out against a less distinct background.

**floor** The level base surface of a room or hall upon which one stands or walks. Also, a continuous supporting surface extending horizontally throughout a building, having a number of rooms and constituting one level in the structure.

**form** The shape and structure of something as distinguished from its substance or material. Also, the manner of arranging and coordinating the elements and parts of a composition so as to produce a coherent image; the formal structure of a work of art.

**fresco** The art or technique of painting on a freshly spread moist plaster surface with pigments ground up in water or a lime water mixture.

**frieze** The horizontal part of a classical entablature between the cornice and architrave, often decorated with sculpture in low relief. Also, a decorative band, as one along the top of an interior wall, immediately below the cornice, or a sculptured one in a stringcourse on an outside wall.

**galleria** A spacious promenade, court, or indoor mall, usually having a vaulted roof and lined with commercial establishments.

**gallery** A long, relatively narrow room or hall, esp. one for public use and having architectural importance through its scale or decorative treatment. Also, a roofed promenade, esp. one extending inside or outside along the exterior wall of a building.

**gestalt** A unified configuration, pattern, or field of specific properties that cannot be derived from the summation of the component parts.

**Gestalt psychology** The theory or doctrine that physiological or psychological phenomena do not occur through the summation of individual elements, as reflexes or sensations, but through gestalts functioning separately or interrelatedly.

**Golden Section** A proportion between the two dimensions of a plane figure or the two divisions of a line, in which the ratio of the smaller to the larger is the same as the ratio of the larger to the whole: a ratio of approximately 0.618 to 1.000.

**ground** The main surface or background in painting or decorative work. Also, the receding part of a visual field against which a figure is perceived.

**hall** The large entrance room of a house or building, as a vestibule or lobby. Also, a large room or building for public gatherings or entertainment.

**harmony** The orderly, pleasing, or congruent arrangement of the elements or parts in an artistic whole.

**hierarchy** A system of elements ranked, classified, and organized one above another, according to importance or significance.

**in antis** Between antae, the rectangular piers or pilasters formed by thickening the end of a projecting wall.

**intercolumniation** A system for spacing columns in a colonnade based on the space between two adjacent columns measured in diameters.

**joist** Any of a series of small, parallel beams for supporting floors, ceilings, or flat roofs.

**lintel** A beam supporting the weight above a door or window opening.

**mass** The physical volume or bulk of a solid body.

**massing** A unified composition of two-dimensional shapes or three-dimensional volumes, esp. one that has or gives the impression of weight, density, and bulk.

**mausoleum** A large and stately tomb.

**megalith** A very large stone used as found or roughly dressed, esp. in ancient construction work.

**megaron** A building or semi-independent unit of a building, typically having a rectangular principal chamber with a center hearth and a porch, often of columns in antis: traditional in Greece since Mycenaean times and believed to be the ancestor of the Doric temple.

**menhir** A prehistoric monument consisting of an upright megalith, usually standing alone but sometimes aligned with others.

**mezzanine** A low or partial story between two main stories of a building, esp. one that projects as a balcony and forms a composition with the story beneath it.

**minaret** A lofty, slender tower attached to a mosque, having stairs leading up to one or more projecting balconies from which the muezzin calls the Muslim people to prayer.

**model** An example serving as a pattern for imitation or emulation in the creation of something.

**module** A unit of measurement used for standardizing the dimensions of building materials or regulating the proportions of an architectural composition.

**monastery** A place of residence for a community of persons living in seclusion under religious vows, esp. monks.

**monolith** A single block of stone of considerable size, often in the form of an obelisk or column.

**mosque** A Muslim building or place of public worship.

**mullion** A vertical member between the lights of a window or the panels in wainscoting.

**mural** A large picture painted on or applied directly to a wall or ceiling surface.

**narthex** The portico before the nave of an early Christian or Byzantine church, appropriated to penitents. Also, an entrance hall or vestibule leading to the nave of a church.

**nave** The principal or central part of a church, extending from the narthex to the choir or chancel and usually flanked by aisles.

**obelisk** A tall, four-sided shaft of stone that tapers as it rises to a pyramidal point, originating in ancient Egypt as a sacred symbol of the sun-god Ra and usually standing in pairs astride temple entrances.

**order** A condition of logical, harmonious, or comprehensible arrangement in which each element of a group is properly disposed with reference to other elements and to its purpose. Also, an arrangement of columns supporting an entablature, each column comprising a capital, shaft, and usually a base.

**orthographic** Pertaining to, involving, or composed of right angles.

**pagoda** A Buddhist temple in the form of a square or polygonal tower with roofs projecting from each of its many stories, erected as a memorial or to hold relics. From the stupa, the Indian prototype, the pagoda gradually changed in form to resemble the traditional multi-storied watch tower as it spread with Buddhism to China and Japan.

**palazzo** A large, imposing public building or private residence, esp. in Italy.

**pantheon** A temple dedicated to all the gods of a people. Also, a public building serving as the burial place of or containing the memorials to the famous dead of a nation.

**parterre** An ornamental arrangement of flower beds of different shapes and sizes.

**parti** The basic scheme or concept for an architectural design, represented by a diagram.

**pavilion** A light, usually open building used for shelter, concerts, or exhibits, as in a park or fair. Also, a central or flanking projecting subdivision of a facade, usually accented by more elaborate decoration or greater height and distinction of skyline.

**pedestal** A construction upon which a column, statue, memorial shaft, or the like, is elevated, usually consisting of a base, a dado, and a cornice or cap.

**pergola** A structure of parallel colonnades supporting an open roof of beams and crossing rafters or trelliswork, over which climbing plants are trained to grow.

**piazza** An open square or public place in a city or town, esp. in Italy.

**pier** A vertical supporting structure, as a section of wall between two openings or one supporting the end of an arch or lintel.

**pilaster** A shallow rectangular feature projecting from a wall, having a capital and a base and architecturally treated as a column.

**pilastrade** A row of pilasters.

**pillar** An upright relatively slender shaft or structure, usually of brick or stone, used as a building support or standing alone as a monument.

**Platonic solid** One of the five regular polyhedrons: tetrahedron, hexahedron, octahedron, dodecahedron, or icosahedron.

**plaza** A public square or open space in a city or town.

**podium** A solid mass of masonry visible above ground level and serving as the foundation of a building, esp. the platform forming the floor and substructure of a classical temple.

**porch** An exterior appendage to a building, forming a covered approach or vestibule to a doorway.

**porte-cochère** A porch roof projecting over a driveway at the entrance to a building and sheltering those getting in or out of vehicles. Also, a vehicular passageway leading through a building or screen wall into an interior courtyard.

**portico** A porch or walkway having a roof supported by columns, often leading to the entrance of a building.

**post** A stiff vertical support, esp. a wooden column in timber framing.

**postern** A private or side entrance, as one for pedestrians next to a porte-cochère.

**promenade** An area used for a stroll or walk, esp. in a public place, as for pleasure or display.

**proportion** The comparative, proper, or harmonious relation of one part to another or to the whole with respect to magnitude, quantity, or degree. Also, the equality between two ratios in which the first of the four terms divided by the second equals the third divided by the fourth.

**prototype** An early and typical example that exhibits the essential features of a class or group and on which later stages are based or judged.

**proxemics** The study of the symbolic and communicative role of the spatial separation individuals maintain in various social and interpersonal situations, and how the nature and degree of this spatial arrangement relates to environmental and cultural factors.

**pylon** A monumental gateway to an ancient Egyptian temple, consisting either of a pair of tall truncated pyramids and a doorway between them or of one such masonry mass pierced with a doorway, often decorated with painted reliefs.

**pyramid** A masonry mass having a rectangular base and four stepped and sloping faces culminating in a single apex, used in ancient Egypt and pre-Columbian Central America as a tomb or a platform for a temple.

**quoin** An external solid angle of a wall, or one of the stones forming such an angle, usually differentiated from the adjoining surfaces by material, texture, color, size, or projection.

**rampart** A broad embankment of earth raised as a fortification around a place and usually surmounted by a parapet.

**ratio** Relation in magnitude, quantity, or degree between two or more similar things.

**reentrant** Reentering or pointing inward, as an interior angle of a polygon that is greater than 180°.

**regular** Having all faces congruent regular polygons and all solid angles congruent.

**repetition** The act or process of repeating formal elements or motifs in a design.

**rhythm** Movement characterized by a patterned repetition or alternation of formal elements or motifs in the same or a modified form.

**roof** The external upper covering of a building, including the frame for supporting the roofing.

**room** A portion of space within a building, separated by walls or partitions from other similar spaces.

**scale** A proportion determining the relationship of a representation to that which it represents. Also, a certain proportionate size, extent, or degree, usually judged in relation to some standard or point of reference.

**semiotics** The study of signs and symbols as elements of communicative behavior.

**shrine** A building or other shelter, often of a stately or sumptuous character, enclosing the remains or relics of a saint or other holy person and forming an object of religious veneration and pilgrimage.

**sill** The lowest horizontal member of a frame structure, resting on and anchored to a foundation wall. Also, the horizontal member beneath a door or window opening.

**solarium** A glass-enclosed porch, room, or gallery used for sunbathing or for therapeutic exposure to sunlight.

**solid** A geometric figure having the three dimensions of length, breadth, and thickness.

**space** The three-dimensional field in which objects and events occur and have relative position and direction, esp. a portion of that field set apart in a given instance or for a particular purpose.

**stair** One of a flight or series of steps for going from one level to another, as in a building.

**stele** An upright stone slab or pillar with a carved or inscribed surface, used as a monument or marker, or as a commemorative tablet in the face of a building.

**stoa** An ancient Greek portico, usually detached and of considerable length, used as a promenade or meeting place around public places.

**stringcourse** A horizontal course of brick or stone flush with or projecting beyond the face of a building, often molded to mark a division in the wall.

**symbol** Something that represents something else by association, resemblance, or convention, esp. a material object used to represent something invisible or immaterial, deriving its meaning chiefly from the structure in which it appears.

**symbology** The study of use of symbols.

**symmetry** The exact correspondence in size, form, and arrangement of parts on opposite sides of a dividing line or plane, or about a center or axis. Also, regularity of form or arrangement in terms of like, reciprocal, or corresponding parts.

**synagogue** A building or place of assembly for Jewish worship and religious instruction.

**technology** Applied science: the branch of knowledge that deals with the creation and use of technical means and their interrelation with life, society, and the environment, drawing upon such subjects as industrial arts, engineering, applied science, and pure science.

**tectonics** The art and science of shaping, ornamenting, or assembling materials in building construction.

**tensile structure** A thin, flexible surface that carries loads primarily through the development of tensile stresses.

**terrace** A raised level with a vertical or sloping front or sides faced with masonry, turf, or the like, esp. one of a series of levels rising above one another.

**tetrastyle** Having four columns on one or each front.

**tholos** A circular building in classical architecture.

**threshold** A place or point of entering or beginning.

**tokonoma** Picture recess: a shallow, slightly raised alcove for the display of a flower arrangement or a kakemono, a vertical hanging scroll containing either text or a painting. One side of the recess borders the outside wall of the room through which light enters, while the interior side adjoins the tana, a recess with built-in shelving. As the spiritual center of a traditional Japanese house, the tokonoma is located in its most formal room.

**topography** The physical configuration and features of a site, area, or region.

**torii** A monumental, freestanding gateway on the approach to a Shinto shrine, consisting of two pillars connected at the top by a horizontal crosspiece and a lintel above it, usually curving upward.

**transformation** The process of changing in form or structure through a series of discrete permutations and manipulations in response to a specific context or set of conditions without a loss of identity or concept.

**trellis** A frame supporting open latticework, used as a screen or a support for growing vines or plants.

**trullo** A circular stone shelter of the Apulia region of southern Italy, roofed with conical constructions of corbeled dry masonry, usually whitewashed and painted with figures or symbols. Many trulli are over 1,000 years old and still in use today, usually located among vineyards to serve as storage structures or as temporary living quarters during the harvest.

**truss** A structural frame based on the geometric rigidity of the triangle and composed of linear members subject only to axial tension or compression.

**uniformity** The state or quality of being identical, homogeneous, or regular.

**unity** The state or quality of being combined into one, as the ordering of elements in an artistic work that constitutes a harmonious whole or promotes a singleness of effect.

**vault** An arched structure of stone, brick, or reinforced concrete, forming a ceiling or roof over a hall, room, or other wholly or partially enclosed space. Since it behaves as an arch extended in a third dimension, the longitudinal supporting walls must be buttressed to counteract the thrusts of the arching action.

**veranda** A large, open porch, usually roofed and partly enclosed, as by a railing, often extending across the front and sides of a house.

**vestibule** A small entrance hall between the outer door and the interior of a house or building.

**villa** A country residence or estate.

**void** An empty space contained within or bounded by mass.

**volume** The size or extent of a three-dimensional object or region of space, measured in cubic units.

**wainscot** A facing of wood paneling, esp. when covering the lower portion of an interior wall.

**wall** Any of various upright constructions presenting a continuous surface and serving to enclose, divide, or protect an area.